MY BIG

QUESTION
and
ANSWER
BOOK

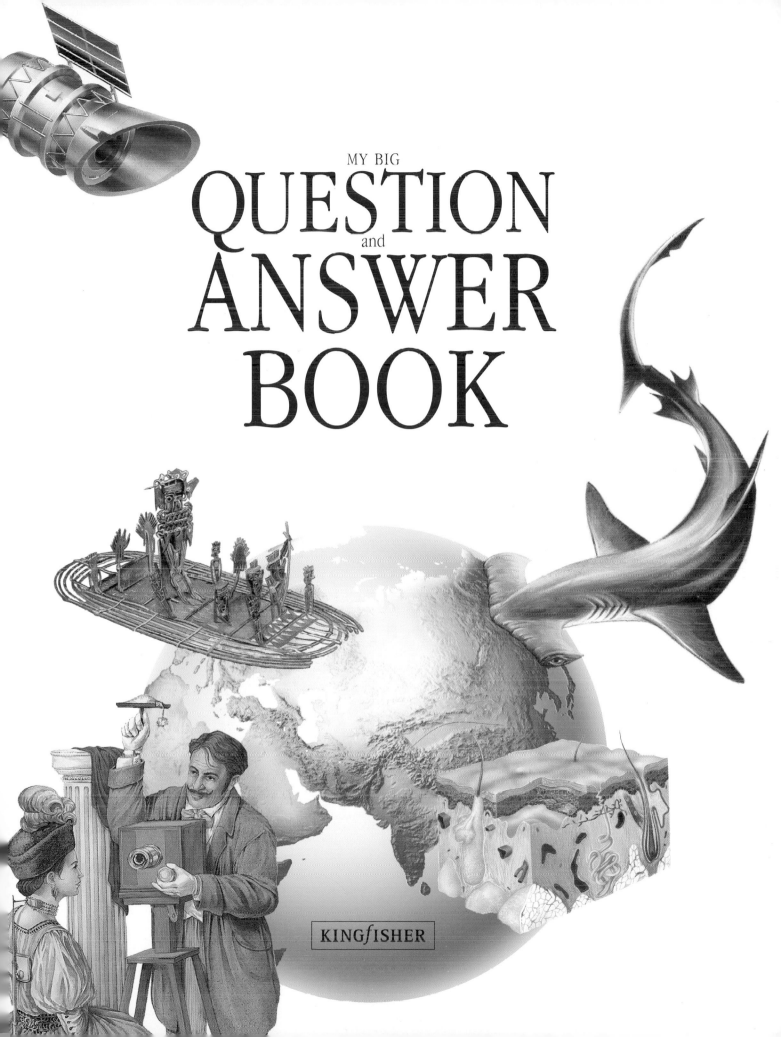

KING*f*ISHER

KINGFISHER
Kingfisher Publications Plc
New Penderel House, 283–288 High Holborn,
London WC1V 7HZ

Material in this edition previously published by Kingfisher Publications Plc
in the *Encyclopedia of Questions and Answers*

First published by Kingfisher Publications Plc 1999
2 4 6 8 10 9 7 5 3 1

1BS / 0699 / TWP / NEW(RNB) / 150AM

A CIP catalogue record for this book is available from the British Library

ISBN 0 7534 0437 0

Produced by Miles Kelly Publishing Ltd.
Designer: Smiljka Surla
Editors: Rosie Alexander, Kate Miles,
Angela Royston
Assistant Editors: Susanne Bull, Lynne French
Indexer: Sue Lightfoot
Picture Research: Yannick Yago

Printed in Singapore

CONTENTS

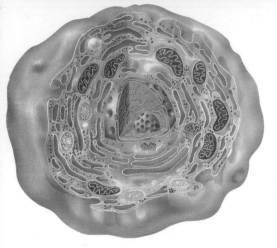

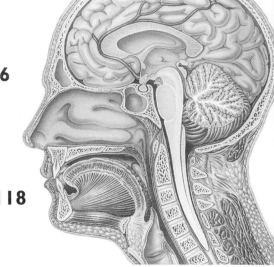

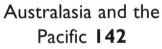

INDEX

EARTH FACTS

How big is the Earth?

The Earth's circumference (the distance around the world) at the Equator is 40,091 kilometres. Its diameter (the distance across the centre of the Earth) at the Equator is 12,756 kilometres. The Earth is slightly smaller when measured between the poles (12,713 kilometres), so it is not an exact sphere. If you could put the world on scales, it would weigh nearly 6,000 million million million tonnes.

▼ This cutaway of the Earth shows the upper rocky layer or lithosphere. The crust beneath the oceans is much thinner than the crust beneath the continents.

What is the Earth made of?

The Earth is a huge ball of rock. The top layer is the crust of the Earth. It is as little as 6 kilometres thick beneath the oceans. Then comes a thick layer of rock called the mantle, which goes almost halfway down to the Earth's centre. As it gets deeper, it gets hotter and beneath the mantle is a layer of hot, liquid rock called the outer core. Finally, at the centre of the Earth is the inner core – a huge ball of hot but solid rock. It begins 5,000 kilometres beneath our feet. At the centre, its temperature is thought to reach 4,500 degrees Celsius. Scientists know about the Earth by studying earthquakes, by comparing the Earth with meteorites and by looking at its size and shape.

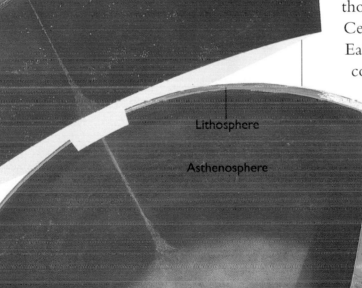

Lithosphere

Oceanic crust

Continental crust

Enlarged section

Lithosphere

Asthenosphere

Outer core

Mantle

Inner core

Crust

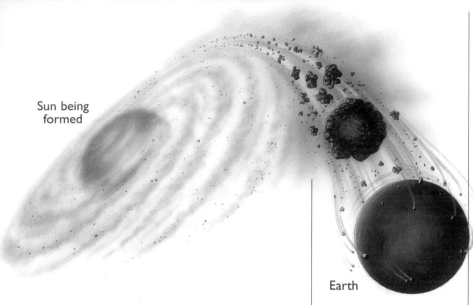

Sun being formed

Earth

▲ **The Earth was formed at the same time as the Sun. Material around the Sun cooled and collided to build up bodies that in time became planets.**

How old is the Earth?

The universe began to form over 15 billion years ago. The Earth is much younger. It is about 4.6 billion years old. Scientists have worked this out by studying rocks in meteorites which have landed on Earth from outer space. Meteorites are lumps of rock which were formed at the same time as the Earth. Scientists have also calculated the Earth's age from the rate at which elements of the radioactive metal uranium decay (break down) into lead.

Why is the Earth round?

The world is round for the same reason that a raindrop and a bubble are round. If possible, a liquid naturally shapes itself into a ball. When the Earth formed, it was hot and liquid. Because it was floating in space, it became round. When the liquid rock cooled and hardened into solid rock, the Earth stayed round.

Actually, the Earth is not perfectly round, but is slightly flattened at the poles. This flattening is caused by the speed of its spin.

The Earth is the only planet known to have enough oxygen for living things. In sunlight, plants give off oxygen, keeping the planet alive.

Is the Earth solid?

The crust is solid, but the rocks of the mantle are so hot that they are partly molten, rather like hot toffee. The outer core is hotter still (between 2,200 degrees Celsius and 5,000 degrees Celsius) and is completely molten and liquid. At the very centre is a ball of hot rock, squashed so tightly that it is solid. The core is far too hot and solid to drill through.

What are rocks made of?

The Earth's crust is made up of rock. Rocks are solid clusters of minerals (chemical substances composed of crystals). The minerals quartz, feldspar and mica are found in granite rocks, for example.

Is the Earth a unique planet?

No other planet orbiting the Sun is like the Earth. Only the Earth has the necessary conditions for life (as we know it) to exist.

What is the biosphere?

The biosphere is the Earth's 'skin' of soil, water and air. Within it live all the planet's plants and animals. No other planet in the Solar System has such a biosphere.

Why does the Earth orbit the Sun?

Like other planets, the Earth is held in a path, or orbit, around the Sun. The Sun's gravity is the force which holds the Earth in place. The Earth travels 958 million kilometres around the Sun in 365 days 6 hours and 9 minutes. This is called a year.

How much land is there?

Less than one-third of the Earth is covered by land. The land is older than the oceans. The rocks of the largest landmasses – the continents – are up to 3.8 billion years old. The oldest rocks in the ocean are less than 200 million years old. The Earth's surface is about 71 percent water. This water includes the oceans, ice and water vapour in the atmosphere.

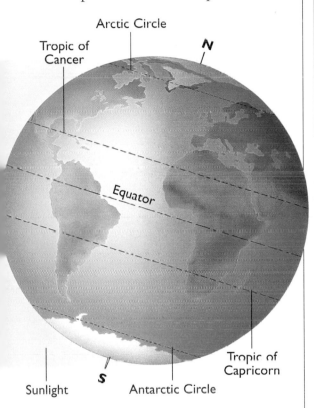

- Arctic Circle
- Tropic of Cancer
- N
- Equator
- Tropic of Capricorn
- Antarctic Circle
- Sunlight
- S

Where is the Equator?

The Equator is an imaginary line around the middle of the Earth. It is the line of 0 degrees latitude. The fattest part of the Earth is just below the Equator where the planet bulges.

Where is the North Pole?

The North Pole is near the middle of the Arctic Ocean. It is the point where all the lines of longitude meet on the map. The South Pole is in the Antarctic continent.

EARTH FACTS

- Diameter: 12,713 km at the poles, 12,756 km at the Equator.
- Circumference: 40,091 km.
- Surface area: 510 million sq km.
- Area covered by water: 71 percent.
- Age: 4.6 billion years.
- Oldest rocks: 3.8 billion years.
- Thickness of crust: 20 km (average).
- Temperature at centre: 4,500°C.
- Distance from Sun: 152 million km (average).
- Distance from Moon: 385,000 km (average).

◀ This picture of the Earth shows the tropics, the polar circles, and the Equator. The Earth turns on its axis (an imaginary line between the North and South poles). More sunlight reaches the Equator than the poles.

▶ The Northern Hemisphere includes Asia, North America and Europe. The Southern includes Australia, southern Africa and most of South America.

Where are the tropics?

The tropics are regions of the Earth that lie north and south of the Equator. Each of the tropics is about 2,600 kilometres wide. The Tropic of Cancer is 23°27′ north of the Equator. The Tropic of Capricorn is 23°27′ south of the Equator. These two lines of latitude (imaginary lines on the Earth's surface) mark the boundaries of a region where the Sun shines directly overhead.

What are the hemispheres?

A hemisphere is half of a globe. On maps and globes, the Equator (0 degrees latitude) divides the planet into two halves – the Northern and Southern hemispheres. An imaginary line around the Earth from the North Pole to the South Pole (the line of 0 degrees longitude) divides the Eastern and Western hemispheres.

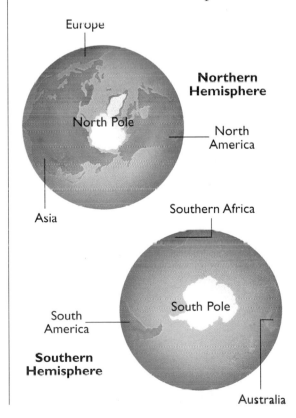

- Europe
- Northern Hemisphere
- North Pole
- North America
- Asia
- Southern Africa
- South America
- South Pole
- Southern Hemisphere
- Australia

What is the Earth's axis?

Take an orange and push a stick through its middle. The stick marks the axis of the orange. There is of course no stick through the Earth — its axis is an imaginary line between the poles. The Earth's axis is tilted about 23.5° from the vertical.

Why do we have day and night?

The Earth turns on its axis as it orbits the Sun, therefore part of the Earth is sunlit (day) while part is in shadow (night). Since the Earth spins all the time, day and night follow each other continually. Sunrise marks the start of day, and sunset the coming of night.

In mid-summer in the Arctic (facing the Sun), it is always daylight and northern Europe and North America have long summer days. In the Antarctic, it is always night. In mid-winter it is the other way round. The Antarctic has permanent daylight, while the Arctic is in darkness, and northern Europe and North America have short winter days.

Axis

▲ We have seasons because of the way the Earth orbits the Sun. The Earth is tilted and so first one pole, then the other, leans towards the Sun.

The Ancient Greeks believed that the Sun was a god called Helios. He rode across the sky in a chariot of flames. This explained sunset and sunrise.

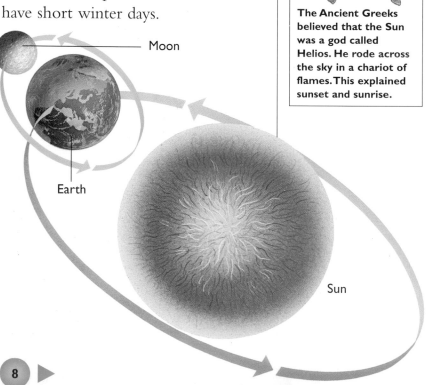

Moon

Earth

Sun

Why do we have seasons?

The seasons (spring, summer, autumn, winter) occur because the Earth is tilted on its axis. As the Earth moves around the Sun, the hemisphere that is tilted towards the Sun gets more of the Sun's rays and so is warmer and has summer. The people in that hemisphere see the Sun passing higher across the sky, and the days are longer. Meanwhile the part tilted away from the Sun has winter because it is less warm. There the days are shorter. At the Equator, the length of a day varies very little.

◄ The Moon moves in orbit around the Earth (green arrow). The Earth travels in orbit around the Sun (blue arrow). All three are spinning like tops at the same time.

Does a compass needle point to the North Pole?

No. The magnetized needle of a compass always turns to point in the direction of the Earth's north magnetic pole. The north magnetic pole is not the same as the geographic North Pole.

Changes in the Earth's magnetic field make the magnetic poles change positions, following circular paths with diameters of about 160 kilometres, but they never stray far from the geographical poles. The north magnetic pole is in northern Canada. The south magnetic pole is in Antarctica. About 450 million years ago the south magnetic pole was in what is now the Sahara Desert.

Every 200,000 to 300,000 years the magnetic poles reverse. North becomes south and south becomes north.

▼ The Earth's magnetic field stretches far into space. Like all magnets, the Earth has north and south magnetic poles.

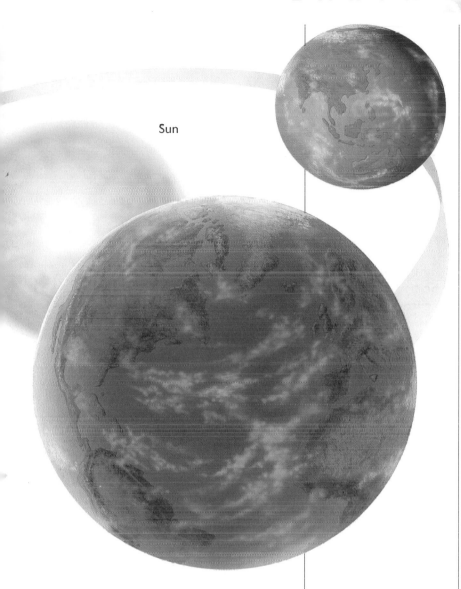

Sun

▲ Since the Earth's axis is tilted, the hemispheres are at different angles to the Sun. In the hemisphere tilted towards the Sun, daylength is longer. This is why days are longer in summer.

How is the Earth like a magnet?

The Earth acts like a giant dynamo. Movements inside it create electrical currents that make a magnetic field with north and south poles, rather like a bar magnet. The Earth's magnetic field stretches far into space for about 60,000 kilometres. The Sun and the other planets also have magnetic fields.

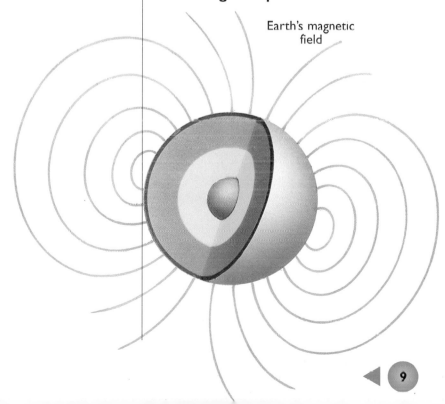

Earth's magnetic field

GEOGRAPHY

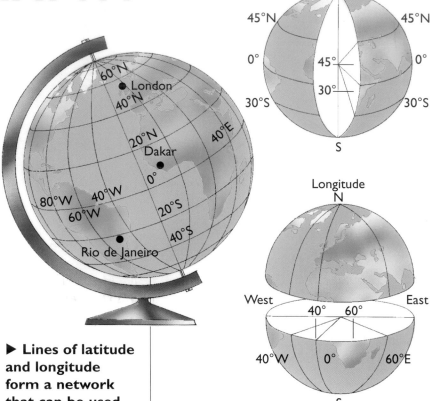

What do geographers do?

Geographers study the Earth, its features and living things. They look at the Earth's landscapes: where people, animals and plants live. They study such features as rivers and deserts. They study where cities are built, what industries produce, how humans and nature alter the landscape. Using survey equipment, they make precise measurements of the Earth's features. From these measurements, accurate maps of various kinds are made. Geographers help plan the cities and countryside in which we live.

When was the Earth first measured?

About 200 BC the Greek scientist Erastosthenes measured the distance around the Earth. He found the angle of the Sun's rays at different places that were a known distance apart. Using geometry, he worked out the Earth's circumference as 252,000 stadia (about 46,000 kilometres). His measurements were a little inaccurate: in fact the modern figure for the Earth's greatest circumference is 40,091 kilometres.

When were the first maps made?

People probably drew rough maps of their own lands over 5,000 years ago. A clay tablet made about 2500 BC in Babylonia (now part of Iraq) appears to show what looks like a river valley with mountains either side.

▶ Lines of latitude and longitude form a network that can be used to pinpoint places. The lines are measured in degrees. Greenwich, in London, is at 0° longitude, the Equator is at 0° latitude.

What are lines of latitude and longitude?

A map has a network of lines across it. The lines running east–west are lines of latitude, or parallels. The north–south lines are lines of longitude, or meridians. The lines make it easier to find a place on the map. The Ancient Greek geographer Ptolemy was the first mapmaker to draw such lines.

◀ The first reasonably accurate maps of the world were drawn in the 1500s. Most were based on the tales of seamen and travellers in distant lands.

When did America first appear on maps?

Before 1500, maps made in Europe did not show America. It was unknown to Europeans until Christopher Columbus sailed across the Atlantic Ocean in 1492. Soon mapmakers began to show the coast of the eastern Americas. The name America was first used on a German map in 1507.

When did sailors first use maps?

The first charts (sea maps) were made in Europe in the 1300s. They were called portolan charts and showed the Mediterranean coast in some detail. Sailors could recognize bays and headlands. A web of lines joined the various ports shown on the map, to help sailors find the right direction.

How is height shown on a map?

Height is difficult to show on a flat map. Colour shading shows areas that are the same height above sea level. Contour lines on a map also show height. The closer together contour lines are, the steeper the slope.

What is a map projection?

No flat map can be entirely accurate because the Earth's surface is curved. A map projection is a means of transferring the curved surface onto a flat map. One map projection can be imagined by wrapping a cylindrical roll of paper around a globe. It was made popular (though not invented) by the Flemish mapmaker Gerardus Mercator (1512–1594).

▶ Taking aerial photographs is one way to make maps. The photos are taken with an overlap, as shown in this picture. Viewing pairs of photos together gives a 3-D image, so contours can be plotted.

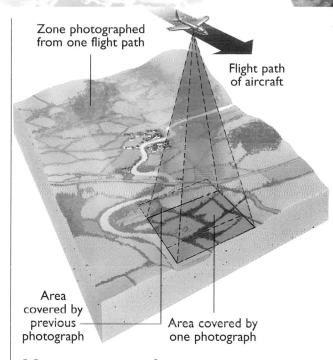

Zone photographed from one flight path

Flight path of aircraft

Area covered by previous photograph

Area covered by one photograph

▼ Two common map projections are Mercator's and the zenithal or azimuthal. In the zenithal projection, the paper is flat and touches the globe at one point.

How are modern maps made?

Most maps are made from photographs taken from aircraft or from satellites orbiting the Earth. They show the land and sea in great detail.

Mercator's projection (cylindrical)

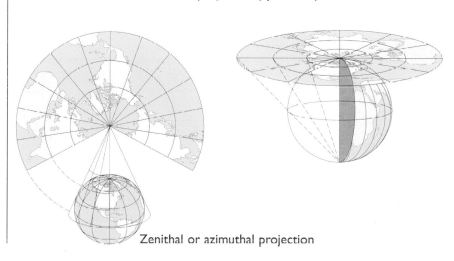

Zenithal or azimuthal projection

EVER-CHANGING EARTH

How is the Earth always changing?

Since the Earth was formed over 4.6 billion years ago, it has changed in many ways. Some changes happen so slowly that they are not noticeable in a person's lifetime. Earthquakes and volcanoes, however, can alter landscapes in hours. Glaciers, rivers and the oceans also alter the face of the Earth but they may take thousands of years.

How can continents move?

The Earth's crust is formed of a number of separate curved plates. The plates float like giant rafts on a thick treacly mass of molten rock. Heat from within the Earth sends currents moving through the 'treacle', and these cause the plates to move. As the plates move, so do the continents resting on them.

All seven continents on the Earth today – Africa, Asia, Antarctica, Australia, Europe, North and South America – were once part of one gigantic super-continent called Pangaea, which later broke up.

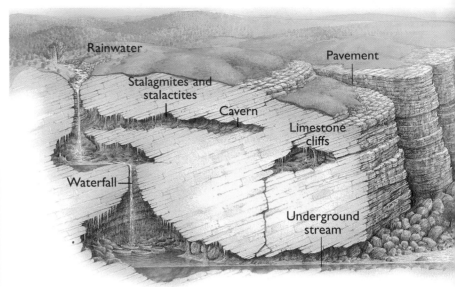

Rainwater · Pavement · Stalagmites and stalactites · Cavern · Limestone cliffs · Waterfall · Underground stream

▲ Caves, caverns and potholes are formed by water wearing away soft limestone rocks. Drips of lime-bearing water form stalactites and stalagmites.

▼ Pangaea began to break up about 200 million years ago, to form the continents we know today.

How are caves made?

Most caves are hollowed out of rock by underground water. The water trickles down from the Earth's surface, dissolving some of the rock to form small passages and openings. Carbon dioxide in the air can make the water slightly acidic, and this acid eats away at the rock. Streams may also flow into and through the cave, making it bigger.

What makes a landslide?

Landslides are falls of rock and mud sent cascading down a mountain or hillside. The cause is often an earthquake or volcanic eruption. The movement of the surface causes loose or wet surface material to break away and slide downhill. A big landslide can bury a whole valley. Heavy rains can send mud slipping down a hillside. The risk of this kind of landslide is greater when trees on mountain slopes are felled – a major problem in some developing countries.

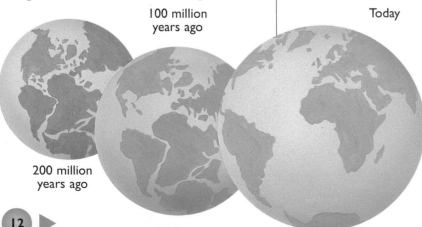

100 million years ago

Today

200 million years ago

How can we tell stalactites from stalagmites?

Stalactites and stalagmites form inside limestone caves. The water that drips steadily from the roof contains a mineral called calcite. The water dries, but the calcite remains and slowly builds into a column. Stalactites grow downwards, from the cave roof. Stalagmites grow upwards, from the cave floor. Sometimes the two columns meet to form a pillar.

Why are high mountain tops covered in snow?

High mountain tops are surrounded by very cold air. For every 1,000 metres in height, the temperature falls by 5 degrees Celsius. The highest mountains are snow-covered all year round. The highest mountains in the

▶ Stalactites and stalagmites look like long icicles of rock. Stalactites grow down from the cave roof, stalagmites grow up from the floor.

ICE AND CAVE FACTS

■ In the mountains of eastern Italy is a cave known as the Room of Candles. It is full of white stalagmites that look like candles.

■ Don't sit and watch a stalactite grow. It can take 1,000 years to get 1 cm longer!

■ During the last Ice Age, 28 percent of the Earth was ice-covered. Today, about 10 percent is covered by ice.

■ The world's longest glacier is the Lambert Glacier in the Antarctic which is over 400 km in length.

■ The world's deepest cave is at Rousseau Jean Bernard in France. It is 1,535 m deep.

■ The longest cave system is beneath Mammoth Cave in Kentucky, USA. It is at least 530 km long.

■ Sarawak Chamber in Indonesia is the world's biggest cavern. It is 700 m long, 300 m wide and 70 m high.

world are found in long ranges such as the Himalayas (Asia), the Andes (South America), the Rockies (North America) and the Alps (Europe).

What is a glacier?

A glacier is a moving 'river' of ice. Glaciers are found in polar regions and in high mountains, wherever more snow falls in winter than is lost through melting and evaporation in summer. The icy mass creeps slowly downhill. Glaciers shape landscapes, flattening hills and carving out valleys. When a glacier reaches the sea in very cold regions, huge blocks of ice break off to form floating icebergs. The largest icebergs in the world are found in the ocean around Antarctica.

Pyramidal peak

Cirque

Crevasses

Movement of glacier

Snout

Terminal moraine

▶ **A glacier wears away a valley. The head of the valley weathers into an armchair-shape known as a cirque. Crevasses or cracks often appear in glaciers. Rocks pushed along by the ice pile up as a moraine.**

What is an avalanche?

An avalanche is a sudden fall of snow and ice down a mountainside. Avalanches are very dangerous because they can bury and kill people. They happen when so much snow falls that the layers of snow on the mountainside become too heavy and suddenly give way and slide or fall down. Avalanches also happen in spring when the warm weather begins to melt the snow so that it slides more easily. Earthquakes, and even sudden loud sounds, can also cause avalanches.

▶ **A volcano may explode violently, blowing out ash and steam and red-hot lava. Sometimes a volcano collapses around its vent, leaving a crater called a caldera.**

What causes earthquakes and volcanoes?

Earthquakes and volcanoes often seem to occur together. They happen most often in parts of the Earth where two of the plates making up the crust meet. Rocks are either pushed up to form mountains or ridges, or sink down into the Earth's mantle to create trenches. This movement makes the Earth's surface unstable, and earthquakes and volcanoes are likely to occur. Scientists can tell where earthquakes and volcanoes are likely to happen, but they cannot predict exactly when.

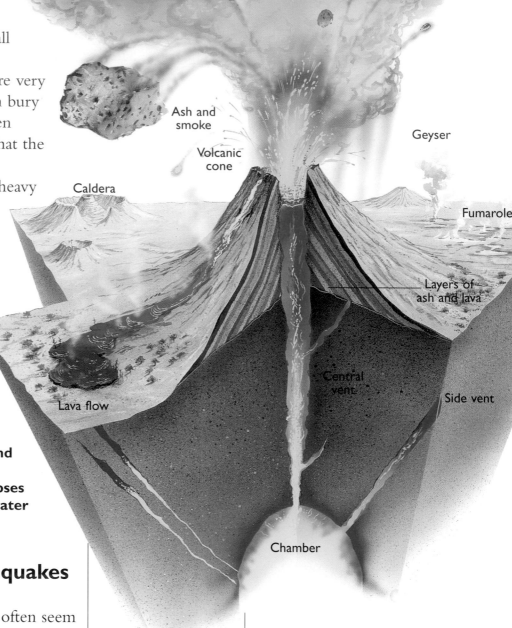

Ash and smoke

Volcanic cone

Caldera

Geyser

Fumarole

Layers of ash and lava

Central vent

Side vent

Lava flow

Chamber

The people of Ancient China believed that the Earth was balanced on the shoulders of a giant ox. Earthquakes happened when the ox shifted the Earth from one shoulder to the other.

Why do geysers spout hot water?

A geyser is a gushing fountain of hot water and steam. Geysers are found in areas of volcanic activity, such as Iceland. Hot volcanic rocks heat underground water, which bubbles up as a hot spring. If water deeper down is heated further, it turns to steam and pushes up the cooler water above it to form a geyser. 'Old Faithful' geyser in the United States has spouted every 76 minutes for the last 80 years.

Why do some volcanoes explode?

When a volcano erupts, magma (molten rock) from deep inside the Earth is pushed up towards the surface. Red-hot lava (the name given to magma when it pours out above ground) flows out of the volcano. Smoke and ash belch upwards, darkening the sky.

An explosive volcano contains very thick lava. The lava is pushed upwards very slowly and may form a plug, sealing the volcano. Pressure builds up inside until gas and ash burst through, blowing the top off the volcano in a huge explosion.

What happens in an earthquake?

In an earthquake, the ground begins to shake. This shaking may last for only a few seconds or for minutes. Buildings may shake, crack and collapse. Surface cracks open up across fields and rocks and whole chunks of land may sink suddenly.

Earthquakes happen in places where there are great cracks, or faults, in the rocks below ground. These places are at the edges of the huge plates, or sections, in the Earth's crust. The plates slowly move past or towards each other. Where two plates meet, the rocks on either side of the gap slide past each other, which can make the ground shake.

Where do the worst earthquakes happen?

Some of the worst earthquakes have happened in China. In 1556, an earthquake at Shensi killed over 800,000 people. Then in 1976, history repeated itself. An earthquake at Tangshan killed about 750,000 people. This is the worst earthquake disaster of modern times.

VIOLENT EARTH FACTS

- The largest volcano is Mauna Loa in the Hawaiian Islands. It measures 119 km across its base.
- When Krakatoa volcano exploded in 1883, the sound was heard in Australia, 5,000 km away.
- There are more than 500 active volcanoes.
- In 1201 there was a terrible earthquake in the eastern Mediterranean. It is possible that over a million people were killed.
- In 1906 the San Francisco earthquake started fires that destroyed much of the city.
- In 1995 an earthquake struck Kobe, Japan. Over 5,000 people died and a third of the city buildings were destroyed.
- Every year there are 1,000 earthquakes strong enough to cause some damage.

Fault line

Epicentre

Hypocentre

Shock waves

▶ **Shock waves radiate from an earthquake's centre. The epicentre is the point where the surface damage is greatest.**

ATMOSPHERE AND WEATHER

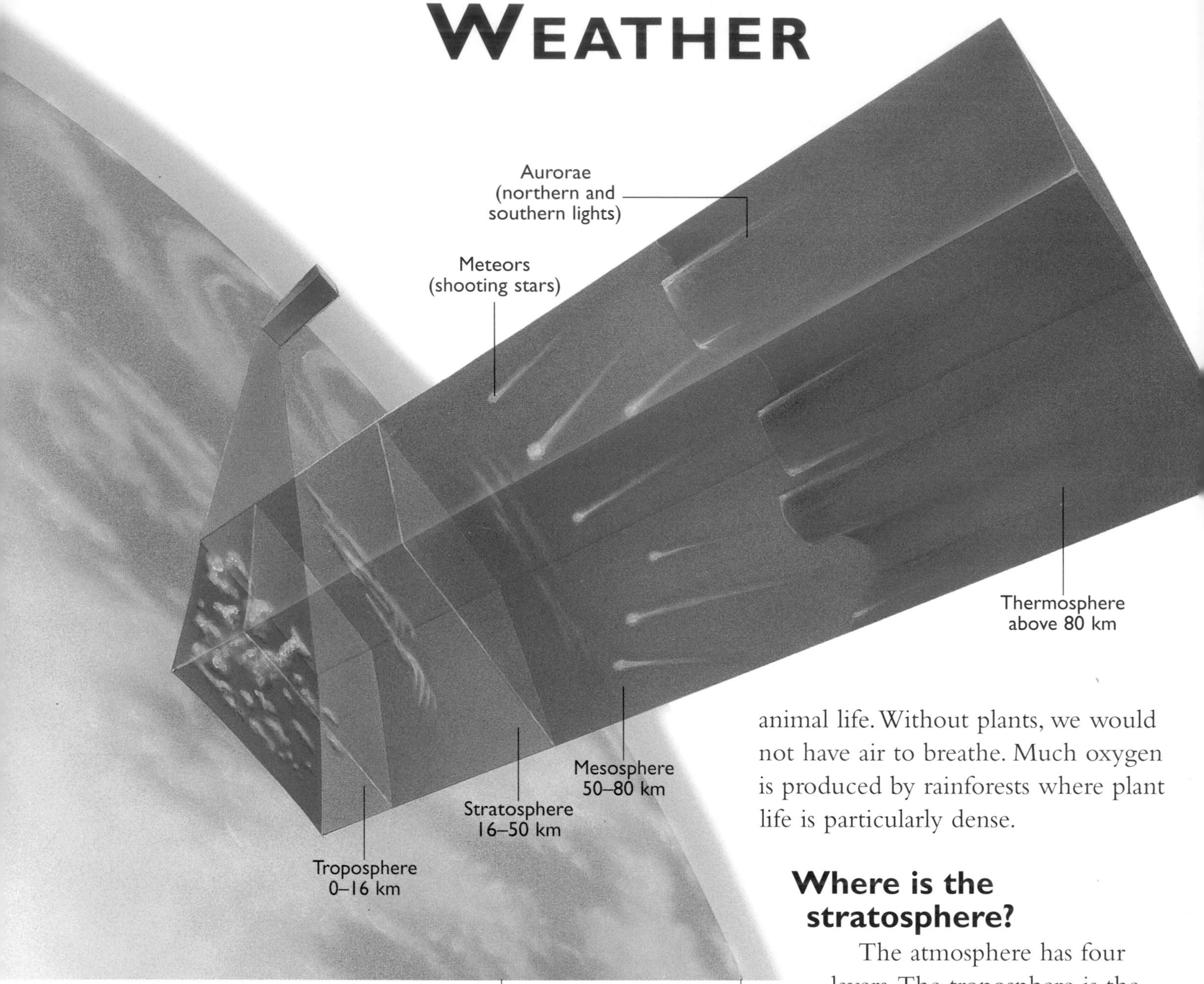

Aurorae
(northern and
southern lights)

Meteors
(shooting stars)

Thermosphere
above 80 km

Mesosphere
50–80 km

Stratosphere
16–50 km

Troposphere
0–16 km

What is the atmosphere?

The atmosphere is the layer of gas surrounding the Earth. The layer is surprisingly thin, yet without it there would be no life on Earth. When the Earth was young, the atmosphere consisted mainly of poisonous gases. Plants (which give off oxygen during photosynthesis) have made the atmosphere capable of supporting

▲ **Air surrounds the Earth like a transparent shell. The layers of the atmosphere shield us from most of the Sun's dangerous rays.**

animal life. Without plants, we would not have air to breathe. Much oxygen is produced by rainforests where plant life is particularly dense.

Where is the stratosphere?

The atmosphere has four layers. The troposphere is the lowest layer. It is up to 16 kilometres thick. Above it is the stratosphere, which reaches to about 50 kilometres high. Higher still is the mesophere, to about 80 kilometres. The upper layer is called the thermosphere. The thermosphere has two parts, the ionosphere and the exosphere. Temperature differences mark the boundaries between the layers.

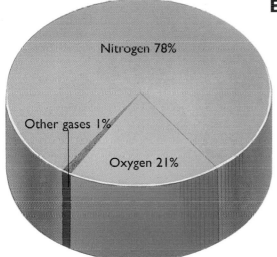

What is air?

Air is a mixture of gases. The most plentiful gases in air are nitrogen (78 percent) and oxygen (21 percent). The remaining 1 percent is made up of water vapour and very small amounts of ozone, carbon dioxide, argon and helium.

Why is the sky blue?

Light reaches the Earth from the Sun. Sunlight looks white, but is actually a mixture of all the colours in the rainbow. When light rays from the Sun pass through the atmosphere, some are scattered by the tiny bits of dust and water in the air. Blue rays are scattered most and reach our eyes from all angles. We see more blue than any other colour and this makes the sky look blue.

Why are sunsets red?

At sunset the Sun is low in the sky and farther away from us as we look towards it. The light rays from the Sun have to pass through more layers of air to reach our eyes. This extra air scatters out all the colours in the sunlight except red. Only the red rays come straight to our eyes and so we see a red sunset.

◀ Our air is mostly nitrogen gas, which makes up nearly four-fifths of the air. About one-fifth of the air is oxygen, the gas we need to breathe. Other gases and water vapour make up the rest.

ATMOSPHERE FACTS

■ The lowest layer of atmosphere is where weather happens.

■ Planes fly above the clouds. Here the skies are clear and the air is thin.

■ Air is heavier than you think. The average roomful of air weighs more than 45 kg – as much as 20 bags of potatoes!

■ The ozone layer is in the stratosphere.

■ In the mesosphere, 50 to 80 km above our heads, it is freezing cold, down to −80°C.

■ The outer layer of the thermosphere is called the exosphere. It extends as far as 8,000 km. Here it is very hot, above 2,200°C.

▶ 'Red sky at night, shepherd's delight.' This old rhyme suggests that a brilliant red sunset (with few clouds) means a fine day tomorrow.

Where is the ozone layer?

Ozone is a form of oxygen. In the atmosphere, ozone forms when oxygen reacts under the influence of sunlight. Most ozone forms near the Equator and is shifted by the winds around the Earth. The ozone layer is an invisible screen. The ozone filters out harmful ultraviolet rays from the Sun. Scientists have discovered holes in the ozone layer, over the Antarctic and Arctic. These holes are believed to be caused by harmful gases given off by aerosol sprays, refrigerators and factories.

Who went up in a balloon to study air?

No one had explored the atmosphere before balloons were invented. The French chemist Joseph Louis Gay-Lussac (1778–1850) made balloon flights over Paris to study the air. He found that air is the same mixture at different heights, although its pressure, temperature and moistness change the higher you go.

What are the northern and southern lights?

The northern lights, or aurora borealis, are marvellous displays of coloured lights in the sky, like an enormous laser show. You can see them in or near the Arctic. The southern lights, or aurora australis, are seen in or near the Antarctic. The lights are caused by electrical particles from the Sun hitting the atmosphere and giving off bursts of light.

Why does sunlight tan the skin?

Sunlight contains ultraviolet rays. We cannot see them, but they are vital to health. They enable skin cells to make vitamin D. However, ultraviolet rays damage the outer layer of skin. The body reacts by making more of a brown pigment called melanin. This darkens the skin. The ozone layer acts as a sun-block, shielding us from most of the ultraviolet rays.

What do we mean by climate?

Climate is the usual weather of a place over a long time. Weather can change from day to day, but climate stays the same. The Earth has five major climatic zones. They are polar (cold); cold forest (cold winters); temperate (mild winters); desert (dry); and tropical rainy (warm and moist).

What makes rain?

Water from the oceans, lakes, rivers and plants is evaporated by the Sun's heat to form water vapour. This vapour, or gas, is held in the air. Air rises when warm, or when forced to

▶ The northern lights produce a brilliant light show in the sky, as energized particles hit the atmosphere.

The melanin pigment that gives us a tan is missing in some people. They are albinos and can be of any race. Their skin and hair are very pale and because the iris of the eye is colourless, blood vessels show through. Albinos cannot develop a protective suntan, so they have to avoid the sun if they can.

WEATHER FACTS

■ Dust and smoke from volcanoes or forest fires can make the Sun and Moon appear green or blue.

■ Every snowflake is a unique six-sided crystal of frozen water molecules.

■ Even in summer, clouds contain ice. Most of the ice melts as it falls, except during occasional summer hailstorms.

■ One of the world's wettest places is Cherrapunji, India, which has nearly 11,000 mm of rain a year.

■ The Atacama Desert in Chile is the driest, with less than 0.1 mm a year. London has about 600 mm a year.

rise over mountains, or when heavier cold air pushes underneath it. As the warm, moisture-laden air rises, it cools. The water vapour condenses back into water droplets, which mass together to form clouds. As the air rises, more vapour turns to water. The clouds grow bigger. When the water droplets are too big for the air to carry, they fall as rain and the cycle begins again.

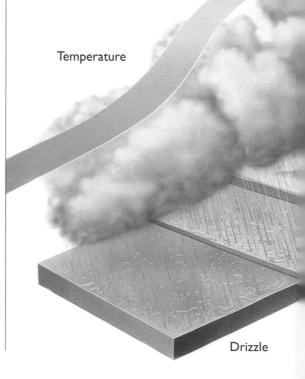

Temperature

Drizzle

What are the highest clouds in the sky?

High clouds include cirrus, cirrostratus and cirrocumulus. These clouds are formed mainly of ice crystals. Cirrus clouds are wispy clouds and can form at heights up to 10,000 metres. The rare nacreous or mother-of-pearl clouds can be over 20,000 metres high.

Why do some lands have monsoons?

A monsoon is a wind which blows from sea to land in summer, and from land to sea in winter. In hot lands near the Equator the air heats up in summer and rises. Cool air, carrying moisture from the ocean, is drawn

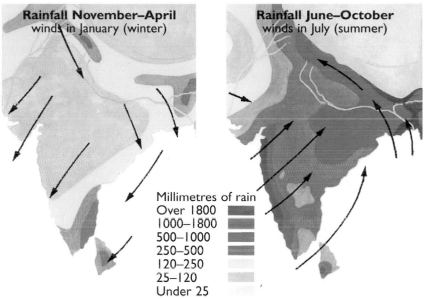

Rainfall November–April winds in January (winter)

Rainfall June–October winds in July (summer)

Millimetres of rain
Over 1800
1000–1800
500–1000
250–500
120–250
25–120
Under 25

▲ **The Indian sub-continent receives rain-carrying winds from the Indian Ocean during the monsoon season. In winter, the winds blow in the other direction.**

inland to take the place of the rising warm air. The cool winds bring rain which is often torrential. In India the monsoon lasts from three to four months, bringing rain in summer. In winter, there is much less rainfall.

What makes a rainbow?

Sunlight is a mixture of colours. When the Sun's rays pass through falling raindrops, the raindrops act like tiny mirrors or glass prisms. They bend and scatter the light into all its colours. We see a rainbow when the Sun is behind us and the rain in front of us. You can make your own rainbow with a water sprinkler or hose on a bright, sunny day.

Wet snow

Dry snow

Sleet

Rain

◄ **Whether water falls as drizzle, rain, sleet (a mixture of snow and rain) or snow, depends on the temperature of the air and the ground.**

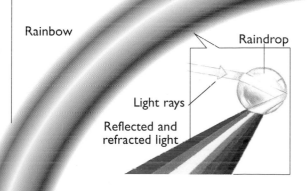

It may not rain cats and dogs, but it can rain frogs and fish! The animals are sometimes sucked up from ponds by extra-strong winds and fall with the rain.

▶ **A rainbow is caused by sunlight shining on a screen of water droplets. Light rays are bent (refracted), reflected and then refracted again as they strike each droplet.**

Rainbow

Raindrop

Light rays

Reflected and refracted light

OCEANS, RIVERS AND LAKES

What is a current?

A current is a stream of water moving through the ocean. There are surface currents and deep water currents. Great surface currents carry warm water from the Equator. The water cools and mixes with colder water as it moves away from the heat of the Equator. When the current turns towards the Equator again, its waters are cold. Offshore currents are caused by tide movement. Winds cause the much larger currents circling in the oceans in regular patterns. The Gulf Stream is a warm water current which begins in the Gulf of Mexico, then runs north-east towards Europe.

▼ **Ocean currents are moved in regular patterns by the winds. Near the Equator, the main currents are blown westwards. Near the poles they are blown eastwards.**

 Warm water

Cold water

How big can waves be?

Each wave in the ocean is made up of water particles moving in a circle. The wind pushes the wave upwards, forming a crest. Then gravity pulls it down again, into a trough. It is the up and down movement of water in waves that has been used to drive generators. Storm waves, driven by high winds, often rise 12 metres or more in an open sea. The highest sea wave seen from a ship and officially recorded was 34 metres high, during a hurricane in 1933. The biggest wave measured by instruments was 26.2 metres high in 1872 in the North Atlantic. Such waves are rare.

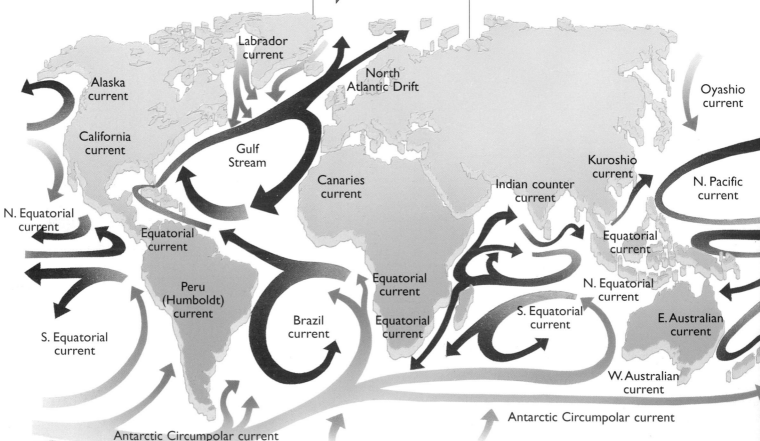

Labrador current
North Atlantic Drift
Oyashio current
Alaska current
California current
Gulf Stream
Canaries current
Kuroshio current
N. Pacific current
Indian counter current
Equatorial current
N. Equatorial current
Equatorial current
N. Equatorial current
Peru (Humboldt) current
Equatorial current
S. Equatorial current
E. Australian current
Brazil current
Equatorial current
S. Equatorial current
Equatorial current
S. Equatorial current
W. Australian current
Antarctic Circumpolar current
Antarctic Circumpolar current (West Wind Drift)

Why is seawater salty?

The saltiness of the sea comes from minerals. Minerals are washed into the sea from the land by rivers, which dissolve minerals from the rocks over which they flow. The most plentiful mineral in seawater is sodium chloride, or common salt.

Why do the tides rise and fall?

Ocean tides rise (flood) and fall (ebb) about twice every 24 hours. Tides are caused by the gravitational pull of the Sun and Moon on the Earth. They pull the oceans towards them. The land is pulled too but water moves more easily, making a giant wave. As the Earth spins, the wave travels around the Earth, causing the tides.

Away from the shore, the ocean plunges to a depth of about 4 km in most places. It's like going down a high mountain!

▼ The sea bed is cut through with valleys (trenches) and also has mountains (guyots) and volcanoes. The continental shelf slopes down gradually.

Where is the deepest point in the oceans?

The deepest point in the oceans is the bottom of a deep trench called the Mariana Trench in the Pacific. Measurements of the trench have varied from 11,034 metres to 10,916 metres below the surface.

Where is the continental shelf?

In most places, land does not stop suddenly at the coast. It slopes gently away beneath the sea to a depth of about 180 metres. This undersea land is called the continental shelf. At the outer edge of the shelf the steeper continental slope begins, leading down to the deep ocean floor known as the abyss.

Coral reef   Volcanic islands   Guyot   Deep ocean trench   Continental slope   Continental rise   Continental shelf

Continental crust   Oceanic crust

Which is the biggest ocean?

The three great oceans are the Pacific, the Atlantic and the Indian. The Pacific Ocean is by far the biggest ocean on Earth. It covers over 166 million square kilometres.

▼ The five world oceans compared: the Pacific is by far the largest.

Atlantic Ocean
106,000,000 sq km

Antarctic Ocean
32,248,000 sq km

Arctic Ocean
14,350,000 sq km

Pacific Ocean
166,242,500 sq km

Indian Ocean
73,500,000 sq km

What is the ocean bottom like?

The deep basins of the ocean floor are formed from heavy rock called basalt. Layers of mud overlie the deep oceanic trenches and level parts of the ocean floor. Some of the muds are filled with the remains of dead plants and animals. Such muds are called oozes. They are hundreds of metres deep in places. There are great mountain ranges too beneath the oceans. Many undersea mountains are volcanoes, the tops of which form islands on the surface.

THE UNIVERSE

Gravity cannot s
the expansion o
universe

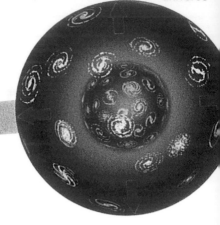

An ever-expanding universe

Big Bang

Galaxies fly apart
after the Big Bang

A finite universe

Big Bang

Gravity stops
expansion of the
universe

What is space?

Space is nothing – or almost nothing. It is the space that lies between the Earth and the Moon, between the planets of the Solar System, and between the stars. Space is almost empty. It does not contain any air. A piece of space the size of a house would contain a few atoms of gases and perhaps some specks of dust.

What holds the universe together?

The same force that keeps your feet on the ground holds the whole universe together. This is the force of gravity. Gravity extends through space between planets, between stars and between galaxies (groups of stars). It keeps the planets together in the Solar System and holds the stars together in huge galaxies.

▲ **The universe may keep on expanding, galaxies flying apart for evermore. Or it may all rush together in a 'Big Crunch' and start a new universe.**

To see how the universe is getting bigger, paint some spots on a balloon (for galaxies) and watch them get bigger as you blow it up.

When did the universe form?

A long time ago, all the galaxies in the universe would have been squeezed into a small space. Perhaps a great explosion happened, causing the galaxies to spread out. This explosion, or Big Bang, would have happened about 15 billion years ago.

How big is the universe?

No one knows for sure how big the universe is. There may be parts of the universe beyond the reach of our telescopes. Also, astronomers are not sure that light comes from the most distant objects in the universe in straight lines. The lines could be curved, making the objects closer than they appear to be. However, they could be as much as 15 billion light years away.

A series of universes
A completely new universe begins

Big Crunch   Big Bang

How do we know the universe is getting bigger?

Astronomers can measure the speed with which stars and galaxies are moving. Most of them are moving away from us. The farther away a galaxy is, the faster it appears to be moving away. This means that the universe is getting bigger. No one knows for certain if the universe will ever stop growing.

Where are we in the universe?

The universe is everything that exists – all the planets, moons, stars and galaxies put together. The universe stretches out in all directions. There may be parts of the universe that we cannot see through our telescopes, and so we cannot tell where exactly we are in the universe.

UNIVERSE FACTS

■ In 1965, scientists found a very feeble warmth in space. This is all that's left of the fantastic heat given off by the Big Bang.

■ Imagine the edge of the universe is a hollow ball the size of the Earth. On this scale, the Milky Way galaxy would be 40 m across. The Earth would be too small to see without a microscope!

■ The study of how the universe began is called cosmology.

■ Scientists think they have found at least one Earth-sized planet orbiting a distant star. The planet is 30,000 light years away.

What is the difference between a planet and a star?

A star is a huge ball of hot glowing gas, like the Sun. A planet is a world like the Earth. The Sun and stars produce their own light. The planets are lit by light from the Sun. In the night sky, you cannot tell the planets from the stars. They all look like tiny points of light, because they are far away. However, the planets are nearer than the stars. Through a powerful telescope, you can see that the planets are other worlds. The stars are so very distant that they still look like points of light, even through the most powerful telescope. Astronomers think that some stars have planets orbiting around them, just like the Sun.

Which star is nearest to the Earth?

The star Proxima Centauri is the nearest to us, at a distance of 4.2 light years. Next closest are Alpha Centauri (4.3 light years) and Barnard's Star (6 light years).

How do astronomers gaze into the past?

Light reaching us from even the closest stars has taken several years to cross the enormous distances of space. The nearest star is more than four light years away, so the light from it takes four years to reach us. This means we see the star as it looked four years ago. Other stars are millions of light years away. So when astronomers study light from these stars, they are seeing them as they were millions of years ago.

THE SUN

How big is the Sun?

The Sun is 1,392,500 kilometres across, 109 times the diameter of the Earth. It weighs 333,000 times as much as the Earth, and its volume is so huge that it could swallow up 1,300,000 Earths. If the Earth were the size of a tennis ball, then the Sun would be as big as a house.

What is the Sun made of?

The Sun is a huge, self-luminous ball of intensely hot gas. Its temperature is so high that it glows white hot, giving out light and heat rays. Most of the gas in the Sun is hydrogen. This is slowly turning into another gas, helium, inside the Sun. As it does so, it produces tremendous amounts of heat. The bright surface of the Sun is called the photosphere.

When did the Sun begin to shine?

The Sun began to shine about 5 billion years ago. It formed from a cloud of gas and dust floating in space. The cloud gradually got smaller and became thicker. As the cloud shrank, the centre heated up. Eventually, it became so hot that it began to glow and the Sun was born. The rest of the cloud formed the Solar System, including planets, moons, asteroids and comets.

▼ If we could cut a slice out of the Sun, we would see layers of hydrogen below the surface. There are sunspots and huge streamers of glowing gas called prominences forming arches of fire.

Earth

Does the Sun move?

The Sun appears to move across the sky from dawn to dusk. However, this motion is caused by the Earth spinning. The Sun only seems to be moving, and it is we who are moving and not the Sun. Nevertheless, the Sun moves in other ways. It spins as the Earth does, though slowly, but because it is made of gas, different parts spin at different rates – its equator spins fastest, the poles are

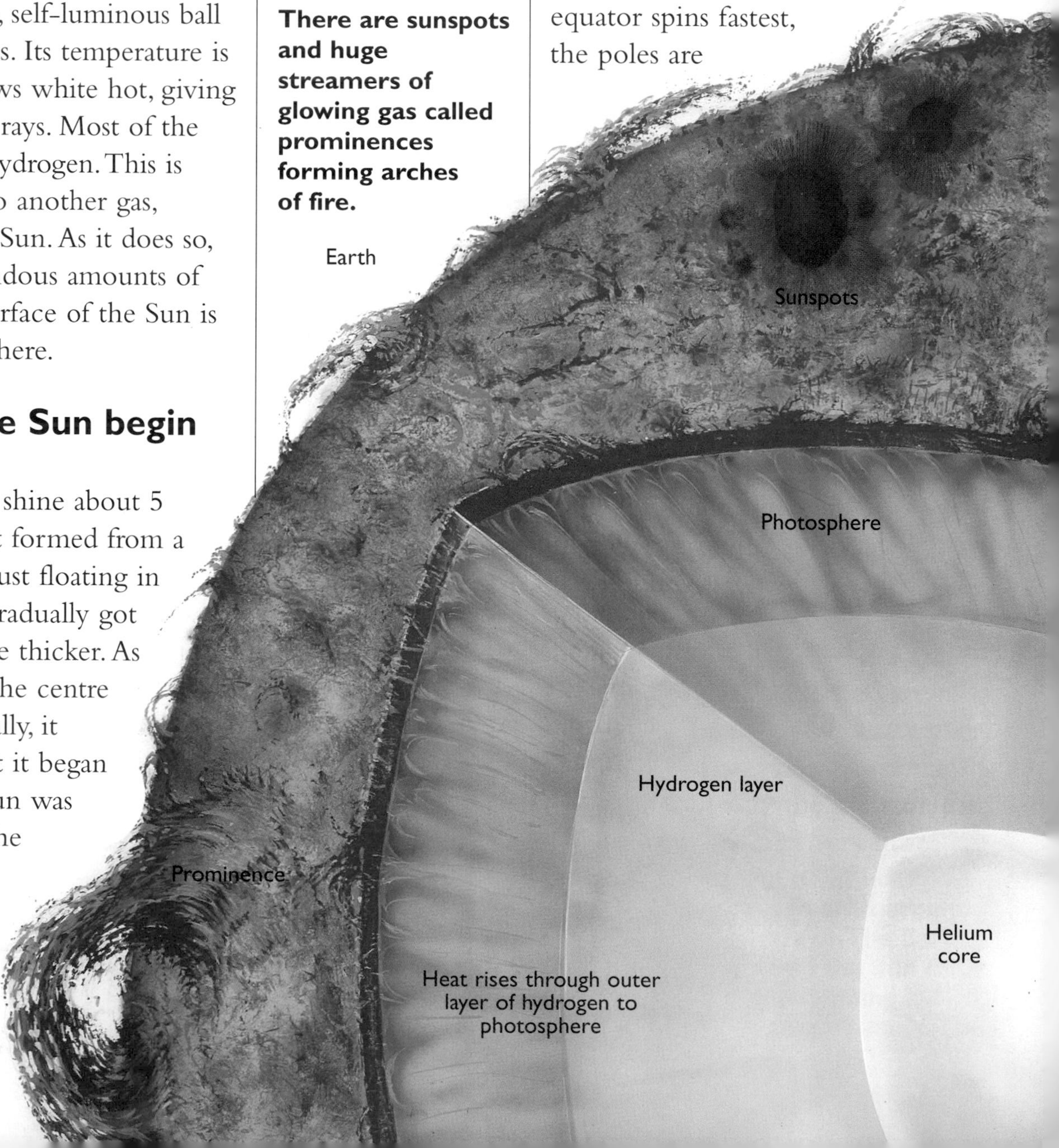

Sunspots

Photosphere

Hydrogen layer

Prominence

Helium core

Heat rises through outer layer of hydrogen to photosphere

slowest. Also, as the Earth moves around the Sun with the Moon, so the Sun moves around the centre of the Galaxy taking the Earth and the rest of the Solar System with it.

What happens during an eclipse of the Sun?

The Moon moves in front of the Sun during an eclipse of the Sun. It gets dim outside and the Sun appears to get smaller, like a new moon. In a total eclipse, the Sun disappears for a short time and it becomes dark and cold outside. During an eclipse of the Moon, the Moon seems to get smaller and may disappear. This is because the Earth moves in front of the Sun, and its shadow falls on the Moon.

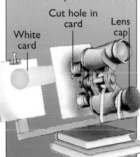

WARNING

■ It is very dangerous to look directly at the Sun.

■ A person who looks directly at the Sun through binoculars or a telescope can be blinded for life.

■ NEVER look at the Sun in this way. Use binoculars to project an image of the Sun onto a piece of card.

Cut hole in card

White card

Lens cap

What are sunspots?

Sunspots, looking like darker patches, appear and disappear on the surface of the Sun. Chinese astronomers studied them as early as 300 BC. European astronomers were puzzled by sunspots. As they believed the Sun was a 'perfect sphere' in the heavens, they could not accept that there were any 'imperfections' on its surface.

Where is the Sun hottest?

At the centre. Here, where the nuclear reactions that keep the Sun shining are going on, the temperature is 15 million degrees Celsius. The surface temperature is only 6,000 degrees Celsius, that is, 60 times the temperature of boiling water!

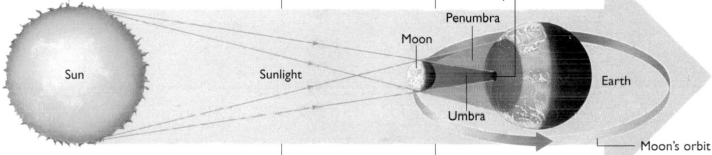

Sun

Sunlight

Moon

Total eclipse seen here

Penumbra

Umbra

Earth

Moon's orbit

Will the Sun grow hotter or colder?

The surface temperature of the Sun is about 6,000 degrees Celsius. The Sun is an 'average' star, in terms of its size and brightness. Billions of years from now, it will swell up to become a 'red giant' perhaps a hundred times its present size. The Earth itself may even be engulfed by the gigantic Sun. In time, the red giant Sun will shrink and become a tiny, very dense star called a 'white dwarf'. As its life ends, it will gradually cool and become invisible.

▲ When the Moon passes between the Earth and the Sun, it casts a shadow and causes an eclipse. Within the central shadow, or umbra, the Sun is completely hidden.

Who first said the Earth travels around the Sun?

The Polish astronomer Nicolaus Copernicus published a book in 1543 that upset many people's ideas about the universe. Copernicus declared that the old theory that the Earth was the centre of the universe was wrong. In his book he showed a drawing of the Solar System, with the Sun at its centre and the six known planets circling it. Many people were alarmed by these new ideas, but modern astronomy was built on the foundations of Copernicus.

THE MOON

How big is the Moon?

The Moon is 3,476 kilometres across – about the same width as Australia. Its total area is less than four times the size of Europe.

Where does the Moon come from?

The Moon formed when the Solar System was formed, at the same time as the Earth. This was about 4.6 billion years ago.

Why is the Moon covered in craters?

There are craters on Earth. They are made by meteorites crashing from space, and also by volcanoes. The same kinds of craters occur on the Moon. The action of the weather smoothes out most of the craters on Earth. However, there is no weather on the Moon so its craters have never changed and never will.

How does the Moon stay up in the sky?

The Moon is pulled by the Earth's gravity, just like anything that falls to the ground. It moves around the Earth in a path, or orbit, that is almost circular. In this way, it keeps about the same distance from the Earth. It is an average of 385,000 kilometres away, or thirty times the diameter of the Earth. If the Earth were an orange, the Moon would be about the size of a cherry 2 metres away.

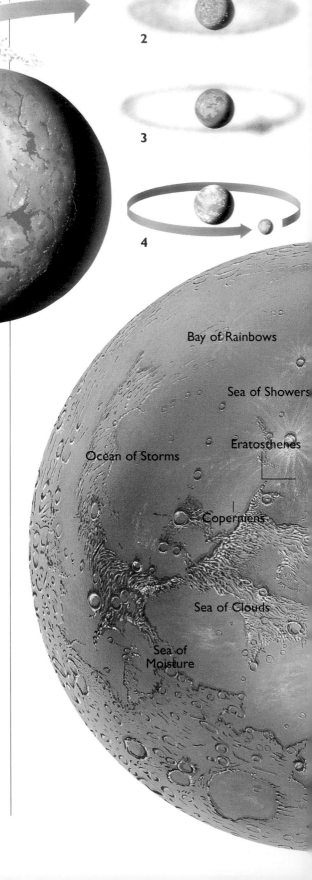

▲ **The Moon may have been made by a space collision, when a planet-sized body smashed into the Earth (1). Debris formed a cloud orbiting the Earth (2 and 3) which finally formed the solid Moon (4).**

▶**The near side of the Moon, the side we see from Earth, has huge plains, called maria ('seas' in Latin). These plains were formed by floods of volcanic lava. There are also huge craters.**

Bay of Rainbows

Sea of Showers

Ocean of Storms

Eratosthenes

Copernicus

Sea of Clouds

Sea of Moisture

Why does the shape of the Moon change in the sky?

Every four weeks, the Moon goes from a crescent-shaped new moon to a round full moon and back again. These changes are called phases. The Moon does not actually change shape. As it moves around the Earth, different parts become lit up by the Sun. We see only the lit-up parts.

How high could you jump on the Moon?

You could jump higher on the Moon than on Earth because your body would weigh six times less there. This is because the Moon's

The Moon's gravity isn't as strong as Earth's. You would be about six times lighter on the Moon. So you could jump six times higher – but only without a spacesuit.

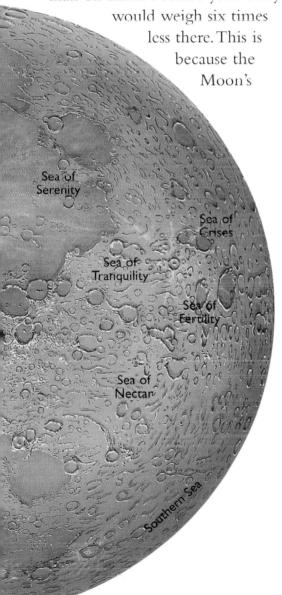

Sea of Serenity

Sea of Crises

Sea of Tranquility

Sea of Fertility

Sea of Nectar

Southern Sea

MOON FACTS

■ Before spacecraft flew around the Moon, no human had ever seen the far side.

■ Because the Moon has no wind or weather, footprints left by astronauts will remain undisturbed for ever.

■ Craters on the Moon were formed by smaller bodies hitting the surface. The far side of the Moon has far more craters than the near side.

■ Moon rock is older than any rock yet found on Earth. The oldest Moon rock found is 300 million years older than any rock found on Earth.

■ The Moon is pretty small. It is only 3,476 km across, less than the width of the United States.

gravity is one-sixth of the gravity on Earth. However, this doesn't mean that you could jump six times as high as you can on Earth, because you would have to wear a heavy and bulky spacesuit to stay alive.

Why is the Moon lifeless?

The Moon is only 3,476 kilometres across. Its gravity is too weak to hold down the gases left in its atmosphere after it formed. They floated away into space, leaving the Moon a dead, airless world.

How fast does the Moon spin?

The Moon spins once each time it goes round the Earth. That means it spins once every 29.25 days – the same time it takes to complete one orbit around the Earth.

Can we see all of the Moon?

One side of the Moon is always turned away from the Earth – the dark side of the Moon. As the newly formed Moon cooled, the Earth's gravity pulled at it. This slowed the Moon's spin and raised a bulge on the side nearest the Earth. Because the Moon spins once as it orbits, this same side always faces Earth.

How does the Moon affect the Earth?

The pull of the Moon causes the rise and fall of the ocean tides. The Moon can also black out the Sun's light during an eclipse. When this happens, a black shadow covers part of the Earth, which darkens.

THE PLANETS

How were the planets formed?

The Sun and its planets were formed at about the same time. A whirling cloud of gas and dust collected in space. It grew denser and denser as gravity squeezed the gas and dust together. Most of the cloud formed the Sun. What was left over became the planets.

Who are the planets named after?

All the planets, except for one, are named after gods and goddesses in Greek or Roman legends. The biggest planet, Jupiter, is named after the Roman king of the gods, for example. The exception is our planet, which we call Earth. This is because the other planets were thought to be in heaven, like the gods, and our planet lay beneath, like the earth. Five of the planets can be seen with the unaided eye and were named thousands of years ago. They are Jupiter, Saturn, Mars, Venus and Mercury. Uranus was found in 1781, Neptune in 1846 and Pluto in 1930.

If the Earth were the size of an orange, then the Moon would be the size of a cherry.

▼ The nine planets of the Solar System move in orbits at different distances from the Sun. By far the biggest are the giant planets Jupiter and Saturn. Four planets have rings.

What is the difference between a planet and a moon?

A planet is a world that goes around the Sun. A moon is a smaller world that goes around a planet. All except two of the planets have moons. The Earth and Pluto have only one, whereas Jupiter has sixteen. Mercury and Venus have none.

What is the Solar System?

The Solar System is made up of the Sun and all the bodies that go around the Sun. These are the planets and their moons, the asteroids or minor planets, meteoroids and comets. Each

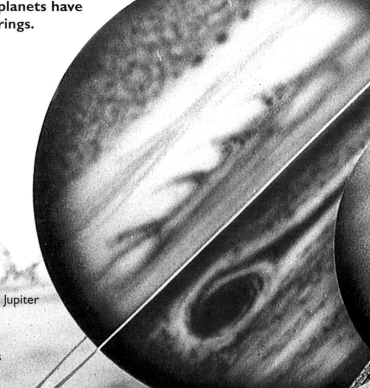

Sun

Mercury

Venus

Earth

Mars

Jupiter

moves in a particular path or orbit around the Sun. The Sun's force of gravity holds all these bodies together in the Solar System because it is bigger than they are.

How many planets are there?

The Sun has nine planets. They are Mercury, which is closest to the Sun, followed by Venus, Earth, Mars, Jupiter, Saturn, Uranus, Neptune and finally Pluto. Pluto is usually the most distant planet, but at the moment it is closer to the Sun than Neptune and will be until 1999.

Which is the smallest planet?

Pluto is the smallest planet. Its diameter is 2,250 kilometres. This is about two-thirds the size of our Moon and only twice the size of the largest asteroid.

▶ **Io is a small moon of Jupiter. It has active volcanoes. Jupiter has 15 other known moons.**

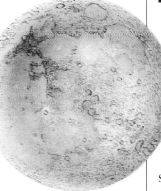

The Moon

Pluto

Which is the biggest planet?

The biggest planet is Jupiter. Its diameter is 142,800 kilometres, more than eleven times the diameter of the Earth. In volume, Jupiter is more than 1,300 times the size of the Earth! Jupiter is so massive that it weighs 2½ times as much as the other eight planets put together.

Which planet has the most moons?

Saturn has at least 18 moons. A moon is a small world going around a planet. It is held in orbit by the planet's gravity.

FACTS ABOUT THE PLANETS			
PLANET	Distance from the Sun in km	Diameter at equator in km	Time taken for 1 orbit
■ Mercury	58 million	4,878	88 days
■ Venus	108 million	12,104	224 days
■ Earth	152 million	12,756	365.25 days
■ Mars	228 million	6,794	687 days
■ Jupiter	778 million	142,800	11.9 years
■ Saturn	1,427 million	120,000	29.5 years
■ Uranus	2,870 million	52,000	84 years
■ Neptune	4,497 million	48,400	164.8 years
■ Pluto	5,900 million	2,250	247.7 years

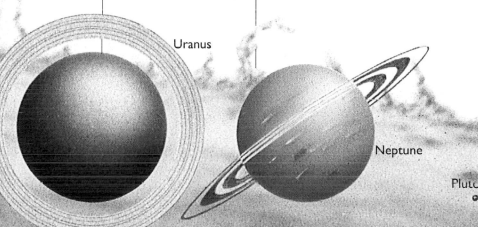

Saturn

Uranus

Neptune

Pluto

Where does the Solar System end?

The most distant planet, Pluto, is often thought to be at the edge of the Solar System. Its orbit takes it an average distance of 5.9 billion kilometres from the Sun. However, some comets are thought to travel halfway to the nearest star – a distance of about two light years. This would make the Solar System about four light years across, which is nearly 40 million million kilometres.

The word planet comes from the Greek word *planetes*, which means wanderer. The Greeks saw 'wandering' stars in the night sky.

Where are the inner and outer planets?

The inner planets are the four planets nearest to the Sun. They are Mercury, Venus, Earth and Mars, all made of rock and metal. The five other planets – Jupiter, Saturn, Uranus, Neptune and Pluto – are farther away from the Sun and are called the outer planets. These, except Pluto, are gaseous.

▼ The planets and asteroids go around the Sun in oval paths, or ellipses.

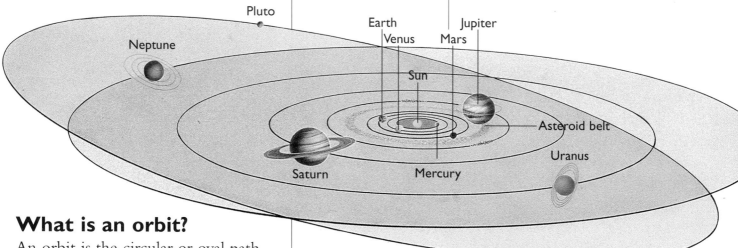

Pluto

Neptune

Earth

Venus

Jupiter

Mars

Sun

Saturn

Mercury

Asteroid belt

Uranus

What is an orbit?

An orbit is the circular or oval path that something follows as it moves through space. The planets move in orbits around the Sun, and moons travel in orbits around planets. Satellites orbit the Earth. To get into orbit around the Earth, a spacecraft has to fly out into space beyond the atmosphere where it is partly free from the Earth's gravity.

Which planets have rings around them?

Four planets have rings around them – Jupiter, Saturn, Uranus and Neptune. The rings are thin belts of rocks orbiting the planets. Saturn's rings make it the most beautiful planet in the sky.

▼ The four giant planets all have rings. Saturn has the biggest ring system.

Jupiter

Saturn

Uranus

Neptune

Which planet is so hot that lead would melt there?

The hottest planet is not Mercury, the planet nearest the Sun. It is Venus, the second nearest. It is very hot on Venus because, unlike Mercury, Venus has an atmosphere. The atmosphere acts rather like the windows in a greenhouse and helps to heat the surface of the planet. The temperature there is about 475 degrees Celsius, which is hot enough to melt several metals, including tin, lead and zinc. No plants or animals could live on the scorching, rocky surface.

Which planet turns so slowly that one day lasts two years?

Mercury is so near the Sun that the Sun has slowed its rotation. It spins so slowly that one complete day on Mercury – from one sunrise to the next – takes 176 Earth days. This is equal to two of Mercury's years, which are 88 Earth days long. On Mercury, you would have two birthdays every day!

Does a planet have to be bigger than a moon?

A moon is always smaller than the planet around which it moves. A smaller body always orbits around a larger body, because the larger body has a greater force of gravity. However, not all moons are smaller than all planets. Our Moon and six other moons of the outer planets are all bigger than the tiny planet Pluto. But Pluto may once have been a moon of Neptune.

PLANET FACTS

■ Mercury holds two records: it is the planet with the longest day and the shortest year.

■ Mars has two small rocky moons, Deimos and Phobos.

■ There are valleys on Mars that look like dried up river beds.

▶ Mars is a rocky planet and seems to be without life. It has an ice cap, mountains and craters.

▲ Mercury is the planet closest to the Sun. It is heavily scarred with craters, probably formed many millions of years ago.

What is the Red Planet?

The Red Planet is the fourth planet from the Sun, Mars. When it nears the Earth, it looks like a bright red star in the sky. Mars looks red because its surface is made of red soil and rock. Even its sky is red, because red dust floats in the atmosphere.

Which planet spins faster than any other?

The planet that spins the fastest is also the largest planet – Jupiter. It spins once around every 9 hours 50 minutes, 2½ times as fast as the Earth. A point on Jupiter's equator is moving around the planet's centre at a speed of more than 45,000 kilometres per hour. This is so fast that it makes Jupiter bulge in the middle.

Where is the highest mountain in the Solar System?

There were once volcanoes on Mars. A volcanic mountain, Olympus Mons, rises 23 kilometres above the surface. This is the highest mountain in the Solar System.

STARS AND GALAXIES

Where do stars form?

Stars form in clouds of gas and dust, as the Sun did. Far away in space, there are huge clouds of gas and dust called nebulae. Some nebulae are luminous and shine with light, and it is there that stars are forming. This process is going on right now.

How far away is the nearest star?

The nearest star to the Earth is the Sun. It is 152 million kilometres away, or nearly 12,000 times the diameter of the Earth.

How far away is the most distant star?

Our Sun is one of about 100,000 million stars that make up the galaxy. The most distant stars on the other side of the galaxy to the Sun are about 80,000 light years away. However, there are millions of other galaxies much farther away, each containing millions of stars.

Which is the brightest star?

The brightest star in the sky is the Sun. It outshines all the other stars because it is so near to us. The brightest star in the night sky is Sirius. It actually produces 25 times as much light as the Sun. Other stars are even brighter, and may be as much as a million times more luminous than the Sun. They look fainter than Sirius because they are much farther away.

▲ An infrared photograph of the Swan Nebula, a cloud of young stars and gas in the constellation Sagittarius.

Did you know that stars are being born all the time? Young stars begin their lives in star-nurseries called clusters.

How many stars are there in the sky?

On a very clear night, far from a town, you could count about 2,000 stars in the sky. From all points on the Earth, about 6,000 stars can be seen in all. With a telescope, many fainter stars reveal themselves. There are millions upon millions of stars in the universe.

Is the Sun an unusual kind of star?

To us on Earth, the Sun looks enormous and very bright. But this is only because we live so close to the Sun. Compared with most stars, it is of average size and brightness and it is not in any way unusual. There are millions of other 'suns', many bigger and much brighter.

ATOMS

Electron

Neutron

Nucleus

Electron orbit

Proton

What is an atom?

An atom is the smallest unit of a chemical element – iron or copper, for example – to have its own recognizable identity. Scientists can tell the atoms of one element from those of another by their structure. Atoms are the building blocks of the elements which make up all matter in the universe.

At the centre of an atom is its nucleus, which is made up of tiny particles called protons and neutrons. Orbiting the nucleus are other particles called electrons, held in place by electrical charges. The arrangement of protons, neutrons and electrons is different for each kind of atom.

How big is an atom?

Atoms are too small to be seen with the naked eye. But scientists using high-powered electron microscopes have photographed atoms. They look like fuzzy white dots.

The nucleus is ten thousand times smaller than the atom itself. Electrons are smaller still.

▲ In an atom, tiny protons and neutrons make up the centre or nucleus. The particles orbiting the nucleus are called electrons.

▼ Atoms are very small. If an atom were as big as your fingernail, your hand could pick up the Earth!

How many different kinds of atom are there?

There are 92 different chemical elements found in nature. Therefore there are 92 different kinds of atom forming these separate elements. A few other elements and atoms have been made by scientists in the laboratory. An atom of uranium is two hundred times heavier than an atom of hydrogen, but in fact all atoms are roughly the same size. There are about two million atoms in the thickness of this page.

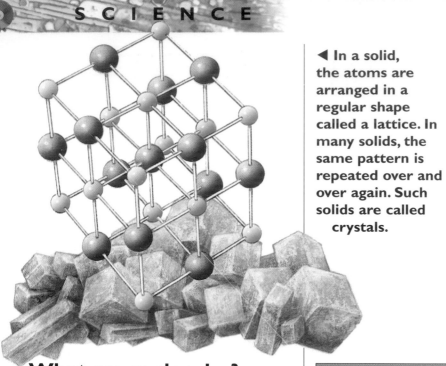

◀ **In a solid, the atoms are arranged in a regular shape called a lattice. In many solids, the same pattern is repeated over and over again. Such solids are called crystals.**

What are molecules?

A molecule is the smallest part of a substance that retains the nature of the substance. Take paper, for example. The thickness of each page of this book is roughly 100,000 paper molecules. If each paper molecule were broken up, it would no longer be paper, just a random group of atoms. Every molecule of a substance is made of exactly the same number of atoms linked together in exactly the same pattern.

Molecules are tiny. There are at least as many molecules in a teaspoon of water as there are teaspoonsful of water in the Atlantic Ocean.

Who first tried to weigh atoms?

The British chemist John Dalton (1766–1844) worked out that a molecule of water always contains the same proportions of oxygen and hydrogen. He thought oxygen atoms must be heavier than hydrogen atoms. In fact an oxygen atom weighs 16 times more than an hydrogen atom.

ATOM FACTS

■ In the 400s BC, the Greek scientist Democritus gave the name 'atom' to what he thought was the smallest particle of matter.

■ In 1818 Jons Berzelius, a Swedish chemist, classified 45 different substances by their atomic weights.

■ Berzelius also suggested naming elements by using the first letter or letters of their names, for example O = oxygen.

■ Atoms are incredibly light. There are about 600 billion trillion hydrogen atoms in a gram!

■ Electrons whizz around at amazing speed. They constantly change positions as they orbit the nucleus, making billions of trips in just one millionth of a second.

Who discovered electrons?

Electrons were discovered in 1895 by Sir Joseph John Thomson, a British scientist. Thomson worked in the Cavendish Laboratory at Cambridge University and was investigating the rays produced when an electric current passed through a vacuum. For this discovery he received the Nobel Prize for Physics in 1906.

Sir Joseph John Thomson

Who first split the atom?

Until the early 1900s, nobody knew how the atom was arranged. Sir Joseph John Thomson thought that the atom looked something like a plum pudding, with electrons scattered around like currants. Ernest Rutherford, in 1911, and Niels Bohr, in 1913, put forward different ideas.

Rutherford, a New Zealander, discovered the nucleus of the atom and proved that the electrons were very light. Bohr, a Danish physicist, devised the 'sun and planets' model of particles orbiting the nucleus of the atom. This theory is accepted by most scientists today.

Rutherford did what the Ancient Greeks thought impossible. He split the atom, and in so doing changed one substance into another. He bombarded atoms of nitrogen gas with alpha particles. This changed them into oxygen and hydrogen atoms. Rutherford first split the atom in 1919, while working at Cambridge University in Britain.

ELEMENTS AND MATTER

What is an element?

An element is a substance made up of only one kind of atom. All the atoms in an element have the same atomic number, and it is impossible to break up an element into parts that have different chemical properties.

There are 92 elements found in nature. Others can be made only in the laboratory during atomic reactions. In all, 109 elements have been officially found, though scientists claim to have discovered two more.

The most common element in the Earth's crust is oxygen (about 50 percent by weight). Next comes silicon (about 28 percent by weight). Each element has a symbol that stands for its name; for example, He (helium), Cu (copper), Zn (zinc), Fe (iron). This makes it easier when writing out long chemical formulas.

▶ Flame tests can identify chemical elements. Platinum wire dipped in compounds of these elements produce a different colour when heated.

▼ The periodic table shows all the elements in order of atomic number. Elements of atoms with similar structures and properties are logically grouped together. The main groups are non-metals, alkali metals, transition metals and the inner transition series metals.

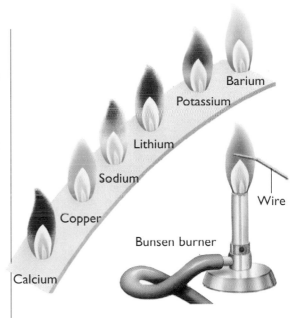

Barium
Potassium
Lithium
Sodium
Copper
Calcium
Wire
Bunsen burner

What is a mineral?

Gold, silver and mercury are examples of pure elements, but most chemical elements react with other elements so readily that they are not found singly on Earth. Instead, they combine (join) with one another as minerals. Some 3,000 minerals are known.

																	2 Helium He
3 Lithium Li	4 Beryllium Be	Alkali metals			Transition metals			1 Hydrogen H		5 Boron B	6 Carbon C	7 Nitrogen N	8 Oxygen O	9 Fluorine F	10 Neon Ne
11 Sodium Na	12 Magnesium Mg	Non-metals			Inner transition series					13 Aluminium Al	14 Silicon Si	15 Phosphorus P	16 Sulphur S	17 Chlorine Cl	18 Argon Ar
19 Potassium K	20 Calcium Ca	21 Scandium Sc	22 Titanium Ti	23 Vanadium V	24 Chromium Cr	25 Manganese Mn	26 Iron Fe	27 Cobalt Co	28 Nickel Ni	29 Copper Cu	30 Zinc Zn	31 Gallium Ga	32 Germanium Ge	33 Arsenic As	34 Selenium Se	35 Bromine Br	36 Krypton Kr
37 Rubidium Rb	38 Strontium Sr	39 Yttrium Y	40 Zirconium Zr	41 Niobium Nb	42 Molybdenum Mo	43 Technetium Tc	44 Ruthenium Ru	45 Rhodium Rh	46 Palladium Pd	47 Silver Ag	48 Cadmium Cd	49 Indium In	50 Tin Sn	51 Antimony Sb	52 Tellurium Te	53 Iodine I	54 Xenon Xe
55 Caesium Cs	56 Barium Ba	57-71 Lanthanide series	72 Hafnium Hf	73 Tantalum Ta	74 Tungsten W	75 Rhenium Re	76 Osmium Os	77 Iridium Ir	78 Platinum Pt	79 Gold Au	80 Mercury Hg	81 Thallium Tl	82 Lead Pb	83 Bismuth Bi	84 Polonium Po	85 Astatine At	86 Radon Rn
87 Francium Fc	88 Radium Ra	89-103 Actinide series	104 Rutherfordium Rf	105 Element 105	106 Element 106	107 Element 107	108 Element 108	109 Element 109									

57 Lanthanum La	58 Cerium Ce	59 Praesodmium Pm	60 Neodymium Nd	61 Promethlcum Pm	62 Samarium Sm	63 Europium Eu	64 Gadolinium Gd	65 Terbium Tb	66 Dysprosium Dy	67 Holmium Ho	68 Erbium Er	69 Thulium Tm	70 Ytterbium Yb	71 Lutetium Lu
89 Actinium Ac	90 Thorium Th	91 Protactinium Pa	92 Uranium U	93 Neptunium Np	94 Plutonium Pu	95 Americium Am	96 Curium Cm	97 Berkelium Bk	98 Californium Cf	99 Einsteinium Es	100 Fermium Fm	101 Mendelevium Md	102 Nobelium No	103 Lawrencium Lr

What are the three states of matter?

The three states in which matter exists are solid, liquid and gas. Solids have both shape and volume; their molecules are held together tightly. Liquids have volume too, but no shape; their molecules are held together less tightly, so that a liquid will flow into a container. Gases have neither volume nor shape; their molecules are free to move about and a gas will fill any container which encloses it.

When you dry your hair, warm air blown from the dryer turns the water on your hair to water vapour, which is absorbed by the air. Washing on a line dries this way too.

Can matter change its state?

Many substances change state quite easily, when heated or cooled. Water is a liquid at normal temperature but changes to a gas (water vapour) when heated. When water is cooled, it becomes a solid (ice). When ice is heated, it changes first to water and then to water vapour (steam).

What is evaporation?

When a liquid is heated, it will change to a vapour. The steam coming from a boiling kettle is water vapour, a gas. The same thing happens when hot sun shines on a wet road: water vapour can be seen rising. This is evaporation. Evaporation can be used to extract salt from salty water. Boiling causes the water to evaporate as vapour and solid salt crystals are left behind.

▲ If you pour hot water (liquid) onto ice (solid), you see water vapour (gas) rising. Water is the only compound that is liquid in its natural form.

▶ These long coloured streamers are crystals growing in a solution of sodium silicate (water glass).

Why does a balloon burst when you squeeze it?

If you blow up a balloon, and then squeeze it, the volume of air inside is reduced, and its pressure increases. Eventually the pressure of air inside becomes so great that the balloon bursts. This is a practical demonstration of one aspect of gases' behaviour discovered in 1662 by the scientist Robert Boyle.

How are crystals formed?

Crystals are solids found in nature in an almost endless variety of sizes and shapes. Most solid matter, including nearly all minerals and metals, are crystalline. You can watch crystals form in a sugar solution. If you add sugar to water, the sugar dissolves to make a sugar and water solution. If you heat the solution to boiling point, the water will begin to evaporate. The remaining solution will contain more and more sugar. Eventually, the water that is left will be 'saturated' with sugar and the sugar will begin to form crystals.

What is a chemical reaction?

When two or more substances are put together, they may mix, as when you mix sand and water in a bucket, but remain separate substances. However, if a chemical reaction takes place, they may undergo a chemical change and become a different kind of substance. For example, when zinc is added to hydrochloric acid, a reaction occurs. The products are hydrogen gas and zinc chloride.

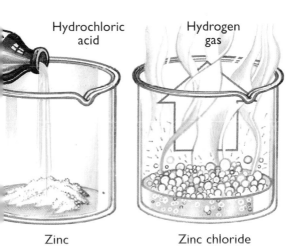

Hydrochloric acid   Hydrogen gas

Zinc   Zinc chloride

▶ An iron chain will rust in air or water. Air and water contain oxygen. Oxygen is very effective at taking electrons from iron atoms to form a compound called iron oxide, seen as brownish-red rust.

◀ Zinc is a metal. Hydrochloric acid is a liquid. When zinc and hydrochloric acid are mixed, the acid reacts with the metal to form a new compound, zinc chloride.

Water

Oxygen

Rusted metal

What is a compound?

A compound is a substance made up of two or more elements which cannot be separated by physical means. For example, water is a compound of hydrogen and oxygen. Each water molecule is made up of two hydrogen atoms joined to one oxygen atom by invisible forces called bonds.

Why does iron go rusty?

When a piece of unpainted iron or steel is left outside in the damp air, it soon goes rusty. Rust can eat into the surface of metal objects, such as car bodies. Rust is an example of a chemical reaction, or combination, between the iron in the car bodywork

Salt speeds up rusting. You can test this by putting pieces of wire wool in two tubes. Fill one tube with plain tap water. Mix salt and water in the other. See which piece of wire wool rusts first. Try the same experiment with boiled water. Boiling removes air from the water. What happens to the wire wool?

and the oxygen in the air. This reaction is called oxidation and produces iron oxide, or rust. A coating of paint, or of a non-rusting metal such as chrome, prevents rust by stopping oxygen reaching the iron.

What did Lavoisier discover?

Antoine Lavoisier, who lived from 1743 to 1794, was a French scientist and one of the founders of modern chemistry. His most important discovery was that matter cannot be destroyed during a chemical reaction, even though it may change its appearance. This is one of the basic laws of science: the law of conservation of mass. It means that the amount of matter produced by a chemical reaction must always be the same as the amount that took part in the reaction. Lavoisier was executed on the guillotine during the French Revolution.

Why are there so many carbon compounds?

Carbon is the only element whose atoms are able to join together to form chains, rings and other more complicated bonds. This means that there is a huge number of organic (carbon) compounds; nearly four million are known.

What are diamonds made of?

Diamond is a form of carbon. It is the hardest substance known. Natural, uncut diamonds look dull and have little lustre. The brilliant gems that are so valuable are made by careful cutting and polishing.

What is an acid?

An acid is a chemical compound containing hydrogen and at least one other element. For example, sulphuric acid (formula H_2SO_4) is made up of hydrogen (H), sulphur (S) and oxygen (O). Acids are normally found as liquids.

Certain acids, known as organic acids, are found in food plants. For instance, citric acids are found in lemons and oranges, and malic acid is found in apples, plums and rhubarb.

Why are some acids dangerous?

In concentrated form, some acids are so strong that they burn skin and even dissolve metals. When diluted with water, they are less harmful.

▼ Carbon occurs in three forms. In diamond, the carbon atoms are arranged in a regular framework called a lattice. In graphite, the atoms are in layers. Amorphous carbon has no regular structure.

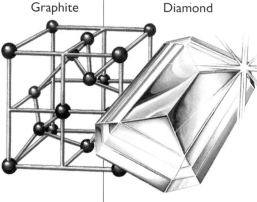

Graphite   Diamond

ACID FACTS

■ Some acids can eat through glass, and so must be kept in special containers.

■ The human body produces weak hydrochloric acid to aid the breakdown of foods during digestion.

■ Sulphuric acid is probably the most important chemical compound. It has dozens of uses, including making fertilizers and drugs.

■ When World War I began in 1914, lots of nitric acid was needed to make explosives such as nitroglycerine. German chemist Fritz Haber invented a new way to make nitric acid by heating ammonia and air.

How can you test for acid?

A simple test for an acid is to dip a piece of blue litmus paper into the liquid. Litmus paper is stained with a blue dye from a fungus which turns red in acid. If acid is present, the litmus paper will turn red.

What is a base?

A base is a substance which reacts with an acid to form a salt plus water. Most bases are the oxides or hydroxides of metals: in other words they are the products of reactions with oxygen or hydrogen. One of the most easily remembered chemical rules concerns acids and bases. It is this: Acid + Base = Salt + Water. When this happens, the acid and base are said to *neutralize* one another.

What is a metal?

Elements can be divided into two basic groups: metals and non-metals. Metals can be made to shine or have a lustre, they conduct heat and electricity easily and they are 'malleable' – they can be beaten into shape or pulled out into wire. More than 70 of the known elements are metals.

What is an alloy?

An alloy is a mixture of metals or of metal and another substance. Copper, for example, is a pure metal. When copper and tin (another pure metal) are mixed together by heating them until they melt, they make an alloy called bronze – the earliest known alloy. Copper and zinc together make brass. Steel is an alloy of iron and carbon.

Which metal most easily conducts heat and electricity?

Silver has the highest conductivity of all known metals. It is also valued for its beautiful appearance. Because it is easily worked, and has a bright, light-reflecting finish, it has been used since ancient times for making jewellery, coins and ornaments.

Which is the most abundant metal on Earth?

The metal found most plentifully in the Earth's crust is aluminium, which makes up about 8 percent of the crust. It is found not as a pure metal but as an ore called bauxite.

Which metals give colour to fireworks?

Strontium burns with a red light, copper green, sodium yellow, barium green and magnesium a brilliant white light.

What is the air around us mostly made of?

About 78 percent (by volume) is nitrogen, about 21 percent is oxygen. Carbon dioxide, water vapour, helium and other gases make up the rest.

Heat never stays still. It is always moving. When you stir a hot drink, heat energy moves from the drink into the spoon. That's why the spoon gets hot.

▶ A fire extinguisher smothers a fire with carbon dioxide gas. Without oxygen, the fire dies.

◀ People who make fireworks know that certain metals will give off different colours when the fireworks are burned.

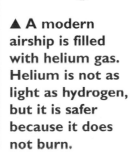

▲ A modern airship is filled with helium gas. Helium is not as light as hydrogen, but it is safer because it does not burn.

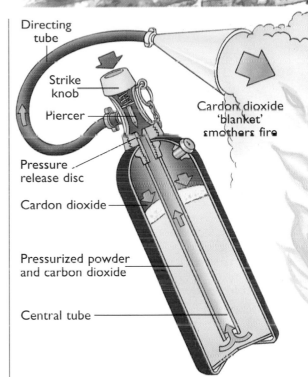

Directing tube

Strike knob

Piercer

Pressure release disc

Carbon dioxide

Pressurized powder and carbon dioxide

Central tube

Carbon dioxide 'blanket' smothers fire

Why will carbon dioxide put out fires?

Carbon dioxide gas will not support combustion. Pure carbon dioxide is also heavier than air. If sprayed on a fire from a fire extinguisher it forms a blanket, cutting off the oxygen which would otherwise feed the flames.

Which gas is most suited for use in balloons and airships?

Hydrogen is the lightest gas and was used in early balloons and airships. But it has the great disadvantage of being highly inflammable and several large airships have exploded with great loss of life. Helium is second to hydrogen in lightness. Because helium does not catch fire, it is much safer and is used in modern lighter-than-air craft. The two gases helium and hydrogen make up most of the matter in the Sun and other stars.

ELECTRICITY, MAGNETISM AND ELECTRONICS

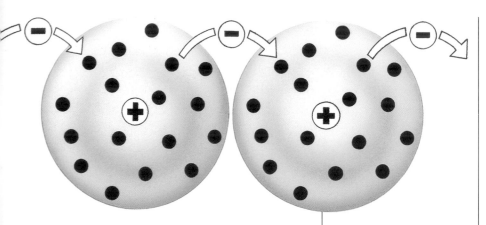

What is electricity?

Electricity is a form of energy. It is produced when electrons, tiny atomic particles, move from one atom to another. Although scientists had known that this mysterious energy existed, its workings were not understood until the secrets of the atom began to be revealed about a century ago.

Without electricity, our lives would be very different. We would have no radios or televisions, no telephones, no computers. Our streets and homes would be lit by oil or gas lamps and we would have none of the gadgets that we take for granted today.

Who proved that lightning was electric?

In 1752, the American scientist Benjamin Franklin determined to find out if electricity and lightning were connected. He carried out a very dangerous experiment. He took a kite and attached to it a metal rod. Then he tied the end of the kite string to a

▲ The positively charged (+) protons of an atom attracts negatively charged (–) electrons. Electricity flows when electrons are free to move from one atom to another.

▼ In Franklin's experiment, lightning sent an electric charge down the kite string to a key, producing a spark.

door key and went out into a thunderstorm. When he flew the kite into a thundercloud, he saw sparks flash and felt a shock as electricity from the cloud passed from the kite down the string to the key. Never try this experiment yourself!

After this, Franklin made and tested the first lightning conductor. Today, all tall buildings are fitted with lightning conductors, which attract lightning more readily than the buildings. The connecting cable safely carries the electricity to the ground, preventing damage to the building.

◄ Rub a balloon against a wool or nylon jumper. This makes static electricity build up on the balloon's skin. Hold the balloon against a wall and it should cling there.

About 100 years ago, few people had electricity in their homes. The first electrical gadgets were dangerous, and servants sometimes risked their lives using them.

How can objects be electrically charged?

All matter is made up of atoms. Normally, each atom has the same number of electrons and protons (see page 57). The positive charge of the protons and the negative charge of the electrons cancel each other out. But if this balance is upset, the object becomes electrically charged. For example, if a balloon is rubbed with cloth, electrons pass from the cloth to the balloon. The balloon becomes negatively charged, and the cloth having lost electrons, becomes positively charged. Unlike charges always attract each other, so the cloth clings to the balloon.

What is a conductor?

A conductor is a material through which electricity can pass. Electricity travels more easily through some materials than others. Metals are good conductors of electricity. Lightning conductors are made of copper, which conducts electricity easily.

► Rubber is a good insulator. It has few free electrons and so does not conduct electricity well. Plastic, ceramics and glass, also poor conductors, are used as insulators in electrical equipment.

What are superconductors?

When made very cold, certain substances have almost no resistance to electricity; they become superconductors. This was first observed in 1911 using mercury. More than 25 other metals, including copper and various alloys, behave in the same way. Superconducting coils that allow current to flow practically non-stop are used in particle accelerators. New materials that superconduct at room temperature are being developed.

What is an insulator?

An insulator is a material that will not conduct electricity. Good insulators are diamond, glass, paper, plastic, rubber and many gases. That is why the wires inside an electrical cable are enclosed in a rubber or plastic sheath. The plug on the end of the wire is also made of rubber or plastic. The insulating material protects us from getting a shock when we touch the cable or the plug because it does not conduct electricity easily.

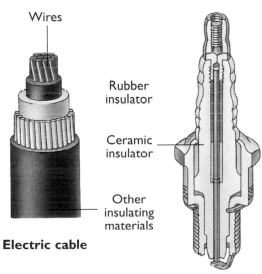

Spark plug

Wires

Rubber insulator

Ceramic insulator

Other insulating materials

Electric cable

LIGHT AND SOUND

What is light?

No one really knows what light is made of. In the 1600s Sir Isaac Newton thought light was made up of bullet-like particles which he called corpuscles. The Dutch scientist Christiaan Huygens thought light was made up of pulses, or waves, travelling through space. Modern science has found some truth in both theories. Light certainly does travel in waves, but it also behaves as if it were made of particles. Scientists now call these light particles photons.

Light is a form of energy, similar to heat. It is the only type of energy we can see. Light comes from a star such as the Sun and travels through space. Stars shine as a result of their immense nuclear energy.

The shortest light waves that we can see are blue or violet. The longest light waves we can see are red. There are other waves, shorter and longer, that we cannot see but some animals can. A bee sees colours beyond violet, but it sees red objects as black.

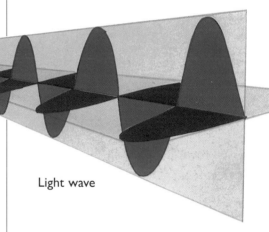

Light wave

▶ **Light is a kind of electromagnetic radiation. It travels as a wave made up of an electric field and a magnetic field at right angles to each other and to the direction of the wave's travel.**

◀ **The three primary colours when mixing light are red, green and blue. Added together, they make white. Paint pigments mix differently. Their primary colours are yellow, blue and red. Mixed together, they make brown.**

How fast does light travel?

Light travels at enormous speed, at roughly 300,000 kilometres a second (186,000 miles a second). At this speed, the light from the Sun still takes more than eight minutes to reach the Earth. The speed of light was first measured accurately in 1676, by Olaf Roemer of Denmark. Nothing travels faster than light.

What are light waves?

If you throw a pebble into a pool, it sends out ripples of waves. Light also travels in waves. In 1873 the British scientist James Clerk Maxwell discovered the wave-structure of light after 20 years' research. He showed that light is made up of vibrating waves of electrical and magnetic fields. The vibrations take place at right angles to the direction of the wave's motion, and to each other. Maxwell was the first to suggest that light was a form of electromagnetic radiation. He went on to state that other kinds of rays must also exist, invisible to the eye.

What makes light bend?

Light is bent when it is bounced back from a surface, such as a mirror. This bending is called reflection. Light is also bent when it travels from one transparent surface to another. This bending is called refraction. It explains why a pencil standing half in and half out of water looks broken.

What makes the colours of the rainbow?

The rainbow is nature's spectrum. Falling drops of rain behave like tiny prisms. They break up white sunlight into the colours of the spectrum.

The first person to show that white light is a mixture of colours was Sir Isaac Newton. Between 1665 and 1666, he carried out experiments in a darkened room. He put a glass prism in a beam of sunlight streaming through a small hole in the wall, and saw it split into the colours of the rainbow: red, orange, yellow, green, blue, indigo and violet. When he placed a second prism in the coloured beam, he saw the light rays bend back and become white again.

▼ When light passes through a glass prism, it splits into the colours of the rainbow: red, orange, yellow, green, blue, indigo and violet. This is known as the spectrum.

▶ When you look in a mirror, your left side looks to be on your left. If you were looking at another person, their left side would be to your right. Light always travels in straight lines. So the mirror reflects light rays from your left side straight back to you on the left.

LENSES AND MIRRORS FACTS

■ The first mirrors were made of highly polished metal, such as bronze.

■ Making glass mirrors, by coating one side of the glass with silver to make it reflect light, was not perfected until the 1600s.

■ A lens that is thinner in the middle than at the edges is said to be concave.

■ A lens that is thicker in the middle than at the edges is convex.

■ A concave lens spreads light passing through it and makes objects looks smaller. A convex lens narrows the light and makes things look bigger.

■ The Arabs knew of the magnifying glass about the year 1000. The first spectacles were made soon after this.

Why do mirrors reflect our images?

Everything reflects light, even the pages of this book. But most surfaces are rough, so the light is diffused, or spread in all directions. We can see the pages of this book from wherever we stand in the room. A mirror's smooth, shiny surface reflects light much more accurately as parallel rays so giving a clear image.

Who invented the telescope?

Lenses are glass or plastic discs that bend light to make objects look larger or smaller. In about 1600 a Dutch spectacle-maker named Hans Lippershey put two lenses together and looked through them at the weather vane on a distant church. He was startled to see how large the weather vane appeared. He had made the first telescope. Soon telescopes were being made all over Europe.

Spectrum

Glass prism

How does a periscope work?

A simple periscope can be made with two flat mirrors, set at an angle of 45°. Light is reflected from the top mirror down to the lower one. In this way, it is possible to see an object over a wall, or above water even when you are in a submerged submarine.

Who invented the microscope?

The microscope was invented in the early 1600s, and there are several claimants for its invention, among them Zacharias Janssen of Holland. What is surprising is that lenses had been known and made in Europe for more than 300 years before this invention, but no one had thought of combining them to make either a microscope or a telescope.

What are the most powerful microscopes?

The best optical microscope cannot magnify an object more than two thousand times. An electron microscope can magnify more than a million times. Electromagnetic fields are the microscope's 'lenses'. A hot wire filament sends a stream of electrons in a beam to hit the object to be examined. The denser areas of the object stop some electrons passing through. The rest travel on and hit a television screen or a photographic plate. The result is a 'shadow picture' of the object.

▶ **In the late 1800s, it took so long to take a photo that people needed a back-rest to help them sit still. Eyes looked blurred if the sitter blinked.**

Submarines have periscopes so people inside can see what is going on above water while the submarine stays hidden. Submarines often cruise with just the periscope showing. But the world's longest periscope is on land. It is 27 metres long and is used at a laboratory in the United States so that scientists can study nuclear reactors without being exposed to dangerous radiation.

When was the first photograph taken?

The earliest known photograph was taken by the French scientist Joseph Niepce in 1826. It was made on an asphalt-coated pewter plate, and shows a view from a window. The exposure took eight hours.

In the 1830s and 1840s two new photographic processes were developed. They were the daguerreotype of the Frenchman L.J.M. Daguerre and the calotype of the Englishman W.H. Fox Talbot. The daguerreotype used a silver-copper plate instead of glass. It took a minute to expose the plate. In 1888 the American George Eastman invented the Kodak camera, which used roll film instead of plates.

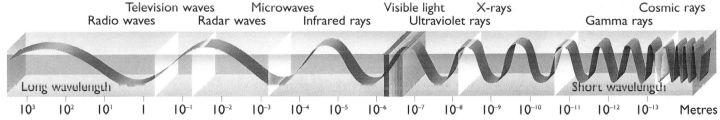

Television waves   Microwaves   Visible light   X-rays   Cosmic rays
Radio waves   Radar waves   Infrared rays   Ultraviolet rays   Gamma rays

Long wavelength   Short wavelength

10^3 10^2 10^1 1 10^{-1} 10^{-2} 10^{-3} 10^{-4} 10^{-5} 10^{-6} 10^{-7} 10^{-8} 10^{-9} 10^{-10} 10^{-11} 10^{-12} 10^{-13} Metres

Are there rays that we cannot see?

In the 1870s James Clerk Maxwell predicted other forms of radiation beyond the visible spectrum – in other words, ones we cannot see. The electromagnetic spectrum is a band of radiation of which light is just one part. The rays travel through space in waves of varying lengths. We can see light rays, but other parts of the spectrum are invisible to the eye. At the red end of the visible light spectrum are infrared, microwaves, radar, television and radio waves. At the other (violet) end of the spectrum are ultraviolet, X-rays, gamma rays and cosmic rays.

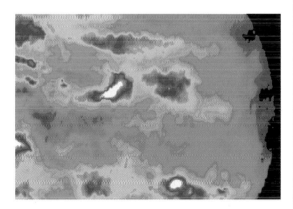

What can infrared photography show up?

We feel infrared rays when we sit in front of an electric fire and feel the 'radiant' heat from its bars. More than half of the Sun's energy comes to us in the form of infrared rays. Infrared photography from space can detect tiny temperature changes on Earth.

▲ The electromagnetic spectrum ranges from long wavelength radio waves through light waves to short wavelength gamma rays. All electromagnetic waves travel at the speed of light.

Because dense cloud covers Venus, radar had to be used to map the planet's surface. In 1990 the *Magellan* spacecraft sent back a radar picture of Venus, revealing its active volcanoes and craters.

◄ A near infrared map of the cloud cover over Venus, taken by the *Magellan* space probe in 1990. Infrared photos of the Earth can reveal diseased crops in fields, and track warm and cold water currents in the oceans.

Who discovered X-rays?

The German scientist Wilhelm Roentgen discovered X-rays by accident in 1895. He was experimenting with a cathode ray tube and noticed that crystals in the same room glowed when the tube was switched on. Even when he moved the crystals to the next room, they still glowed. Roentgen realized that invisible rays were causing the glow. The rays could even penetrate solid walls. He called them X-rays (X = unknown).

How was radar invented?

Radar was invented in the 1930s. It worked by transmitting a radio beam from the ground. Any object crossing the beam (such as an aircraft) produced an 'echo', and this could be received on the ground and used to work out the height and position of the aircraft.

How did the laser get its name?

The first laser was made in 1960 by an American scientist, Theodore H. Maiman. Its name comes from a set of initials that stand for Light Amplification by Stimulated Emission of Radiation. A laser produces a powerful beam of light, so powerful it can burn a hole through metal. Unlike the light from a torch, a laser beam spreads hardly at all.

What is a hologram?

The Greek word *holos* means 'whole'. A hologram is a 'whole picture', or a three-dimensional picture. A hologram is made by illuminating an object with laser light. The three-dimensional picture is viewed by shining a laser of the same colour or wavelength through the hologram. The principle of the hologram was worked out by the Hungarian-born physicist Dennis Gabor in 1948, but making holograms was not possible before the invention of the laser.

How can light be used to send telephone calls?

In a telephone, sounds are changed into electrical signals and sent through wires. In 1966 scientists succeeded in using lasers to carry telephone calls by changing the electrical signals into light-pulses. Instead of wires, they used optical fibres – very long, thin glass rods. The light-pulses travel inside the rods, kept in by the mirror-like sheath. At the end of the cable the pulses are changed back into sounds.

▼ **A single optical fibre can carry hundreds of telephone conversations as pulses moving along strands of glass.**

Dennis Gabor

Bank and credit cards contain holograms to make the card design more difficult for forgers to copy. Holograms are used to make jewellery and in advertising displays. They can also detect faults in lenses, tyres, and aircraft wings.

▶ **The loudness of sound is how strong it seems when the soundwaves hit our ears. Loudness is measured in decibels. Noises louder than about 140 decibels can cause pain!**

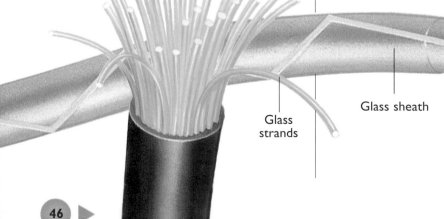

Glass strands

Glass sheath

What causes sound?

Sounds can be very different – the roar of a jet engine, the music of an orchestra, the song of a bird – but all sounds are made in a similar way. When an object vibrates (moves backwards and forwards), it produces sound.

Sound is a form of energy. Like light, it travels in waves. But sound needs something to travel through. Sound cannot travel in a vacuum such as space.

Rocket lift-off
150–190 decibels

Jet lift-off
120–140 decibels

Thunder
95–115 decibels

Motorbike
70–90 decibels

Vacuum cleaner
60–80 decibels

Orchestra
50–70 decibels

Talking
30–60 decibels

Whispering
20–30 decibels

Falling leaves
20 decibels

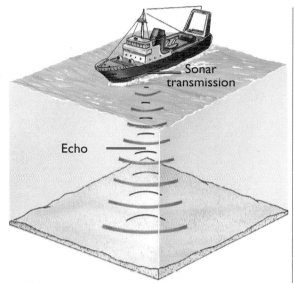

Sonar transmission

Echo

What causes an echo?

Have you ever stood inside an old cathedral and heard your voice echoing from the thick, stone walls? The same thing happens inside a cave, or where there are cliffs or high walls. The echo is caused by the sound waves bouncing off the hard wall. The sound is reflected back to your ear and you hear an echo of your voice.

Ships use echo-sounders, devices that send out pulses of sound, to tell how deep the water is. This technique is known as sonar, which is short for SOund Navigation And Ranging.

Why is the Moon a silent world?

You can hear sounds underwater. In fact, sound travels faster through water than through air. Sound can also travel through metal, such as steel. But no sound can travel across the airless surface of the Moon. The astronauts who explored the Moon talked to one another by radio. There were no other sounds, not even when they hit a rock with a hammer. It is impossible for sound to travel through the vacuum of outer space.

◄ Ships use sonar to tell how deep the sea bed is. The echoes bounce back from the bottom. Using this method, a survey ship can chart the sea bed.

▼ A sound's frequency is the number of vibrations per second, and is measured in Hertz (Hz). We can hear sounds between about 16 Hz and 20,000 Hz. Some animals emit and receive frequencies far beyond those we can hear.

Is there really a sound barrier?

Before the late 1940s no aircraft had flown faster than sound. People wondered if there was a mysterious 'sound barrier', but the invention of jet planes proved it could be broken. Jets flew faster than sound without being shaken apart and without harm to their pilots. Today the supersonic airliner Concorde regularly carries passengers across the Atlantic at twice the speed of sound.

Are there sounds we cannot hear?

Human ears are most sensitive to sounds at around 2,000 Hertz (Hz). The lowest sound we can hear is about 16 Hz and the highest is about 20,000 Hz. Dogs can hear higher-pitched sounds. Some dog owners use whistles that make a sound too high for them to hear, but which is heard perfectly well by their pet.

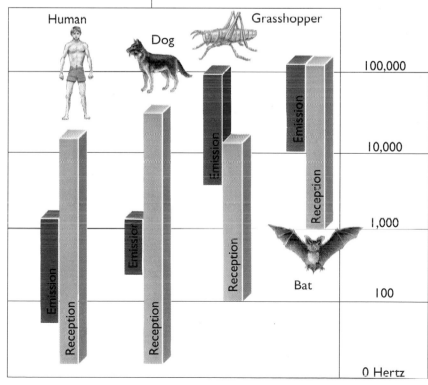

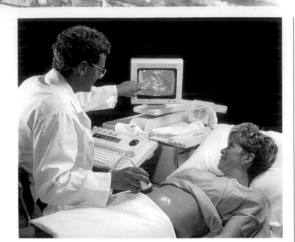

◄ An ultrasound scanner shows how an unborn baby is developing inside the womb of a pregnant woman.

◄ The 'tape recorder' invented by Valdemar Poulsen did not look much like a modern portable stereo. The sound was stored on metal wire, not on plastic tape.

How do doctors examine unborn babies with the help of sound waves?

Ultrasonic waves penetrate flesh and other soft body parts, just like X-rays, and they can be used to produce pictures of the inside of the body. Because the sound waves have no harmful effects, doctors use ultrasonic scanners to examine pregnant women. The scan shows if the unborn baby in the womb is healthy and growing properly.

When were sounds first recorded?

The first sound recording was made by the American inventor Thomas Alva Edison in 1877 on a machine he called the phonograph. Sounds were picked up by a vibrating membrane, and the vibrations made a needle cut spiral grooves on a cylinder covered with tinfoil. When a second needle was moved along the grooves, the sounds were reproduced by means of another vibrating membrane and amplified through a horn.

▼ Edison's phonograph of 1877 recorded sounds as grooves cut into a foil-covered cylinder. Flat records were invented in 1887.

► In digital recording the signals are changed into off-on electrical pulses. Analogue recording builds up a continuous sound 'image'.

When was recording tape first used?

The first experiments with sound recording on tape were made in 1898 by the Danish inventor Valdemar Poulsen, using magnetized metal wire. In the 1930s paper tapes were developed and reel-to-reel tape recorders appeared in the 1940s. Today's cassette players use plastic tape coated with magnetic material.

What is digital recording?

In older recording systems, the electrical signals are stored as a continuous wave pattern. These build up a replica or analogue of the original sounds. In digital recording, as used on music CDs, the sound waves are converted into electrical pulses which are coded as a series of numbers (digits) in binary form. Digital recordings give more accurate reproduction, because they store much more information about the sounds being recorded.

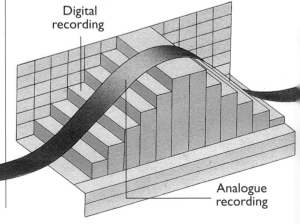

Digital recording

Analogue recording

ENERGY AND MOTION

What is energy?

Energy is the ability to do work. When you walk upstairs, or even when you are resting, your body is working, and uses energy. The spring inside a clockwork motor provides the energy to drive the mechanism. A torch battery provides the energy needed to light up the bulb. The Sun's energy enables plants to grow. In fact, all living things depend on the Sun for their energy. Energy can neither be created nor destroyed.

Where does energy come from?

Energy comes from matter. Everything in the universe is made up of matter, so in some form energy is found everywhere. Even the tiniest atomic particles can be changed into energy. Matter can be changed into energy and energy can be changed into matter.

Are there different kinds of energy?

Energy that is stored up is called potential energy. Water stored behind a dam, an archer's bow drawn and ready to fire, both of these are examples of potential energy. Falling water and an arrow shot from a bow each have kinetic energy. Potential and kinetic energy are both forms of mechanical energy. There are other kinds of energy too: thermal or heat energy, chemical energy, nuclear energy and radiant energy.

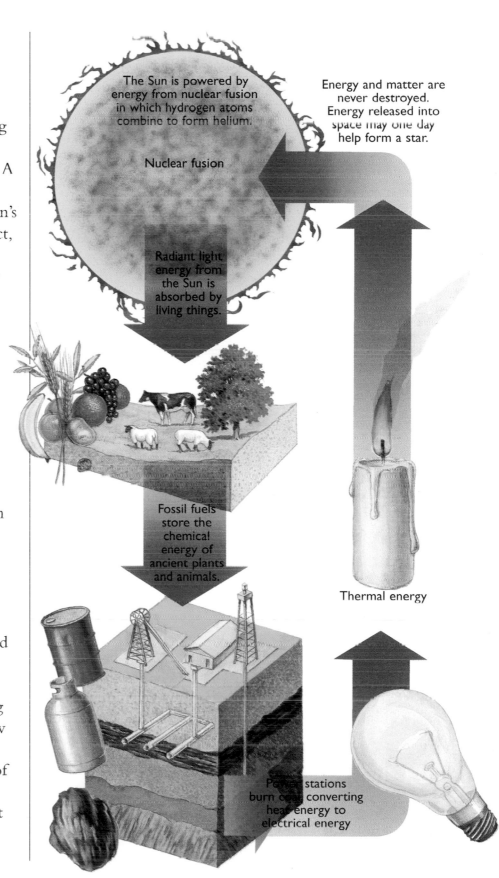

The Sun is powered by energy from nuclear fusion in which hydrogen atoms combine to form helium.

Nuclear fusion

Energy and matter are never destroyed. Energy released into space may one day help form a star.

Radiant light energy from the Sun is absorbed by living things.

Fossil fuels store the chemical energy of ancient plants and animals.

Thermal energy

Power stations burn oil, converting heat energy to electrical energy

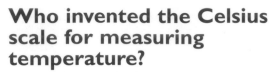

What are fossil fuels?

Much of the energy we use at home and at work comes from the burning of so-called fossil fuels such as coal, oil and gas. These fuels were formed millions of years ago from the remains of plants and animals.

Why do things become hot?

Heat is the transfer of energy from one substance to another. If you rub a piece of cloth with your hand, the cloth will begin to feel warmer. The rubbing has produced heat, as a result of friction.

How can heat travel?

Heat travels in several ways. The heat you feel when you hold a saucepan handle is carried by conduction. The heat energy inside an electric kettle is carried by convection. An electric fire with a shiny reflector sends out heat waves by radiation. Substances that carry heat well are called good conductors of heat. Metals are the best conductors – that is why we use metal cooking pots.

In the Celsius or Centigrade scale, the boiling point of water is 100 degrees. Scientists use another scale, the Kelvin scale, in which the boiling point of water is 373 degrees. On this scale, water freezes at 273 degrees.

▼ The air above a warm radiator (left) rises and cool air moves in creating a convection current. Heat from a match (centre) sets molecules of air moving, causing heat rays. As a metal spoon gets hot (right), molecules at the heated end move faster and collide with their neighbours, setting them moving.

Who invented the Celsius scale for measuring temperature?

The earliest scale for measuring temperature was invented by a Dutchman called Gabriel Fahrenheit in the early 1700s. This scale, named after him, has the freezing point of water at 32 degrees, and the boiling point at 212 degrees. In 1742 a Swede named Anders Celsius suggested a scale in which the freezing point of water would be fixed as 0 degrees.

What is the coldest anything can be?

When a substance is warmed, its molecules move about faster. When it is cooled, they move more slowly. The coldest that anything can get is when its molecules stop moving. This is at a temperature of minus 273 degrees Celsius (−273°C), or 'absolute zero'.

Scientists have not yet achieved zero, but they have managed temperatures close to it.

Conduction

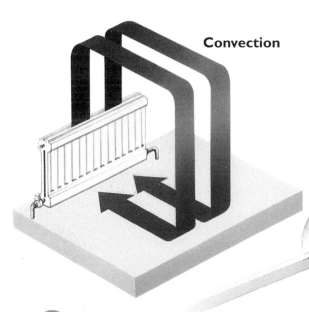

Convection

Radiation

◄ The ice in an iceberg is less dense than the surrounding water, so it floats. Water expands (and so becomes less dense) when it becomes colder than 4°C.

Why does an iceberg float?

Unlike most liquids, water expands (gets bigger) when it freezes and becomes less dense as a result. An ice cube will therefore float in a glass of water and not sink. This fact explains why huge icebergs float and also why rivers do not freeze solid in winter. Ice forms as a floating layer on top, and this layer stops further freezing beneath. If the ice sank to the bottom, the river would quickly freeze solid.

What are the oldest known machines?

A machine is a device for doing work, and the oldest known machines are the simplest: the wedge, the lever and the inclined plane. These were used by Stone Age people 100,000 years ago. Their inventors are unknown. The wheel was a later discovery, and was not in common use until about 5,000 years ago.

ICE FACTS

■ Salt water freezes at a lower temperature than fresh water.

■ The thickest ice in the world covers the Antarctic continent to a depth of 4,800 m.

■ Only the tip of an iceberg shows above water. About 80 percent of an iceberg (or even more) is hidden beneath the water's surface.

■ The largest icebergs break off the Antarctic ice cap. The biggest was 320 km long and 97 km wide.

How does a lever work?

The lever is a simple machine that moves objects. The commonest kind is called a first-class lever. The object to be moved is known as the load, and the force needed to move it is call the effort. The lever needs a pivot, or fulcrum. Using a branch as a lever and resting it on a small rock (the fulcrum), it is possible to lift a much heavier weight. When Stone Age people discovered this, they had invented one of the basic machines: the lever.

▼ Three simple machines, the crowbar, hammer and wheelbarrow, are used on building sites. The crowbar is a lever. So is the wheelbarrow. The hammer acts as a lever too. The fulcrum is the worker's shoulder joints and the load is the hammer head.

Hammer

Load

Fulcrum

Crowbar

Wheelbarrow

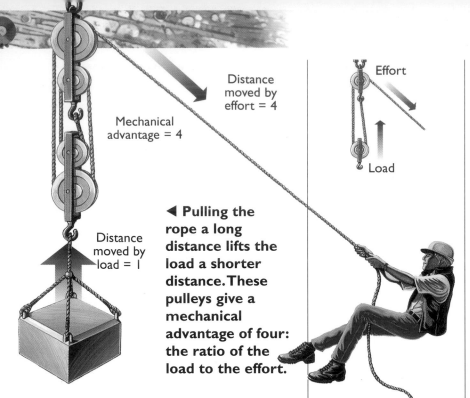

Distance moved by effort = 4

Mechanical advantage = 4

Distance moved by load = 1

Effort

Load

◀ **Pulling the rope a long distance lifts the load a shorter distance. These pulleys give a mechanical advantage of four: the ratio of the load to the effort.**

How do more pulleys make less work?

A pulley is a useful machine for changing the direction of a force. For example, by pulling downwards on a rope running over a pulley wheel, you can lift a load upwards. The more pulleys there are, with one continuous rope running through them, the greater the mechanical advantage and so the greater the load that can be lifted with the same effort.

When were building cranes first used?

The Romans introduced the crane, a machine for lifting loads using the principle of the pulley. Their cranes were worked by treadmills. Slaves trudging inside the treadmill produced the effort needed to lift the load of building stone.

More than 2,000 years ago King Hieron of Syracuse challenged Archimedes to show what simple machines could do. The Greek scientist built a system of pulleys. Unaided, he lifted a ship out of the water and onto the land!

▼ **Inertia in action. A car stays still or moves steadily in a straight line unless it is stopped by another force – such as the brick wall in this picture.**

How do gears work?

A gear is a wheel with teeth along its rim. The teeth fit, or mesh, with teeth on other wheels. As one wheel turns, so do the others. Gear wheels can be used to change the direction of a movement, and also to increase the speed and power of a machine. A big wheel with forty teeth, for example, will turn at a quarter the speed of a wheel with ten teeth, if they are connected. But it will have four times as much power. A car in low gear moves slowly, but has more power for starting and going uphill.

What is inertia?

To start an object moving, a force is needed. When you kick a ball, the ball begins to move. It keeps moving until some other force stops it. The ball has inertia. It rolls on until stopped by another force (your foot perhaps, or a wall, or the friction of the ground). All moving objects have inertia: they try to keep moving until a force opposes them. Have you ever been standing on a bus when it pulled up suddenly? People are thrown forwards, because of the inertia affecting their bodies.

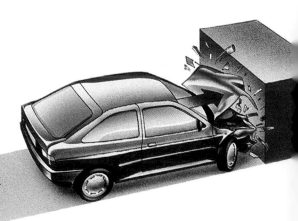

Why does a pendulum swing?

You can make a simple pendulum by fastening a weight to the end of a length of cord. Hold the cord so that the weight hangs vertically. When you give the pendulum a push, it swings away from you. The force of your push gives it motion. When it reaches the lowest point of its swing, the pendulum does not stop but swings on, this time upwards. Inertia keeps it going until a stronger force (gravity) halts it and the pendulum swings back down towards the vertical again.

The Italian scientist Galileo Galilei (1564–1642) made many discoveries. One of them was that the time it takes for a pendulum to swing (known as its period) depends not on its weight, but on its length. Galileo is said to have made this discovery after watching a chandelier swinging.

How can an iron ship float?

A hollow object has low density because it is mostly filled with air. Even an iron ship will float in water because of the air inside. However, if the vessel is holed, water pours in and pushes the air out. The overall density of the ship becomes greater than that of water and the ship sinks.

How can objects float in air?

Air is fluid, like water, but it has such a low density that few objects will float in it. Hydrogen gas is lighter than air, so a balloon filled with hydrogen is less dense than air and will rise upwards. Eventually, it will reach a height where the air is so thin that the hydrogen no longer has a lower density, and can rise no higher.

Why do things fall to Earth?

Gravity is a force which pulls us, and everything else, towards the Earth. Gravity is what makes rain fall downwards and not upwards. Gravity explains why if you throw a ball into the air, it will fall back to Earth again.

Gravity is one of many forces which act on objects on Earth. A plane flying through the atmosphere is thrust forward by its engines, but held in place above the ground by air pressure under its wings acting against the pull of gravity.

The planet Earth exerts a gravitational force on everything. But much smaller bodies also produce a similar effect. Between any two objects there is a gravitational force.

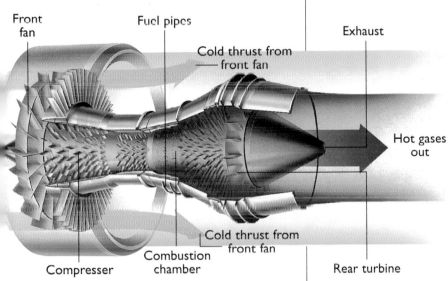

Front fan / Fuel pipes / Exhaust / Cold thrust from front fan / Hot gases out / Compresser / Combustion chamber / Cold thrust from front fan / Rear turbine

How does a jet engine work?

A jet engine is an action-reaction engine. It shoots out a mass of hot gas, and the force of this gas pushing in one direction produces another equally strong force in the opposite direction. For every action (here the hot gas shooting out backwards), there is an equal and opposite reaction (the jet plane flying forwards). Sir Isaac Newton knew this, long before jet planes. This was his Third Law of Motion.

▲ A jet engine sucks in air with a fan. The air is compressed and forced into the combustion chamber where fuel is sprayed in and burns. Hot, expanding gases spin a rear turbine that drives the compressor and the fan. Finally, gases shoot out of the exhaust, producing thrust.

Why do the planets keep moving in their orbits?

The planets have been moving ever since the formation of the Solar System. They were given their starting 'push' then, millions of years ago, and have kept moving around the Sun ever since. The Sun's massive gravitational force holds the planets in orbit around it. They keep moving because there is no force in the Solar System powerful enough to stop them and no friction force opposing them.

How much would you weigh on the Moon?

The weight of an object is the force of gravity acting upon it. Weight is really measured in newtons (the newton is a unit for measuring force). Mass is measured in kilograms (or pounds). The mass of an object never changes, but if you travelled to the Moon, you would weigh less than on Earth, because the Moon has only one-sixth of the Earth's gravity.

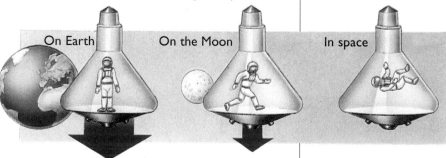

On Earth   On the Moon   In space

What is it like to be weightless?

People inside a spacecraft orbiting the Earth float about inside, as if swimming in air. There is no gravity from Earth to pull them down. If an astronaut lets go of a tool, it drifts about instead of falling to the ground. Imagine eating food from a plate!

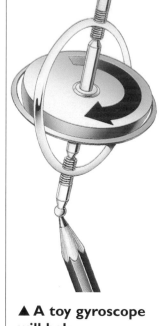

▲ A toy gyroscope will balance so long as it keeps spinning fast enough. The wheel's axle points continuously in the direction it is first set at.

▲ As they escape Earth's gravity, astronauts become weightless. On the Moon, there is very little gravity so an astronaut can bounce around. In space, an astronaut floats.

How can a gyroscope balance on a pencil point?

A gyroscope looks like a spinning-top inside a wheel-like frame. Once set spinning, it will not alter its direction. If balanced on a pencil point, it will not fall off so long as it keeps spinning. The pull of gravity (which tries to upset the gyroscope) is countered by another force called precession, found in spinning bodies. This makes the gyroscope move around the point of the pencil as if it were in orbit.

What causes friction?

Friction is produced when two surfaces rub against each other. Even a smooth-looking surface is actually covered with tiny holes and bumps, as can be seen by looking through a microscope. The rubbing together produces heat. This is why a match struck on a matchbox bursts into flame. There is friction between even the most insubstantial surfaces such as air and water.

Why don't trains have rubber tyres like cars and trucks?

Running a vehicle on rails is actually more efficient than running it on a road. This is because a solid wheel, like that of a train creates less friction than an air-filled tyre (as on a car), since a solid wheel does not flatten out under pressure. So it is easier to pull a heavy load along a train track than along a road. But without some friction to 'stick' the wheels to the rails, a train's wheels would spin helplessly and not grip at all.

SPACE AND TIME

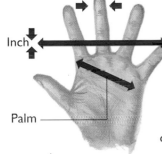

The width of a digit became the inch

Inch

Palm

From thumb to little finger (stretched) was a span.

The yard was the length of a man's arm from nose to fingertip.

Two palms = one span
Four palms = one cubit

The cubit was the length from fingers to elbow

A fathom was a man's armspan

When was zero first used in sums?

We could not count without a figure for nothing, or zero. One way is to leave a blank, but early mathematicians soon found they needed a special symbol: 0. The zero was used by the 7th century AD in India and South-East Asia, and may have been used in China even earlier.

Who invented the decimal system?

We have ten fingers and ten toes, so counting in tens (the decimal system) seems sensible. But counting can be done in lots of other ways. As early as 1400 BC the Chinese used decimals. They wrote the number 365 as 'three hundred plus six decades (tens) plus five days'. Decimals did not reach Europe until the 10th century AD.

How was the human body used in measurement?

Ancient civilizations relied on 'body-measurement'. The smallest unit of length was the 'finger' or 'thumb'. A cubit (the distance from a person's elbow to their fingertips) was equal to 30 fingers (roughly 50 centimetres in modern terms). A hand's width, normally taken as four inches (10 centimetres), is still the unit used to measure the height of horses.

Where was the metric system first made official?

The metric (decimal) system of weights and measures was adopted in France after the French Revolution of 1789. Before then, people in Europe had used various old measures. The metric system is now used throughout the world.

▲ In the ancient world, parts of the body were used as measuring units including the digit, span and cubit. According to the Bible, Goliath was six cubits and one span high, so he was 3.25 m tall.

A pace = one yard

One foot

What is geometry?

Geometry is the branch of mathematics that has to do with the study of shapes and sizes. The name comes from Greek words meaning 'Earth measurement', and it was by using geometry that Greek mathematicians first calculated the size of the Earth. Every advance in science has been aided by geometry, for without it we could not make accurate measurements. In about 300 BC the Greek mathematician Euclid wrote a book called *Elements* in which he brought together many geometrical discoveries made by the Greeks. Euclid's textbook has inspired mathematicians ever since.

How often can you expect to throw a six when playing dice?

Mathematicians have long sought ways of solving problems involving unpredictable factors, such as the fall of dice. The Frenchman Blaise Pascal worked out the basic 'laws of probability' in 1642, using dice. The simplest problem is this: a die has six sides, each with a different value. When you throw it, each side has an equal chance of falling uppermost. The probability that one side will do so is therefore 1 in 6.

The probability of throwing a number greater than two

Possible outcomes

Successful outcomes

Probability of throwing greater than two is therefore four out of six

---

MATHS FACTS

■ As long ago as 3000 BC, the Egyptians used geometry for land surveys and for building.

■ Arabs invented algebra in the 9th century AD.

■ Negative numbers, such as -1, -2, -3 and so on, were unknown in Europe until the 1500s, though the Chinese used them long before.

■ The acre is still used as a field measurement by many farmers. In the Middle Ages, an English acre was the area of land an ox could plough in a day – 22 furrows (lengths) or 'furlongs'.

■ The 17th-century French mathematician Pierre Fermat had a secret test for finding prime numbers. He could give almost instant answers.

■ There is an endless number of prime numbers. There are more than 660,000 between 1 and 10 million.

Euclid thought 6 was a 'perfect' number. 1, 2 and 3 divide exactly into 6. Added together, they make 6. Euclid knew of three more perfect numbers: 28, 496 and 8,128. After that, perfect numbers get very big indeed!

Where did Arabic numerals come from?

The Arabic numerals we use today were first used in India and reached Europe about the year AD 1000. A book written in 1202 by an Italian mathematician named Leonardo Fibonacci did much to persuade Europe's scientists that they must use Arabic numerals in order for the science of mathematics to progress.

Who first proved that the angles of a triangle always add up to 180 degrees?

The Ancient Greeks were fascinated by geometry. They knew that a circle is made up of 360 degrees, a number probably chosen by the Babylonians. No matter what its shape, a triangle has angles that always add up to 180 degrees. This was first proved by Euclid about 300 BC.

Why do mathematicians hunt for prime numbers?

A prime number is one that can be divided only by itself and 1. For example, 12 is not a prime number because it can be divided by 1, 2, 3, 4 and 6. On the other hand, 11 is: it can be divided only by 1 and 11. What mystifies mathematicians about prime numbers is that they can find no pattern. A Greek named Eratosthenes worked out a slow, but effective, method of finding prime numbers. That was in the 3rd century BC.

◀ **If you roll a die, what is the chance of rolling a number higher than 2? Four of the six possible numbers are greater than 2, so the probability of rolling one of them is 4/6 or 2/3.**

Who counted in suns and nights?

People have measured time in a number of ways. Early people counted the days (from sunrise to sunset). But not all used the 'day' as their unit. The Comanche tribe of North America counted in 'suns' and Greenlanders counted in 'nights'.

Who first worked out how long a year is?

More than 3,000 years ago, the priests of Babylon were skilled in astronomy and kept accurate records of the passing of the seasons. They calculated how long it took the Earth to complete one year's cycle around the Sun, and worked this out as 365 days 5 hours 42 minutes and 14 seconds. The modern calculation is only 26 minutes and 55 seconds longer.

▲ Hundreds of years ago, the Aztec people of Mexico made a calendar. It was a huge stone shaped like the Sun. Signs for the days were carved around the edge.

People born in a leap year on 29 February have to wait four years for their next 'special' birthday. A leap year can always be divided by four with nothing left over. The years 1996, 2000 and 2004 are all leap years.

Why were leap years found necessary?

The Romans based their calendar on the Moon's monthly phases. The Roman calendar started off with 360 days, but was then reduced to only 355. It became clear that the calendar was gradually getting out of step with the seasons. So Julius Caesar ordered a new calendar of 365.25 days. Every fourth year an extra day was added, to use up the quarter-days. This became a leap year. Before the new calendar could begin, an extra-long year was needed to put things straight. The year 46 BC had 445 days and, not surprisingly, was known as 'the year of confusion'.

When did people protest at having 11 days stolen?

Julius Caesar's calendar, named the Julian calendar, was used until the 1500s. By then, it too was out of step. Easter was falling in summer instead of spring. Pope Gregory XIII, head of the Roman Catholic Church, ruled that there should be a new calendar from 1582. Britain kept to the old calendar until 1752. That year, September 2 was followed by September 14. People took to the streets protesting that they had had 11 days stolen from their lives!

Who had two calendars?

People of the Maya civilization in Central America (from about AD 250 to 1500). One calendar had 365 days, divided into 18 months of 20 days, with five 'unlucky' days at the end of the year. Maya fortune-tellers used a sacred calendar with 260 days.

Water clock

Sundial

When were sundials and water clocks used?

Sundials were used as 'shadow clocks' more than 3,000 years ago in Babylon. An upright stick casts a shadow as the Sun's rays alter position during the day. (Remember, this is because the Earth is moving, not the Sun.) Around the stick is a dial marked out with the hours.

The Ancient Egyptians and Greeks used water clocks. There were various types, but they all worked on the same principle. Water dripped slowly out of a container. As the water level fell, so did a float on the surface. To the float was attached a pointer which marked the passing of the hours on a scale.

When were mechanical clocks invented?

Medieval monks needed to know the times for prayers during the day. They wanted a clock that would ring a bell at regular intervals. The machinery that made this possible was invented in the 1300s. Falling weights provided the force needed to ring a bell, and the fall of the weights was regulated by a mechanism known as an 'escapement'. The movement of the escapement gave the clockwork its familiar 'tick-tock' sound.

▲ In an Egyptian water clock, water poured slowly from one pot to another. The Egyptians also had sundials. In Babylon, people marked the face of the sundial into 12 hours. The dial shown here has Roman numerals.

▲ John Harrison made the first reliable chronometer, or ship's clock, in the 1700s. It had a slowly unwinding spring inside, so it kept time accurately.

▶ The cross-staff and backstaff, early navigational instruments.

Were there hands on the first clocks?

Early clocks were intended only to 'strike' the hours, with a bell. They were very inaccurate, losing perhaps 15 minutes a day. But people were not worried about minutes, they needed to know only what hour it was. Clocks struck every quarter-hour, and that was precise enough. After all, there were no trains or buses to catch. Not until the 1600s were clocks with minute hands and faces marked into 12 hours common.

How did the early sailors find their way?

Few seamen in ancient times ventured out of sight of land. The Greeks invented a sundial-like device, the astrolabe, for finding longitude (east-west position) and calculating the time of day. The astrolabe did not reach northern Europe until much later, in the 14th century. Later, sailors made use of instruments called the simple cross-staff and the improved backstaff (1595) to discover their latitude (north-south position) by measuring the precise angle of the Sun above the horizon.

Cross-staff

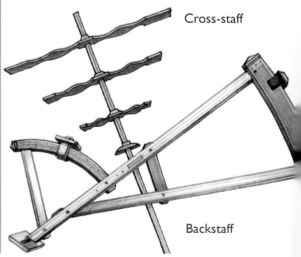

Backstaff

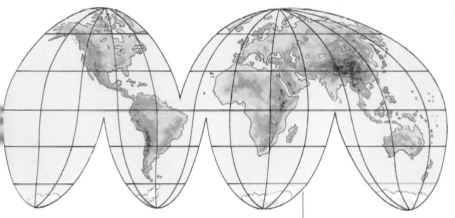

Why is a flat map never really accurate?

A map in a book is flat. But the Earth is round, and its features cannot be drawn accurately on a flat surface. Try peeling an orange, and you will find you cannot lay the skin out flat on a table without it breaking. Every map is drawn in a way that makes some feature (such as area) accurate, but other features (such as shape) less so. This is called a projection.

Why do air travellers have to alter their watches?

The world is divided into 24 time zones. The time in each zone differs by one hour from the time in the next. East of Greenwich in England (where it is Greenwich Mean Time, or GMT), the time is later. West of Greenwich, the time is earlier. Noon in Greenwich is 7am (5 hours earlier) in New York and 3pm (3 hours later) in Moscow. The United States covers five time zones: Atlantic, Eastern, Central, Mountain and Pacific. Travellers flying west put their watches back on landing. Flying east, they must put their watches forward. So if a flight from London to New York takes five hours, you land at the same time as you set off.

▲ To make a map on a flat surface, a section of the world's surface has to be shown as if it were flat. It is as if the peel of an orange were cut off and then laid out flat on the table.

▼ Since 1884, the world has had a standard time: Greenwich Mean Time. In each time zone, time differs by one hour. Travellers crossing the International Date Line gain or lose a day.

When was BC and AD dating introduced?

There are many different systems for dating. Muslims begin their calendar from the Hegira, the flight of Muhammad from Mecca in AD 622. The Christian calendar, now widely used worldwide, begins with the birth of Jesus. Dates before then are followed by the letters 'BC' ('Before Christ'). Dates after then are prefixed by the letters AD (Latin 'Anno Domini' or 'Year of Our Lord'). AD dating was suggested by a monk-mathematician named Dionysius Exiguus in AD 525. It was much later that BC was used, in the 1600s.

How do archaeologists measure time?

Archaeologists uncover the past, layer by layer. Objects can be dated by the radiocarbon method (measuring the amount of radioactive carbon-14 left in charcoal, wood or animal bones). Tree growth-rings also help them, especially using the bristlecone pine of California, which can live as long as 4,600 years. Tree-ring dating has helped to correct errors in radiocarbon dates.

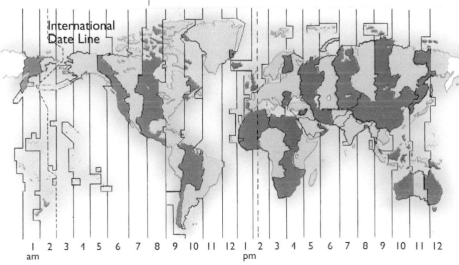

International Date Line

| 1 | 2 | 3 | 4 | 5 | 6 | 7 | 8 | 9 | 10 | 11 | 12 | 1 | 2 | 3 | 4 | 5 | 6 | 7 | 8 | 9 | 10 | 11 | 12 |
am   pm

DISCOVERIES AND INVENTIONS

When were the first tools made?

Long before human beings had evolved, there were ape-like creatures that scientists have named *Australopithecus*, whose remains have been found in southern and eastern Africa. They used sticks and stones as weapons. Scientists have discovered some simple pebble-tools these primitive creatures made more than two million years ago.

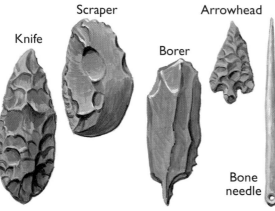

Knife
Scraper
Borer
Arrowhead
Bone needle

How did people discover fire?

Primitive people feared fire, as animals do. A forest fire, started by lightning, sent them fleeing. Someone, somewhere must have plucked up courage to seize a burning branch. He or she used it to start a small fire for warmth and protection against fierce animals. These first fires were kept burning constantly, for no one yet knew how to make fire using simple tools.

▲ Before the wheel was invented, people used logs as rollers to move heavy stones for building, so perhaps it is not surprising that the first wheels were wooden.

◄ Early people used flint for making tools such as knives, scrapers, borers and arrowheads. They made needles from animal bones.

Who invented the wheel?

No one knows when or where the wheel was first used, but it was one of the most important of all human inventions. The wheel seems to have been invented before 3000 BC, probably in several different places. It may be that wheels were first used by potters to turn clay pots, before they were fixed to carts and revolutionized transport. The first carts had two solid wheels, made from pieces of wood fastened together. Spoked wheels, as used on chariots, were much lighter and a great improvement.

◄ People made fire using a bow drill. As the point of the drill turned rapidly, friction produced enough heat to start wool or dry moss smouldering.

When did the first farmers harvest crops?

Archaeologists in Israel have found flint sickles (tools used for cutting grain) thought to be 13,000 years old. Microscopic examination of the sickle blades shows they were probably used to harvest cultivated, not wild, cereals. If this is so, farming began much earlier than was previously thought. Scientists had previously found evidence of cereal planting in Syria some 11,000 years ago.

How is iron smelted?

Iron was first made by heating iron ore in a furnace with charcoal and limestone. As the charcoal burned, the molten iron ran down and cooled into a solid mass. This 'bloom' was then hammered and reheated to purify the iron. The process of melting down iron ore is called smelting. The 'Iron Age' began about 1500 BC, in the Near East.

One of the most important inventions of all time was the eyeglass. The first recorded statement came from Roger Bacon in 1268 when he wrote about the use of lenses in glasses.

▶ Tipping out a furnace of molten steel. All metals come from ores dug up from the ground. The ore is heated until the metal melts. It is poured into moulds to cool and harden.

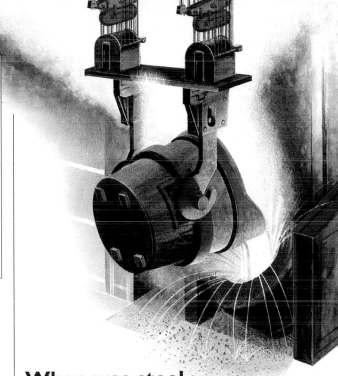

When was steel first made?

The Romans knew how to make steel of a kind, and metal smiths in China and elsewhere probably also made steel by accident. During the Middle Ages, Toledo in Spain was famous for its steel swords. Large-scale steel production was not possible until the invention of an industrial steel-making process. This was done by Sir Henry Bessemer, who invented his 'converter' to make steel in 1856.

When were candles first used?

Candles have been in use for at least 3,000 years, and probably longer. They are mentioned in the Old Testament of the Bible and the Romans burned candles made from flax coated with wax and pitch. Beeswax and tallow (animal fat) were also often used.

◀ More than half the world's steel is made by the basic oxygen process, illustrated here. The electric arc and open hearth are two other common steel-making processes.

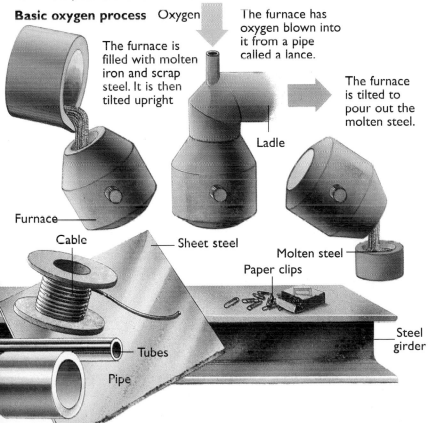

Basic oxygen process Oxygen

The furnace is filled with molten iron and scrap steel. It is then tilted upright

The furnace has oxygen blown into it from a pipe called a lance.

The furnace is tilted to pour out the molten steel.

Ladle

Furnace

Cable

Sheet steel

Molten steel

Paper clips

Steel girder

Tubes

Pipe

Who enjoyed central heating 2,000 years ago?

Wealthy Romans lived in large houses with under floor heating, known as a hypocaust. Slaves fed fuel onto a fire which sent hot air circulating beneath the raised floor of the house. Hot air also made its way through flues in the walls, which allowed smoke to escape. Romans living in parts of their empire far from sunny Italy (such as Britain) must have been grateful for this luxury. The fire also heated water for the bathroom.

How long have people used weighing machines?

Accurate scales or weighing machines are vital for science, and also for trade and business. The Ancient Egyptians had equal arm balances, much the same as are still used today. Such balances have been in use for some 7,000 years!

In Ancient Egypt, few people went to school. Some boys trained as scribes. A scribe's job was writing. He had to learn more than 700 hieroglyphs. Spelling tests were a nightmare!

▼ **Egyptians making papyrus. Papyrus is made from a kind of reed. The stages of the process turned the reeds into a smooth paper-like writing material.**

Who were the first people to use paper?

Paper was first made in China about 2,000 years ago. Before the invention of paper-making machines in the 1800s, each sheet of paper was made separately by hand. The only machines involved were trip hammers, driven by water wheels. These ground rags mixed with water into a pulp. The pulp was then put in a vat, and a wire screen was dipped into it. The screen picked up a thin coating of pulp. It was lifted out, shaken, and laid on felt, and was put in a screwpress to press out the moisture. Each sheet was then peeled off the felt and hung up to dry.

COMMUNICATING

■ Prehistoric people sent messages by using drumbeats, fires and smoke signals.

■ The first writing was picture-writing, so people drew pictures to tell a story.

■ The people of Sumer in Mesopotamia invented a form of picture-writing about 3500 BC.

■ Long scrolls were awkward to carry. So for sending messages, people used wax tablets. They wrote on the soft wax with a pointed stick.

■ People in Ancient Rome were able to read the news. A handwritten news sheet of 59 BC was a forerunner of the newspaper.

1 Paper-makers cut and peeled the reeds.

2 They cut the reed stems into thin slices and laid them in rows, one on top of the other.

3 They hammered them until the sticky plant juices glued them together.

5 Finally, all the pieces of papyrus paper were glued into a long strip and rolled into a scroll.

4 Next they used a smooth stone or a special tool to rub the surface of the papyrus paper smooth.

When were cannon first used in battle?

The Chinese invented gunpowder rockets, but cannon were not used for battle in Europe until the 1300s. The early guns were clumsy and fired solid cannon balls. Often their metal barrels exploded under the force of the gunpowder, doing more damage to their own side than to the enemy.

Why did Leonardo's flying machine never fly?

The Italian Leonardo da Vinci, who invented between 1452 and 1519, dreamed up inventions that were centuries ahead of their time. He drew plans for a submarine, a parachute, an armoured vehicle something like a tank, a helicopter and a flying machine. His flying machine was never built, for no engine existed to power it. The age of light, powerful motors was still several hundred years away.

What was the first steam engine used for?

In 1698 an English engineer named Thomas Savery devised 'an engine for the raising of water and occasioning motion to all sorts of mill works'. His engine was put to work pumping water from the shafts of tin mines in Cornwall. It worked by cooling steam so that it condensed, creating a partial vacuum which 'sucked up' water through a pipe.

▶ James Watt improved Newcomen's steam pumping engine, making it more powerful. This is his 1775 version, which was soon at work in factories throughout Britain.

▲ This early cannon of the 1400s fired solid stone balls. It could not shoot far, but it could knock down castle walls.

In 1482 Leonardo da Vinci wrote to the Duke of Milan that he could build portable bridges, cannons, ships, as well as armoured vehicles and catapults!

Who was called 'Father of the Steam Age'?

The Scottish engineer James Watt (1736–1819) is said to have been inspired to improve the steam engine by watching a kettle boil. In 1764 he was trying to repair a model steam engine of the kind invented by Thomas Newcomen (1663–1729). Realizing how inefficient this kind of steam engine was, Watt added a separate condenser to make it more powerful. He also worked out how to change the up and down motion of the beam engine into rotary motion, suitable for driving machinery. These improvements earned James Watt fame as the 'Father of the Steam Age'.

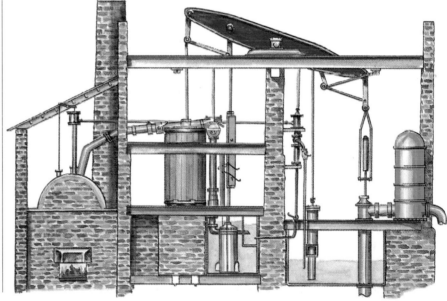

Who built the first reaping machine?

In the 1830s Cyrus Hall McCormick of the USA invented a horse-drawn machine to cut grain. The mechanical reaper was followed in the 1850s by the first combine harvester.

When were fertilizers first used?

Farmers have always used animal manure to restore the goodness in the soil. It was not until the 1800s that they began applying chemical fertilizers. In 1842 John Bennet Lawes of Britain found out how to produce super-phosphate from rock and this was the beginning of the chemical fertilizer industry.

How deep was the first oil well?

The Chinese were able to extract oil from below the ground 2,000 years ago, but the first modern oil well was drilled in Pennsylvania, USA, in 1859. The pioneer driller was Edwin L. Drake, who bored through 21 metres of rock to strike oil. This was 30 years before the first car. The oil was burned in oil lamps.

Who was the most inventive inventor of all time?

This title probably belongs to the American inventor Thomas Alva Edison (1847–1931), with more than a thousand inventions to his credit. Among them were the electric light bulb, the film camera and the phonograph, which was an early form of record player.

The best-attended single-day sports event in the world is a car race – the Indianapolis 500. It is called 500 because the cars must cover 500 miles. The oval track was made from 3.2 million bricks which earned it the name the Brickyard, as it is still called.

▼ Cars rolling off one of the first assembly lines in the United States.

When were cars first built on an assembly line?

Until 1914 cars were built one by one, as wagons had always been. A group of workers finished one car before starting on the next. The American industrialist Henry Ford changed all this by introducing the first assembly line into his factory. Cars moved along an automated conveyor system. Each part (seats, engine, wheels and so on) was put on in turn as the conveyor moved along carrying the car bodies. Instead of taking 13 hours to build a Ford Model T car, it took only one and a half hours using the new assembly line. So the cars cost less.

▶ The Model T Ford first appeared in 1908. It became America's most popular car.

TRANSPORT AND COMMUNICATION

What was the earliest vehicle?

The most ancient of all vehicles is perhaps the sledge. This was used in Stone Age times, and not just in snow. Putting a load (such as an animal killed for food) on a sledge made it easier to drag, because the smooth wood produced less friction as it rubbed against the rough ground. Putting runners on the sledge made it even easier to drag. One day someone added wheels and made the first cart.

Who built the first steam-driven vehicle?

A French soldier named Nicolas Cugnot built a carriage driven by a steam engine in 1763. It had three wheels and Cugnot thought it would be useful for hauling heavy cannon. Unfortunately, it was very slow and after a few test runs, it went out of control and somehow overturned. His superiors decided to stick with horse-drawn artillery and Cugnot's ill-fated machine was locked up for safety.

How did the *Rocket* outstrip its rivals?

Steam locomotives that could run under their own power on road or rails were developed in the early 1800s. In 1829, British pioneers gathered to race their steam locomotives at the Rainhill trials.

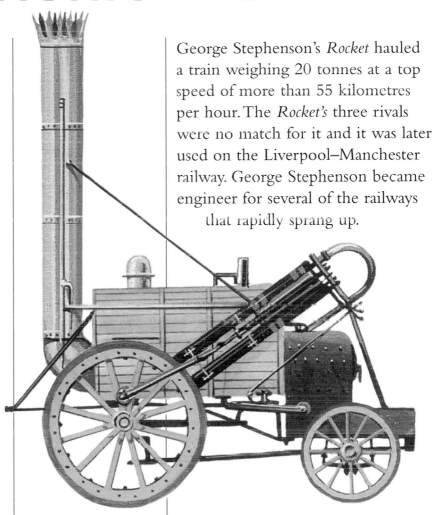

▲ **Stephenson's *Rocket* was the fastest steam locomotive of its day. Inside its boiler were five tubes, so more water was heated. This meant more steam drove the *Rocket*'s pistons.**

George Stephenson's *Rocket* hauled a train weighing 20 tonnes at a top speed of more than 55 kilometres per hour. The *Rocket*'s three rivals were no match for it and it was later used on the Liverpool–Manchester railway. George Stephenson became engineer for several of the railways that rapidly sprang up.

When was the world's first electric railway opened?

In 1879 a 274-metre stretch of electric tramway was opened in Berlin, Germany. It was the brainchild of Werner von Siemens. Four years later, his brother Wilhelm opened an electric railway in Northern Ireland. By the 1920s electric lines were operating throughout the world. Electric trains are now so advanced that the French TGV train has exceeded 500 kilometres per hour.

When did the modern bicycle appear?

Several improvements in bicycle design in the 1800s brought about the shape we know today. The pedals were moved from the front wheels to a position between the wheels and a chain drive was added. Wire-spoke wheels, sprung saddles, gears, ball-bearings and a free-wheel device were other important changes made by the 1880s. Last to be added was the pneumatic (air-filled) tyre.

Who built the first internal combustion engine?

In 1863 a Frenchman named Etienne Lenoir designed an engine which burned coal gas. He used it to drive a cart. In 1864 the Austrian Siegfried Marckus built a similar engine that used petrol vapour, and designed an electrical ignition system.

When did the first motor vehicle take to the road?

The first motor vehicle powered by a petrol engine was a three-wheeler built in 1885 by Karl Benz, a young German engineer. His first trial run in his 'horseless carriage' ended in an accident, when he drove it into a wall. The same year as Benz tested his machine, Gottfried Daimler, working less than 100 kilometres away, built a motor cycle. By 1886 Daimler had produced his first car. It had a single cylinder engine and a top speed of 29 kilometres per hour.

▶ **Karl Benz built his first car in 1885. It had three cart-style wheels and was steered by moving the front wheel.**

Induction	Compression	Power	Exhaust

Fuel and air mixture in	Mix squeezed; spark causes ignition	Combustion (explosion)	Waste gases out through valve

▲ **Inside a four-stroke petrol engine. The up-and-down piston movement is changed to a round-and-round movement of the drive shaft linked to the wheels.**

In 1865, just after the first steam coaches appeared on the road, the 'Red Flag Act' ruled that any car should have someone walking in front of it carrying a red flag!

What makes a car engine go?

The power of the car engine comes from an explosion. If petrol is mixed with air and then ignited by a spark, it explodes. In the internal combustion engine, the explosions are controlled inside cylinders. Each explosion pushes a piston downwards. The pistons are connected to a series of shafts which in turn are connected to the wheels of the car.

▶ A cutaway of the 1983 recordbreaking jet car *Thrust 2*. It was really an engine on wheels, with a small space for the driver.

How fast can a car travel?

Cars fitted with rocket and jet engines can travel much faster than those with ordinary petrol engines. In 1997 Andy Green set a new record in the jet-engined *Thrust SSC* with a top speed of 1,149 kilometres per hour.

What were the first boats like?

The earliest boat was probably a floating log. Then people learned how to build rafts by lashing together logs or bundles of reeds. They hollowed out tree trunks to make canoes. The first boats were driven by paddles. Sails came later.

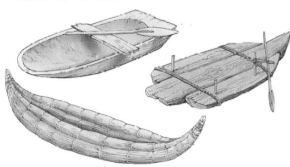

▲ The first boats were dug-out canoes made by hollowing out tree trunks, reed boats and rafts made from planks of wood.

The very first car to go faster than 100 km/h did not run on oil but was battery-powered. It was called *La Jamais Contente*. Amazingly, it did this about 100 years ago in 1899.

Surface-piercing hydrofoil

Fully submerged hydrofoil

▲ Hydrofoils can skim over water at more than 110 km/h. There are two types of hydrofoil, each having a different foil shape.

When did ships first have rudders?

Early ships were steered by a large oar hung over the stern. Chinese vessels were probably the first to be fitted with a rudder, and by the 1200s ships with rudders had appeared in Europe.

Who built the first steamboat?

By the late 1700s inventors in several countries were experimenting with the new power of steam to drive ships. In 1783 a French nobleman, the Marquis de Jouffroy d'Abbans, built a boat whose paddles were worked by a steam engine. He called it the *Pyroscaphe* (meaning 'fire-craft') and tested it successfully on a river. It was the first steamboat.

Who invented the steam turbine?

The high-speed steam engine was made possible by Sir Charles Parsons, a British engineer who invented the turbine in 1884. Steam was passed through the blades of a series of spinning rotors, which converted the steam's energy into fast circular motion. Parsons built a steam turbine-powered launch *Turbinia* that startled naval experts in 1884.

Why can a hydrofoil travel faster than an ordinary speedboat?

A hydrofoil has special legs, or foils, beneath its hull. When motionless, the hydrofoil floats low in the water like a normal craft. But at speed it lifts up on its foils. This reduces the friction between the hull and the water.

Who were the first people to fly?

Over the centuries, many brave but misguided experimenters have tried to fly. We know of nobody who succeeded before November 21, 1783 when two men, Pilatre de Rozier and the Marquis d'Arlandes, flew in a Montgolfier hot-air balloon above Paris. Their historic flight lasted 25 minutes.

Why did Orville Wright lie on his stomach during the first aeroplane flight?

The Wright brothers, Wilbur and Orville, made the first sustained flight in a powered craft when their *Flyer 1* took to the air on December 17, 1903. It had a home-made petrol engine set on the right-hand wing. To keep the plane stable, the pilot (Orville, on the first historic flight) had to lie on the left-hand wing.

Can aircraft fly without engines?

A glider is an aeroplane without an engine. It stays aloft by diving at a very flat angle, or by soaring on rising currents of warm air.

▲ Two brothers, Joseph and Etienne Montgolfier, built the world's first hot air balloon to carry people into the air.

The parachute may have been used as long ago as the 1400s. Drawings made then show cone-shaped canopies, with people dangling underneath.

When did jets first fly?

Piston engines were found not to work well at high altitude, where the air is thin, nor at very high speeds. A new type of engine was needed. As early as 1930 a British engineer called Frank Whittle had patented a jet engine design, but the first jet plane to fly was German. This was the Heinkel He 178 which was tested in 1939. British and American jets flew soon afterwards, during World War II.

How does a helicopter fly backwards?

A helicopter's rotor blades act both as wings and propellers. To hover, or to fly upwards, the blades are kept flat. To fly forwards, the blades are tilted forwards so that they 'bite' into the air. To move backwards, the rotor blades are tilted towards the tail.

How does a jump-jet hover in mid-air?

The *Harrier* is an example of a vertical take-off or 'jump-jet'. It has four swivelling nozzles which direct exhaust gases from the jet engines.

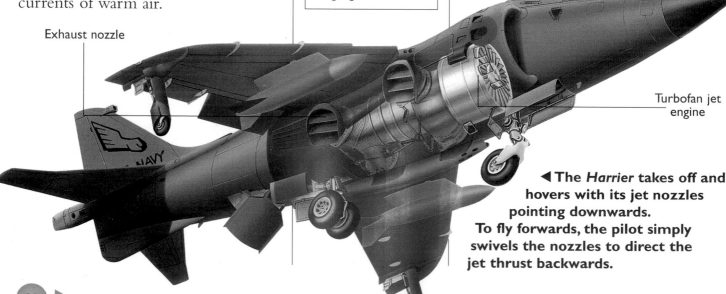

Exhaust nozzle

Turbofan jet engine

◀ The *Harrier* takes off and hovers with its jet nozzles pointing downwards. To fly forwards, the pilot simply swivels the nozzles to direct the jet thrust backwards.

THE ANIMAL KINGDOM

How did life on Earth begin?

The Earth had existed for at least 1 billion years before the first signs of life appeared. As the fiery planet cooled, its atmosphere formed. Rains filled the seas, and in the seas life began. How it began is not known for sure. Maybe lightning provided the energy to start chemical reactions in the primeval 'soup' of elements on the young planet. Perhaps minerals from the rocks formed and reformed new chemical combinations innumerable times. However it happened, an unusual chemical combination appeared: a living cell which could feed itself, and reproduce copies of itself. Over millions of years living cells slowly evolved into plants and animals.

All animals move, even the limpet which moves about two centimetres in its lifetime. Animals take advantage of their ability to move by eating plants.

▼ **The evolution of animal species has shaped the 'family tree' of life. The prehistory of the Earth is marked into eras, each one lasting many millions of years.**

What is the difference between an animal and a plant?

The main difference is that an animal can move and a plant stays in the same place all the time. Another difference is that animals eat other animals or plants for food, but most plants make their own food.

What is a family of animals?

When animal experts talk about a family of animals, they do not just mean parents and young. Different animals with similar bodies are said to be in the same family. Wild cats, such as lions, tigers and leopards, and pet cats all belong to the cat family. The bear family includes polar bears, brown bears, honey bears and so on.

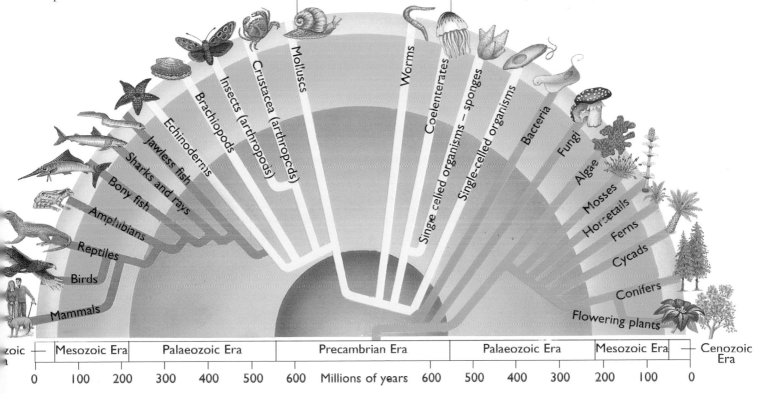

Molluscs · Crustacea (arthropods) · Insects (arthropods) · Brachiopods · Echinoderms · Jawless fish · Sharks and rays · Bony fish · Amphibians · Reptiles · Birds · Mammals · Worms · Coelenterates · Single-celled organisms – sponges · Single-celled organisms · Bacteria · Fungi · Algae · Mosses · Horsetails · Ferns · Cycads · Conifers · Flowering plants

zoic	Mesozoic Era	Palaeozoic Era	Precambrian Era	Palaeozoic Era	Mesozoic Era	Cenozoic Era

| 0 | 100 | 200 | 300 | 400 | 500 | 600 | Millions of years | 600 | 500 | 400 | 300 | 200 | 100 | 0 |

What are fossils?

Fossils are found in rocks such as sandstone which were once soft sand or mud. Fossils are the hardened remains of plants and animals that once lived on Earth. The most common fossils are the shells, teeth or bones of animals or the tough outer skins of plants. Soft parts of living things are not often preserved.

What were the first land animals?

The early animals were invertebrates – animals with no backbones. They were either soft (jellyfish) or shelled (trilobites). The first animals with backbones (vertebrates) were fishes. The first creatures to move to the land were the ancestors of today's insects and spiders. They fed on the first land plants and on one another. Amphibians – animals that can live on land and in water – appeared about 900 million years ago. They probably developed from fish that crawled out of water onto land and breathed air. Their bony fins evolved into legs and feet.

▶ **Early fish were covered in bony armour. Dunkleosteus was a giant flesh-eater with large teeth to grab its prey.**

▲ **Extinct sea animals such as ammonites are found as fossils. The hard shell was buried by mud and sand that hardened into rock. Millions of years later, the fossil is exposed.**

Dinosaurs ruled the Earth for a very long time. The first ones appeared about 225 million years ago and the last ones we know about died out some 160 million years later.

When did dinosaurs rule the Earth?

For about 160 million years (from 225 million years ago to 65 million years ago) a group of reptiles called dinosaurs were the most successful animals on Earth. Some were small but others were giants.

Which were the most fearsome dinosaurs?

The most terrible of the meat-eating dinosaurs were creatures such as Allosaurus, which lived in Jurassic times (180 to 130 million years ago) and Tyrannosaurus rex of the Cretaceous Period (130 to 65 million years ago). These animals were up to 12 metres long and their jaws were lined with razor-sharp teeth. Some other hunting dinosaurs had huge, knife-like claws.

What happened to the dinosaurs?

There are no living dinosaurs today. They seem to have died out at the end of the Cretaceous Period (65 million years ago). Maybe the plants the plant-eating dinosaurs ate died out. Another answer may be that a comet or meteorite hit the Earth, causing an explosion that threw clouds of dust into the atmosphere. The dust blotted out the Sun, plants died – and so did the dinosaurs.

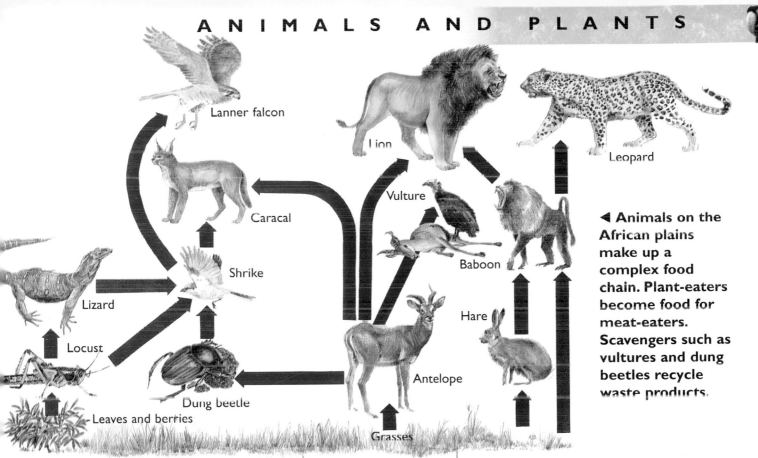

Lanner falcon

Caracal

Lion

Vulture

Leopard

Shrike

Baboon

Lizard

Hare

Locust

Dung beetle

Antelope

Leaves and berries

Grasses

◀ **Animals on the African plains make up a complex food chain. Plant-eaters become food for meat-eaters. Scavengers such as vultures and dung beetles recycle waste products.**

What is a species?

A species is the smallest group of animals which are able to breed among themselves and not with members of another species. Their offspring must also be able to breed successfully. Members of the same species usually look very similar. Human beings are all members of the species *Homo sapiens*.

What is a food chain?

A food chain is a simple way to describe how energy passes from one living thing to another. Here is one example: the grass on the North American prairie grows using energy from the Sun. Grazing animals, such as rabbits and field voles, eat the grass. Coyotes and hawks then eat the rabbits and voles.

▶ **A giraffe can reach higher than other leaf-eating animals. It can also spot danger a long way off.**

ANIMAL FACTS
■ There are about 1.3 million species of animals on Earth today.
■ About 96 percent are invertebrates (animals without backbones).
■ Some experts think there are up to 30 million more species.
■ There are about 4,000 mammals. Compare this to more than 50,000 species of spiders and their relatives!
■ There are about 8,600 species of birds.
■ There are about 6,000 species of reptiles.
■ There are about 2,300 amphibians and over 20,500 species of fish.
■ The longest-lived animal may well be the quahog clam, a shellfish that can live 220 years.

Which is the biggest animal in the world?

The biggest animal that has ever lived is the blue whale. It may grow to more than 30 metres in length, and weighs about 160 tonnes when fully grown. Blue whales have been hunted by whalers and are now rare.

Which is the tallest animal?

The tallest animal in the world is the giraffe. A giraffe may look down from a height of as much as 6 metres – as high as a two-storey house.

Giraffe

How many different kinds of animal can fly?

Three: birds, bats and flying insects. There was one other group of flying animals in the past, the pterosaurs or pterodactyls. They were reptiles but they are all extinct now. There are also animals that glide rather than fly. They can travel a long way like this, but they don't flap their wings as true fliers do. Gliding animals include the flying squirrels, the flying lemurs, a flying lizard and even a flying frog. They all have large flaps of skin that help them to glide slowly down.

What is a predator?

A predator is an animal that lives by killing and feeding on other animals. The animals it hunts are its prey. An animal that eats other animals is also called a carnivore. Animals that eat plants are called herbivores. Those that eat all sorts of different food, as people do, are called omnivores.

Which animals give birth to live young?

Mammals – animals such as dogs, cats, monkeys and kangaroos – are the main groups of animals to do this. But other animals give birth to live young as well, including some fish, snakes, insects and starfish. These species are all exceptions to the rule.

The pitcher plant digests insects. It produces a honey-like substance which attracts insects. They slip and fall into the plant. The plant then digests them.

▼ Molluscs are animals with soft bodies, often protected by hard shells. The octopus is a mollusc without a shell.

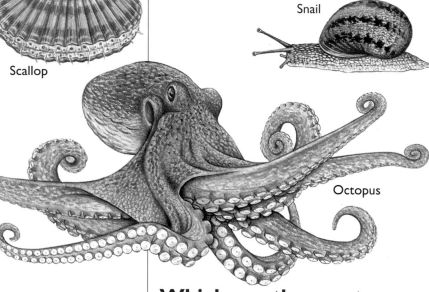

Scallop

Octopus

What is the simplest kind of animal?

A protozoan – it is made up of just one cell. One drop of pond water, when viewed through a microscope, can contain hundreds of these tiny creatures. More than 50,000 different kinds of protozoans are known to exist, and there are probably more!

What is a mollusc?

A mollusc is an animal whose soft body is covered by a thick skin called a mantle. The mantle often secretes a shell, which may lie outside the body, as in snails, or inside, as in cuttlefish. As the mollusc grows, it secretes more shell accordingly.

Snail

Which are the most numerous animals in the world?

Of the animals large enough to be seen without a microscope, insects are by far the most numerous. Some estimates have put the number of insects at around one billion billion. For every human being alive in the world, there are about 200 million insects!

Mice

◄ Humans and mice are mammals. The young are fed with milk from their mother. Only mammals feed their offspring in this way.

Humans

MAMMALS

How many mammals are there?

There are about 4,000 species of mammal in the world. A mammal is a warm-blooded animal, which means that it uses some of its food to keep itself warm. Its body is either wholly or partially covered in hair. Female mammals give birth to live young, and feed them on milk produced in glands called mammary glands (from which mammals get their name).

Why do some mammals sleep through winter?

During the winter, many animals in cold countries hide away and sleep. This sleep is called hibernation. Frogs, toads, lizards, snakes and insects, such as butterflies, all hibernate. So do some mammals, including bats, mice, ground squirrels, chipmunks and even bears. They do so because food is so hard to find in winter that they would starve. In their deep sleep, their bodies cool down and their heartbeat slows down. They use little energy and live off fat they stored in their bodies before they went to sleep.

Squirrel

Beaver

Teeth never stop growing

▶ Rodents are animals with large teeth that they use for gnawing. They can crack nuts (squirrel) or chop down small trees (beaver). Their teeth keep growing and are worn away with use.

Porcupine

What is a rodent?

Rodents are the most common group of mammals alive in the world, and include rats, mice, voles, squirrels, beavers and porcupines. They are small to medium-sized animals with chisel-shaped front teeth which are good for gnawing. Their success must partly be due to the fact that they breed quickly and have large families. Many have several litters a year.

Common poorwill

Bats

Bear

Dormouse

◀ Animals that hibernate eat enough before hibernation to last through winter. The poorwill of North America is the only bird known to hibernate.

Why do tigers have stripes?

The tiger is the largest of the big cats, and usually hunts alone at dusk. Its coat is striped to enable it to blend in with the background vegetation as it stalks its prey – usually deer, wild cattle or pigs. Often a tiger will pounce on its victim as it pauses to drink at a waterhole.

▲ The tiger is the biggest of the big cats. It hunts alone, often lying in wait in the undergrowth. A female tiger guards her cubs fiercely.

How are monkeys suited to a life in the trees?

Monkeys are adapted to their treetop life because they have a pair of forward-facing eyes (enabling them to judge distances) and long arms with grasping hands. Monkeys are therefore able to move about easily in the trees without having to descend. They move quickly and fluently through the tree tops swinging from branch to branch, or climbing between trees in the dense forest canopy. They live in groups and keep in touch with howls, gibberings and other noises.

What is a primate?

A primate is the most highly developed of all mammals: it has a large brain, and good hearing, touch and vision. There are 179 species of primate, falling into two groups: the prosimians, or primitive primates, including lemurs, aye-ayes and bushbabies: and the higher primates, including monkeys, apes and humans.

▲ The chimpanzee is the most intelligent of the apes. Young chimps are playful and can learn simple skills.

Camouflage is used by animals to protect them from their enemies. Many are coloured to match their background.

How do apes differ from monkeys?

Orang-utans, gorillas, chimpanzees and gibbons are apes. They look like monkeys but have no tails. Apes also walk in a more upright position than monkeys, though still on all fours.

▼ The spider monkey uses its strong tail, as well as its hands and feet, to cling onto the branches of trees.

BIRDS

How many species of birds are there?

There are about 8,600 species of birds and they live in, on or above almost every part of the Earth's surface, except for the deep oceans. Different from one another in size, shape and colour, the one charactcristic that unites all birds is the presence of feathers. This is what makes birds unique. No other member of the animal kingdom has feathers.

Can all birds fly?

Not all birds can fly. Penguins cannot fly but use their wings as flippers for swimming under water. Some species of cormorant, too, have lost the power of flight. Their bodies are so well adapted to swimming and diving that their wings have become too small to support their weight in flight. Some flightless land birds, such as the Australian emu, have powerful hindlegs. These birds can walk great distances and flee rapidly from danger. The kiwi from New Zealand has such small wings they don't even show through its feathers.

Most birds can fold their wings close to their bodies. But penguins can't. They hold their wings stiffly out to the side.

▼ The penguin and kiwi are two examples of flightless birds. Penguins use their wings for swimming. Kiwis creep about in thick undergrowth.

Kiwi

Penguin

▲ The ostrich has long, powerful legs and can run very fast. It has wings, but is not able to fly.

Which is the largest living bird?

The African ostrich, standing 2.5 metres tall and weighing up to 135 kilograms, is the largest bird alive. It is too big to fly but is the fastest creature on two legs, achieving speeds of up to 70 kilometres an hour.

Why do birds have feathers?

There are two main reasons why birds have feathers: to keep them warm and to help them fly. Feathers may also provide birds with beautiful plumage to make them attractive to the opposite sex.

Why do birds preen?

Birds keep their feathers in condition by preening. The bird smears its beak with oil from a gland and runs its beak through its feathers like a comb.

What are feathers made of?

Feathers are made of a horny protein substance called keratin. This is the same substance from which our hair and fingernails are made, the difference being in the way the feather is constructed. Keratin combines lightness with strength and flexibility, and this makes it an ideal building material for feathers.

Why do birds moult?

A bird drops worn out feathers and replaces them with new ones. Most birds lose only a few feathers at a time so they can still fly and keep warm. Winter coats are thicker for warmth. In the breeding season, birds tend to grow more brightly coloured plumage.

How are birds able to fly?

Almost every part of a bird's body is designed for flight. Their wings and body shape are streamlined and their bones are light. Because flying uses up huge amounts of energy, their lungs have become very efficient and their internal digestive system is able to release energy from food very quickly.

How do birds keep flying without getting tired?

Birds use up lots of energy when they flap their wings. To reduce the amount of energy used many have evolved ways of flying, such as soaring and gliding, which don't involve flapping. When they need to flap their wings, as during a rapid take-off, their special breathing system ensures that they are supplied with extra oxygen.

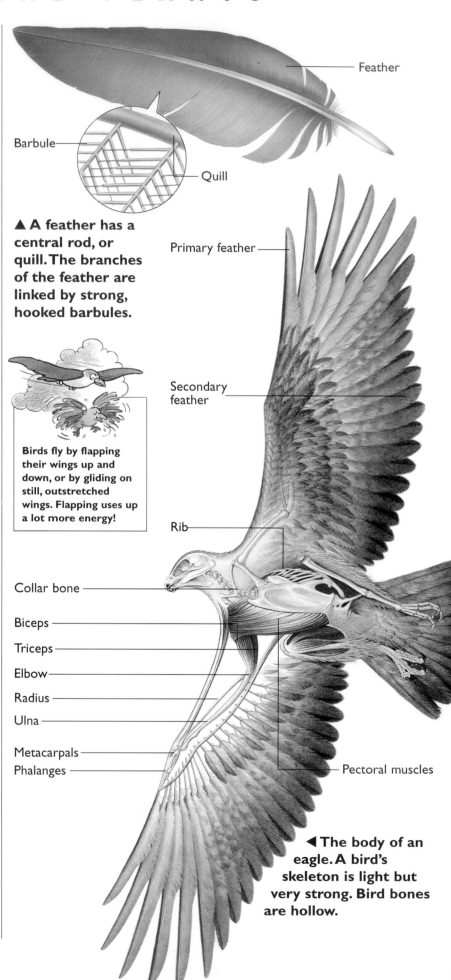

Feather

Barbule

Quill

▲ A feather has a central rod, or quill. The branches of the feather are linked by strong, hooked barbules.

Birds fly by flapping their wings up and down, or by gliding on still, outstretched wings. Flapping uses up a lot more energy!

Primary feather

Secondary feather

Rib

Collar bone

Biceps

Triceps

Elbow

Radius

Ulna

Metacarpals

Phalanges

Pectoral muscles

◄ The body of an eagle. A bird's skeleton is light but very strong. Bird bones are hollow.

Woodpecker
(drill)

Crossbill
(nutcracker)

Kestrel
(tearing)

Spoonbill
(detector/sieve)

Oystercatcher
(probe)

Why do birds lay eggs?

Birds lay eggs because their reptile
ancestors laid eggs, and because it
has suited them to retain this
characteristic. If a female gave birth
to live young or carried a developing
egg around inside her body, then she
would probably be unable to fly
because of the extra weight. So birds
lay their eggs as soon as possible
after mating.

Why do birds build nests?

Birds build nests to protect their eggs
and young from the weather and from
any marauding predators. Nests also
help retain the warmth of the parent
bird during incubation. Bird nests vary
greatly in size and shape: they can be
massive structures of loose branches,
or tiny cup-like containers warmly
lined with hair and feathers.

How do baby birds hatch?

A baby bird chips its way out of
the shell using a special egg tooth
on its beak. It pecks away from the
inside until the shell cracks and it
can escape.

**▶ The woodpecker makes
a hole in a tree for its
nest. The chaffinch makes
a nest of moss and feathers.
Storks build big nests
of twigs, sometimes
on rooftops.**

**▲ You can
sometimes tell
what kind of a food
a bird eats from the
shape of its beak.
Birds use their
beaks as tools, and
five different ones
are shown here.**

BIRD FACTS

■ The ostrich lays the
biggest egg of any bird,
weighing about 1.7 kg.

■ The smallest bird is
the bee hummingbird of
Cuba, which weighs less
than 1.6 g.

■ Depending on its
species, a bird has
between 940 and
25,000 feathers.

■ The world's fastest
animal is a bird. The
peregrine falcon can reach
300 km/h in a dive.

■ The bird with the
longest wings is the
wandering albatross:
over 3 m across.

Why are birds' beaks all so different?

Birds' beaks are so different because
they all eat different kinds of food.
Seed-eaters tend to have short, strong,
wedge-shaped beaks for picking and
cracking seeds, while insect-eaters
have thinner, pointed beaks which
they use like tweezers to extract small
prey. Birds that catch insects on the
wing often have short beaks and wide
gaping mouths which they use like
fishing nets as they fly along. The
beaks of flesh-eating birds are usually
strong and hooked, suitable for
ripping flesh off their prey.

Why do birds sing?

Birds sing to attract other birds of the
same species or to warn them off.
Males sing to attract females as mates.
The song also warns other males
that the singer has its own territory
and will defend it. Parents and
chicks recognize each
other's voices.

Stork

Woodpecker

Chaffinch

◄ Two great crested grebes dance to show that they are a pair. Many birds choose new mates (often more than one) each season, whereas others pair for life.

Why do some birds dance?

Dances form part of the mating displays of certain birds. Great crested grebes perform an elegant courtship dance on the water to establish a firm pair bond. Often their display includes head-shaking and taking turns to preen each other. The display ends in an exchange of weed where two birds rise up out of the water facing each other and present their gifts.

Why do birds migrate?

Birds migrate as the seasons change in order to find the food and living conditions which suit them best at different times of the year. Each year songbirds, seabirds, waterfowl and waders all make long, difficult journeys from their summer breeding quarters to their winter feeding grounds. They do this to take advantage of the seasonal variations in climate and food supply.

► The Arctic tern is the champion long-distance flier. Its amazing migration takes it across the world and back again.

DID YOU KNOW?

■ Treecreepers nest under the bark of trees. They find a loose piece of bark and make a nest behind it.

■ Perching birds, or songbirds, can sleep without falling off branches. They have three forward-pointing toes and one backward-pointing toe, for a firm grip.

■ Jays happily sit on ant nests. Angry ants crawl among the bird's feathers, squirting stinging formic acid. The acid gets rids of lice and fleas which make the bird itch.

■ Woodpeckers use their stiff tail feathers as supports when climbing trees.

■ Owls fly silently. Soft fringes on the feathers muffle the sound of the owl's wingbeats.

Which bird flies from the North Pole to the South Pole (and back again)?

Arctic terns spend months continuously on the wing at sea. They breed within the Arctic Circle during the summer months, and then head south for the Antarctic to take advantage of the summer season there. They cover more than 35,000 kilometres on the round trip.

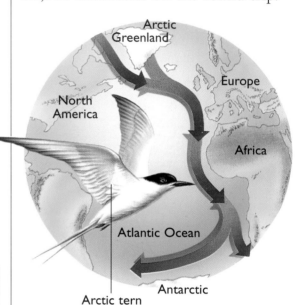

Which birds carry water in their breast feathers?

Sandgrouse are birds which live in dry and desert areas in Africa and the Middle East. The males have special breast feathers that soak up water like a sponge. The males carry water to their chicks.

Why do woodpeckers peck wood?

They feed on insects which burrow in wood and under bark. They also nest in trees and will peck out holes if they can't find a suitable nest hole. Some woodpeckers drum their beaks loudly against trees to attract a mate.

REPTILES AND AMPHIBIANS

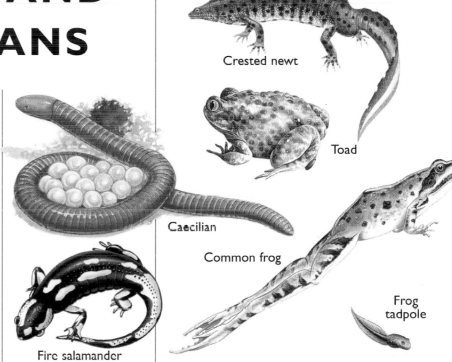

Crested newt

Toad

Caecilian

Common frog

Fire salamander

Frog tadpole

What is an amphibian?

An amphibian can be thought of as the half-way stage between a fish and a reptile. Most amphibians spend the first part of their life in water and the adult phase on dry land. They have soft, moist skins and lay their eggs in water or very damp surroundings. They live in wet places, such as swamps and marshes, although they cannot survive in the sea.

How many species of amphibians are there?

Compared to fish, reptiles, birds and mammals, the total number of living amphibian species is rather small. Some 2,300 species are known, and these can be divided into three groups: frogs and toads (amphibians without tails); newts and salamanders (amphibians with tails); and caecilians (burrowing, limbless amphibians confined to the tropics).

What do frogs and toads eat?

All frogs and toads are flesh-eaters and, as a rule, eat only living prey. Their diet is usually made up of insects, spiders, slugs and worms. Frogs and toads have long, sticky tongues which they shoot out to catch their prey. Some larger frogs, notably the horned frogs and bullfrogs, are able to eat small mammals, such as voles or shrews, and other amphibians.

▲ Amphibians are found all over the world, except in places that are very dry or cold. Most amphibians have four legs, but caecilians are legless amphibians.

How do tadpoles turn into frogs?

When tadpoles first hatch out, they bear little resemblance to their frog or toad parents. Breathing through gills and swimming by means of fish-like tails, these tiny black creatures cannot leave the water. They grow back legs, and then front legs, and their tails shrink. They develop lungs and, now looking like frogs, leave the water.

Adult

Fertilized eggs

16 weeks old

2–3 days old

12 weeks old

6 days old

▶ The life cycle of the frog.

Why do snakes shed their skins?

In fact all animals, including humans, shed their skins, due to natural wear and tear. A snake's tough skin doesn't grow as the snake gets bigger so the snake has to shed it from time to time, like taking off a tight coat.

How does a chameleon catch its food?

Chameleons are highly specialized tree lizards and their ability to change colour to match their surroundings is well known. They capture their prey by means of an extremely long and sticky tongue, which is catapulted out with such speed that few insects stand a chance of escaping. On spotting a suitable prey, both eyes then work separately to give the chameleon a clearer picture of its victim. In this way the chameleon can be said to have the best all-round vision of any reptile. Chameleons change colour when angry or excited, as well as to hide from enemies. Some kinds go black with rage!

► **A snake's old skin begins to split at the lips, and the snake wriggles out head first, turning the skin inside out as it goes.**

Chameleons are masters of disguise. They can change their colour to match their surroundings – well, almost!

Does the Komodo dragon breathe fire?

Unlike the fabulous winged monsters of popular myth, the Komodo dragon does not breathe fire, nor does it fly. This solidly built animal with a huge head and long thick tail is the largest of all living lizards. It lives on a few islands in Indonesia and preys on animals such as deer and wild pigs.

Komodo dragon

▲ **The chameleon's sticky tongue is longer than its body! It shoots it out in a twinkling and reels it back with an insect meal.**

FISH

Water out
past gills

Blood vessels

Water in
through mouth

Gill filaments

Gill arch

Water flowing past

Oxygen-rich
blood

Oxygen-poor blood

◀ **Feathery filaments in a fish's gills take in oxygen from the water. The oxygen passes into the fish's blood and is carried around the fish's body.**

Seahorses are not strong swimmers, so they hang on to seaweed with their tails to avoid being swept away.

How many fish are there?

Fish are the most numerous of all vertebrates. There are estimated to be over 20,500 different types of fish, of which about a third live in fresh water and two-thirds in the sea. Scientists classify fish into three groups: jawless fish (of which there are about 60 species); sharks and rays (about 600 species); and bony fish (20,000 species). The bony fish are the most successful and have colonized almost every body of water on Earth.

How do fish swim?

Most fish swim using a side-to-side movement, the thrust forward being powered by a wave of muscular contraction spreading down the body. The strong muscles which run down either side of the fish's body may sometimes account for up to 75 percent of the fish's weight, and are the part of the fish we like to eat. The fish uses its fins for steering, braking and balance. Some fish also fan their fins to keep themselves in one position. The fastest fish, the blue-finned tunny, can swim at 60 kilometres per hour.

Why do fish die if taken out of water?

Like all animals, fish need oxygen to live. Unlike land-living animals, fish can only take in oxygen from water. When a fish is removed from water, it is removed from its source of oxygen and soon dies if not put back. Fish gulp in water through their mouths, forcing it over their pink gills and out through openings on either side of the head. The water keeps flowing over the gills, bringing fresh oxygen.

▶ **Fish swim by using their muscles to ripple their bodies along. Wiggling their tails from side to side gives them some extra push.**

How does the stickleback build its nest?

The male stickleback builds his nest using small pieces of water plants, gluing them together with a sticky secretion from his kidneys. Once he has assembled a small heap, he then burrows through the middle to make a tunnel, thereby completing the nest. Displaying a bright red belly, the male entices a female into the nest to lay eggs. The male stickleback guards the nest until the eggs hatch and the young are ready to leave. The males do not learn this behaviour but all perform exactly the same actions.

How do some fishes make electricity?

About 250 kinds of fish can produce electric shocks. They do this to find their way in muddy water, and also to kill their prey. The most powerful electric fish can produce shocks of several hundred volts – enough to stun a person. Special muscles work like batteries.

▲ The male seahorse looks after the eggs. He keeps them in a pouch on his body until the young hatch and can look after themselves.

▼ Deep-sea fish look weird, with gaping mouths, stomachs that stretch, and baitlike lures to attract a meal.

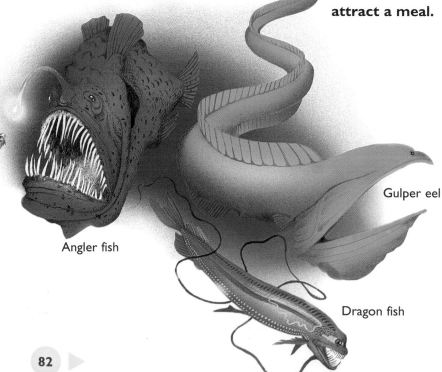

Angler fish

Gulper eel

Dragon fish

What kind of animal is a seahorse?

A seahorse is a very strange animal. It lives in the sea, and its head looks like a horse's head. But it is much smaller than a horse, being no more than 15 centimetres long. It has a curly tail, no legs and swims in an upright position, using a fin on its back. The fin gives it away, for the seahorse is in fact a very unusual kind of fish.

Why is the coelacanth called a living fossil?

Coelacanths are large, heavy-bodied fish which were thought to have died out 70 million years ago. When a living coelacanth was caught off the coast of South Africa in 1938, it was as if someone had discovered a living dinosaur! Living coelacanths bear close similarities to their fossilized ancestors. Their lobed fins have fleshy bases which look like the beginnings of limbs, and they are known to give birth to fully-formed live young. Scientists believe that some of the first vertebrates to live on land looked like coelacanths that walked on their fins.

What is life like for a deep-sea fish?

The world of the deep-sea fish is black and cold. Beyond a depth of 750 metres, no sunlight filters through, so no plants are able to grow. Food is scarce, and deep-sea fish have to rely on other animals for their food. To cope with these difficult conditions, deep-sea fish have evolved special mechanisms, which give them strange and often frightening appearances. Most have huge jaws.

INSECTS

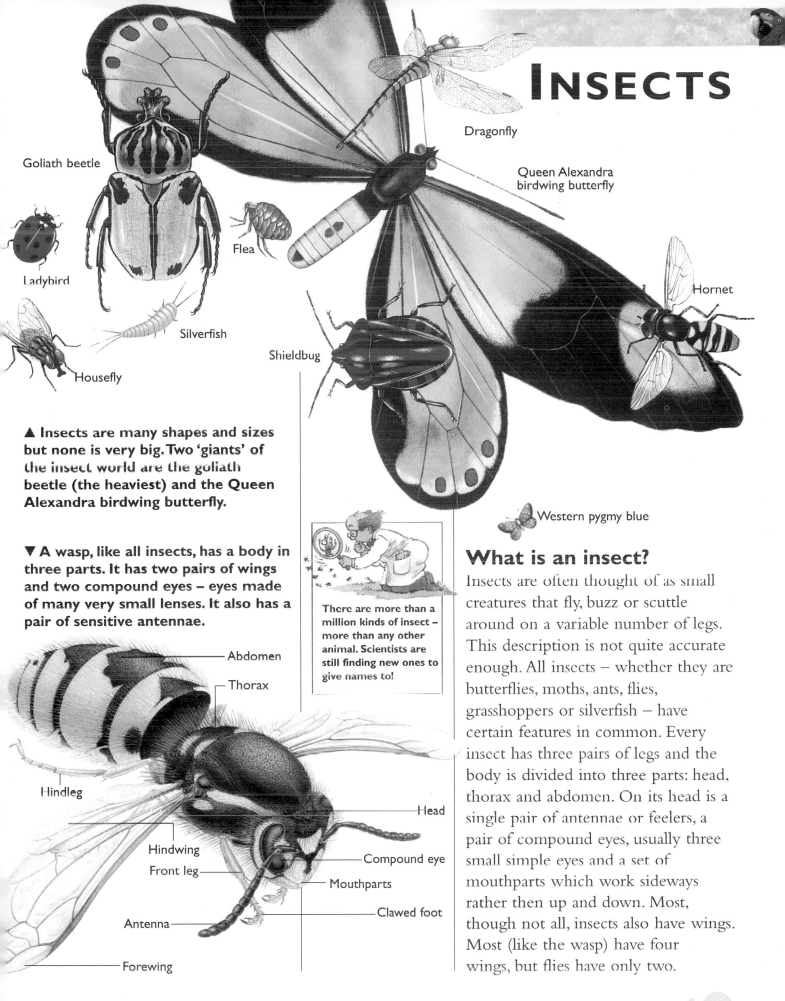

Goliath beetle

Ladybird

Flea

Silverfish

Housefly

Dragonfly

Queen Alexandra
birdwing butterfly

Hornet

Shieldbug

Western pygmy blue

▲ Insects are many shapes and sizes but none is very big. Two 'giants' of the insect world are the goliath beetle (the heaviest) and the Queen Alexandra birdwing butterfly.

▼ A wasp, like all insects, has a body in three parts. It has two pairs of wings and two compound eyes – eyes made of many very small lenses. It also has a pair of sensitive antennae.

There are more than a million kinds of insect – more than any other animal. Scientists are still finding new ones to give names to!

Abdomen

Thorax

Hindleg

Hindwing

Front leg

Antenna

Forewing

Head

Compound eye

Mouthparts

Clawed foot

What is an insect?

Insects are often thought of as small creatures that fly, buzz or scuttle around on a variable number of legs. This description is not quite accurate enough. All insects – whether they are butterflies, moths, ants, flies, grasshoppers or silverfish – have certain features in common. Every insect has three pairs of legs and the body is divided into three parts: head, thorax and abdomen. On its head is a single pair of antennae or feelers, a pair of compound eyes, usually three small simple eyes and a set of mouthparts which work sideways rather then up and down. Most, though not all, insects also have wings. Most (like the wasp) have four wings, but flies have only two.

Life cycle of a butterfly

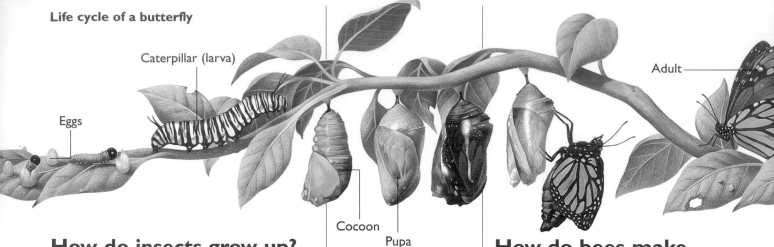

Caterpillar (larva)

Eggs

Cocoon

Pupa

Adult

How do insects grow up?

Insects go through changes as they grow from the egg to the adult. These changes are called metamorphoses. There are two types: insects such as grasshoppers pass through three stages, each resembling the adult more closely. This is incomplete metamorphosis. Complete metamorphosis, as in the butterfly, involves four stages: egg, larva, pupa and adult. The intermediate stages bear no resemblance to the adult. You could not guess that a caterpillar would turn into a butterfly. Inside the pupa an amazing change takes place – and a butterfly comes out.

Which ant grows its own food?

Like other ants, leafcutter ants of Central and South America are 'social' insects – they live together in groups called colonies. These ants strip leaves from trees and use them as a basis for growing fungi in underground 'gardens'. The workers chew the leaves and compress them into fungus beds, fertilizing the growth of the fungus with their droppings. The growing fungus is used to feed the whole ant colony.

▲ **Butterflies lay eggs that hatch into caterpillars. Each caterpillar spins itself a cocoon and becomes a pupa. Finally an adult butterfly emerges.**

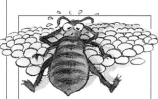

A queen bee lays up to 3,500 eggs a day for several weeks at a time. She is the only mother in the beehive!

▶ **A bee feeding from a flower becomes dusted with pollen. It carries the pollen to other flowers, perhaps a long distance away, and so fertilizes them.**

How do bees make honey?

Honey is made from nectar, the sugary liquid present in flowers. It is sucked up by bees using their long tongues and stored in their honey stomachs. When the bee's honey stomach is full, it returns to the hive and passes the nectar to other workers as a thin runny fluid. The hive bees then mix the nectar with secretions from their mouths before depositing it in open cells in the honey comb. Within about three days the nectar compound is transformed into honey. The finished honey is then sealed with a wax cap until needed for future use, to feed young bees or as winter food for all.

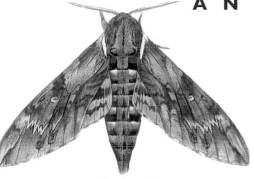

Hawkmoth

Peacock butterfly

What is the difference between a butterfly and a moth?

People tend to think of moths as dull-coloured, night-flying insects with fat, furry bodies, and butterflies as brightly coloured, day-flying insects. In fact there are many brightly coloured moths which fly by day. The six-spot Burnet moth and the emperor moth are two examples. To a scientist, the real difference lies in the shape of their antennae and the linkage between the forewings and hindwings. A butterfly's antennae are long and slender, and tipped with knobs, while the moth's antennae are thin and feathery. At rest, most butterflies fold their wings over their bodies, revealing their underside pattern, while moths hold their wings either spread out flat or at an angle to each other.

How does the grasshopper sing?

A grasshopper produces its familiar chirping sound by rubbing its hindlegs over the ribs of its forewings. On the inner side of the femur, or 'thigh' of each hindleg, is a row of tiny, evenly spaced pegs, and these are stroked over the prominent veins on the forewings. Usually it is only the male who sings.

▲ **Moths look rather like aircraft, with swept back or delta wings. Most butterflies fold their wings when they are resting.**

▶ **The termite queen lays thousands of eggs, attended by the king. Soldiers defend the nest while workers gather food.**

INSECT WONDERS

■ Insects breathe through tiny holes in their bodies.

■ Many insects can drag an object 20 times their own body weight.

■ A caterpillar has from 2,000 to 4,000 muscles – six times as many as you!

■ A tiny midge holds the record for fast wingbeats: more than 62,000 times a minute.

■ Ants lay scent trails to food so other ants can follow them.

Why are termites called white ants?

Termites are pale, soft-bodied insects and, like ants, they live in large, underground colonies. They also have a caste system to separate the different functions of its members. But those are the only similarities. Termites have straight antennae, but an ant's antennae are bent. An ant's body has a 'waist' between the thorax and abdomen, but the termite does not. Ants and termites evolved along similar lines, but in fact, termites are more closely related to cockroaches than to ants.

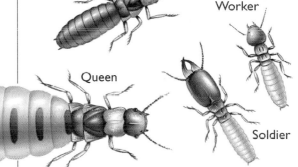

King

Worker

Queen

Soldier

Why are stick and leaf insects so called?

It is not hard to see why stick and leaf insects are named as they are. Practically indistinguishable from a background of twigs, leaves and branches, the stick and leaf insects are camouflage experts. They rest motionless during the day, their long twig-like bodies blending perfectly with the surrounding branches, and move and feed only at night. Even their eggs are camouflaged to look like the seeds of the plant on which they live. These curious insects occur mainly in the tropical regions of Asia and live in trees and shrubs.

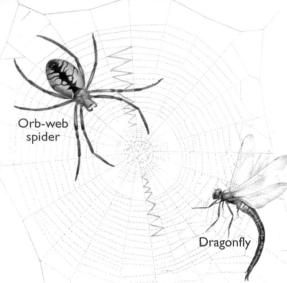

Orb-web spider

Dragonfly

Is a spider an insect?

Spiders are not insects but arachnids. Unlike an insect, which has six legs, a spider has eight legs. Spiders do not have wings, nor do they have antennae, although a pair of slender palps at the front of the head may sometimes be mistaken for these. A spider's body is usually hairy and is divided into two main parts – a combined head and thorax, and an abdomen. The two are linked by a narrow waist. All spiders have a pair of poison fangs with which they kill their prey, and all are capable of producing silk, although they don't always use it to make webs.

Do all scorpions have a deadly sting?

Scorpions are related to spiders. The sting of a scorpion is located at the tip of its long curvy tail, which is either held to one side or arched over the scorpion's back. Some scorpions only have a mild sting, while others can be deadly to human beings. Scorpions live in hot, dry regions, and hunt at night.

◄ **This orb-web spider feels the dragonfly's efforts to escape and rushes to wrap its prey in silk to add to its food store.**

▼ **Lobsters and crabs are crustaceans. Hermit crabs take over the shells of other animals.**

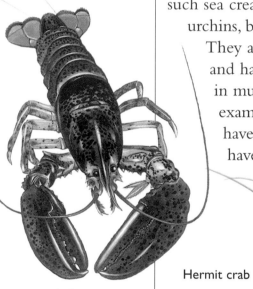

Lobster

▼ **The scorpion is a relative of the spider. It uses its sting for defence and to paralyze its prey.**

Do centipedes really have a hundred legs?

Although 'centipede' literally means a hundred feet, no centipede has exactly that number. Some may have more, some less, but the most familiar garden centipedes have only 15 pairs of legs. Centipedes like to live in dark, damp places such as under logs and stones.

What are echinoderms?

The echinoderms are a group of spiny-skinned animals, which include such sea creatures as starfish, sea urchins, brittlestars and featherstars. They are usually symmetrical and have their organs arranged in multiples of five. For example, starfish normally have five arms but some may have as many as 50.

Hermit crab

What is a crustacean?

Crustaceans have sometimes been described as the water-breathing insects of the sea. They do in fact belong to the same phylum (Arthropoda) as insects, and comprise an enormous variety of species, most of which live in the sea. All crustaceans have hard shell-like outsides, and two pairs of antennae, and some kinds have claws. Crabs, lobsters, prawns, shrimps, waterfleas and barnacles all belong to this group of animals.

THE PLANT KINGDOM

What are the simplest plants like?

The first plants appeared about 3.5 billion years ago. They were single-celled algae and diatoms. Such plants are very tiny. A single drop of water can contain 500 diatoms.

Which are the most successful plants?

The flowering plants are the biggest and most successful plant group. There are more than 250,000 different kinds. They include grasses, cacti, trees, peas and beans, vines, potatoes, spices and many garden and wild flowers. All these plants have flowers which play a part producing seeds to grow into new plants.

PLANT RECORDS

■ The oldest known plant is the creosote plant of California. It is around 11,700 years old.

■ The fastest-growing plant is bamboo. It can grow at 1 metre a day.

■ The Welwitschia, a desert plant of South Africa, lives for over 100 years but grows only two leaves.

■ A wild fig in South Africa had roots 120 m long – the longest roots ever measured.

■ The smallest plant is an Australian floating duckweed. This tiny water plant is just 0.6 mm long and 0.3 mm across.

▼ **Flowering plants bring colour and scents to summer days. They make sure their seeds are spread, either by animals or by the wind.**

Why are flowers coloured?

Many flowers have brightly coloured petals to attract insects. These flowering plants rely on insects to carry pollen from flower to flower. Plants that flower at night often have pale-coloured flowers so that they show up in the dark and the night-flying moths can see them. Many flowers give off scent to attract insects to pollinate them.

Why do most plants have flowers?

Flowers help plants to reproduce themselves. The flower produces male and female cells (pollen and egg cells). The egg cells must be fertilized with pollen from another flower of the same kind. Some plants, such as holly, have separate male and female flowers. The flower also protects the egg cells as they grow into seeds.

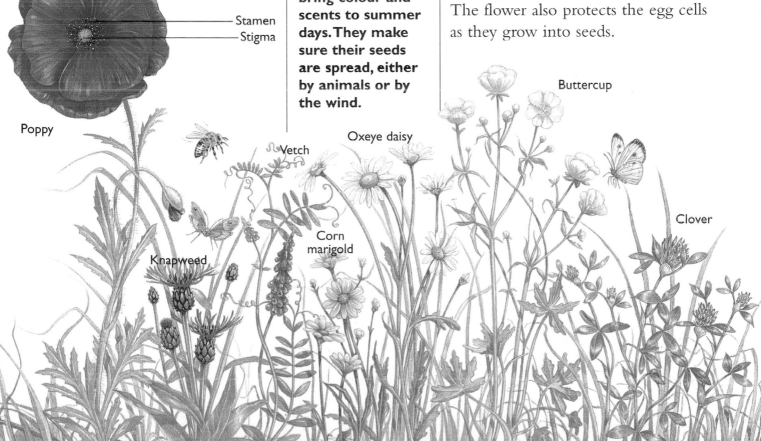

Petal

Stamen

Stigma

Poppy

Buttercup

Oxeye daisy

Vetch

Clover

Corn marigold

Knapweed

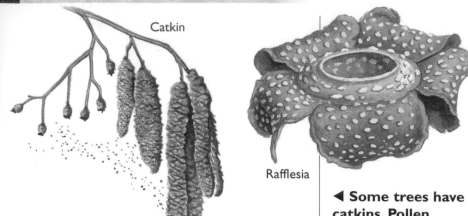

Catkin

Rafflesia

Do all flowers have petals?

No. Some plants are pollinated by the wind or by water. They do not need to attract insects and so their flowers often do not have petals. Many of these plants bloom in early spring, so that leaves do not get in the way of the wind blowing through the branches. The catkin flower of the hazel does not have petals nor does the giant rafflesia.

Do all flowers close up at night?

Many, but not all, flowers close up at night or when the weather is cold. The daisy closes its flowers when the light begins to fade in the evening. Crocuses are even more sensitive, and will open when the sun is shining and close when it goes behind a cloud. Wood sorrel even closes its leaves at night. Some flowers, like the evening primrose, close their petals during the day and open them at night.

Does grass have flowers?

Grass plants do have flowers, but they are not brightly coloured because they do not need to attract insects to pollinate them. The flowers do not

◄ **Some trees have catkins. Pollen grains from male catkins are blown to the female catkins, so male sex cells and female egg cells are mixed. The giant rafflesia flower smells like rotting meat, to attract flies.**

▼ **Cacti soak up water during the rainy season and store it in their stems. The cactus shrinks as it uses up water during the dry season.**

have petals and when the pollen is ready it is just blown away by the wind. Grasses, such as wheat, oats and barley, are the most important source of food for people. The first farmers found that wild grass seeds scattered as easily as the pollen. Modern farmers have managed to grow crops with tighter flowering heads so that the seeds, or grain, do not fall out.

Do all plants have leaves?

Most, but not all, plants have leaves, though they do not always look like leaves. The blades of grass are leaves. Algae such as seaweed do not have leaves, but they have chlorophyll and can make their own food.

How do plants survive in the desert?

Desert plants such as cacti can live for months or even years without water. They have evolved ways of storing moisture in thick stems or swollen fleshy leaves. Other desert plants store water in their roots. A desert plant may remain dried up and appear dead for years. When rain eventually falls, the desert blooms. The plants spurt into growth. They flower, pollinate, make seeds and spread them in only a few weeks.

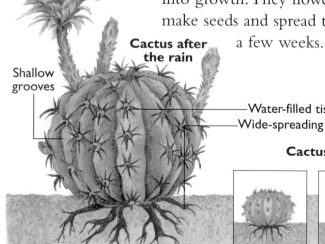

Cactus after the rain

Shallow grooves

Water-filled tissue

Wide-spreading roots

Cactus during drought

Why do some plants have wings and parachutes?

The wind can spread a plant's seeds over long distances. Some seeds are light enough to blow about easily. Dandelions and thistles have fruits crowned with hairy plumes that act like parachutes. The seeds drift away on the wind. The fruit of some trees such as the birch, maple and ash have wings. These spin like the blades of a helicopter as they carry the seed away.

Which fruits explode?

A plant needs to spread its seeds to give each one the best possible chance of growing into a new plant. One way to spread seeds is to shoot them out from an exploding capsule or pod. Laburnum trees and other plants of the pea family have seeds in pods. When a laburnum pod dries out, it splits. The two halves twist, flinging out the seeds to spread them so the seedlings can find space to grow. Incidentally, never eat the seeds (or any part) of the laburnum tree, because they are poisonous.

◄ Some plants parachute their seeds. The dandelion's plume of hairs slows its fall so it can drift on the wind.

▶ There are about 10,000 kinds of ferns (like Adder's tongue) and about 8,000 kinds of liverworts, small plants that grow in damp places (like *Marchantia polymorpha* and *Pellia epiphylla*).

◄ The European squirting cucumber shoots out its seeds in a jet of water from its balloon-shaped fruit. Water pressure inside forces the seeds out suddenly.

Why do some plants have no flowers?

Mosses and ferns have no flowers because they do not produce seeds. Instead they produce spores. The spores of ferns form on its leaves and fall. The spore develops into a heart-shaped structure called a prothallus which produces male and female cells. When the female cell is fertilized, it grows into a new fern.

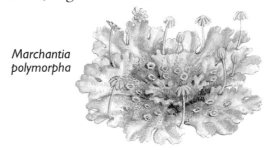

Marchantia polymorpha

Adder's tongue

Pellia epiphylla

HOW PLANTS GROW

Sunlight

Oxygen

Carbon dioxide

Water

Water

Can plants live without sunlight?

All green plants need sunlight because they use the Sun's energy to make their food. The food-making process, called photosynthesis, takes place mainly in the leaves using a substance called chlorophyll. If a green plant is kept in darkness, it soon loses its green colour, withers and dies.

How do plants feed?

Plants have to feed themselves to stay alive, just as people and animals do. However, green plants are able to make their own food. They make sugars and starches by absorbing carbon dioxide through their leaves, and water from the soil and rain through their roots and leaves. They use energy from sunlight to change the gas and water into food, which they can store if necessary. This food-making process is called photosynthesis. Oxygen is given off, keeping the air supplied with oxygen. The plants also take up minerals through their roots.

Fungi such as mushrooms and toadstools are not classed as plants because they do not make their own food. They feed on other plants, or the remains of plants, and can live in darkness.

◄ In photosynthesis, plants use energy from sunlight to turn water (from the soil) and carbon dioxide (from the air) into glucose. Leaves give off oxygen.

How are insects useful to plants?

Insects are useful to plants because they carry pollen from one flower to another. A plant must be pollinated before it can form seeds. Insects are attracted to flowers by their bright colours, or by their scent, and by the sweet nectar many flowers produce. Some flowers even look like the insects they want to attract to them. As the insects reach for the nectar, they brush against the flower's stamens and stigmas and the pollen falls onto them. When they go to another flower, the pollen is brushed onto its stigmas.

Why do plants need water?

Over 90 percent of a plant is water. Without water a plant cannot make food by photosynthesis. Water helps to keep the plant's cells rigid. If there is not enough water, the cells become limp and the plant wilts. Most plants need a constant supply of water from their roots.

◄ Cactus plants are adapted to life in hot deserts. They make use of the smallest drop of moisture.

▶ When a bee lands on a flower, it dips its tongue into the flower to suck up the sweet nectar. At the same time pollen from the stamens sticks to its body and rubs off onto another flower's stigma.

MORE PLANT FACTS

■ Some giant waterlilies of South America have leaves 1.5 m across.

■ The giant saguaro cactus of the American desert reaches a height of well over 15 m.

■ Plants usually need sunlight. But some plants manage to live at ocean depths where there is no sunlight.

■ The maidenhair tree or gingko of China is the earliest surviving plant species. It appeared about 160 million years ago.

■ The true fruit of an apple is the core, not the juicy bit that you eat.

■ The taproot is a plant's main root, the bit that is hard to pull up when you are weeding.

Why do desert plants spread out?

Desert plants do not grow close together. If they did they would compete for the scarce food and water. Instead they spread out. Desert plants usually have long roots, which spread to catch as much moisture as possible. When it rains, the roots of the plant soak up all the water they can reach from the ground. The plant stores the water in its fleshy stem.

How do plants keep cool?

Plants lose water through tiny pores, or stomata, under their leaves. This loss is called transpiration. At the same time the plant draws up water from the soil into its roots. The water lost through the leaves helps keep the plant cool. The flow of water up the stem from the roots brings with it vital minerals from the soil.

Can a plant reproduce itself without making seeds?

Yes. Plants can reproduce in several other ways. They can split into two, they can grow buds that develop into new cells, they can make spores (as ferns do) or they can reproduce by vegetative propagation. This happens in strawberry plants. The plant sends out a long stem, called a runner, which sprouts roots. If the runner is then cut, its rooted part will grow into a new plant. Similarly, if you cut the eye, or bud, from a potato and plant it, it will send out a shoot to make a new potato plant.

Why are some plants parasites?

Some plants, such as ivy or tropical lianas, use other plants as supports. This avoids spending energy on making their own stem stiff. However, they make their own food. Mistletoe is a part-parasite. It takes some food from the tree it clings to by piercing the bark with root-like tubes, but it also has green leaves to make some food on its own. Other parasites take all their food from the 'host' plant and make none of their own. They are true parasites.

How do climbing plants climb?

Plants climb in different ways. Some, like clematis, are very weak and have twisting stems which climb up other stronger plants. As the stems touch the other plants they grow more quickly on one side and so curl around the other plant. Some plants, like ivy,

The first land plants evolved on Earth just over 400 million years ago. Unlike the limp aquatic seaweed that they come from, they had tubes to draw up water and stiff stems to help them stand erect in the open air. But unlike today's plants, they had no leaves, roots or flowers.

grow small roots on their stems and these help them to grow up walls. Peas and marrows have special coiled tendrils which wind around a support. Virginia creeper has little pads like suckers which cling to a wall or other surface. Climbing roses and blackberries use their sharp spines to hold on to surfaces or other plants.

How do the leaves of a waterlily float?

Waterlilies often have large leaves with many air spaces on the underside. The air trapped beneath the leaf makes it float on the water. Also, the leaves usually have strong stems which help them to keep upright. In this way, the waterlily exposes its leaves to the light it needs to stay alive.

Why do some plants have thorns?

Thorns, prickles and sharp spines help to protect a plant from hungry animals. They may also stop insects boring into the plant. Cows in a meadow will eat grass but not thistles, because they have too many spines. Sometimes seeds are prickly so that they will cling to an animal's fur and so get spread around. They are carried by the animal to a new patch of ground, brushed off, and fall to the earth where they can start to grow.

Honeysuckle

Hop

Earth nut pea

Ivy

Bramble

◄ Some plants twist around stronger plants as they climb. Others have small roots or spines to cling on with.

Why does a stinkhorn stink?

A stinkhorn is a kind of fungus which stinks in order to attract flies. It may smell nasty to us, but flies like it. They feed on the slime which contains spores and then they carry the spores away on their legs. In this way stinkhorns can spread over a large area – aided by flies.

Why does moss grow in a thick mat?

Moss grows from spores. When the spore starts to grow, it sends out a thin green thread which grows branches. Buds form on the branches and grow into new moss plants. The young plants therefore grow very close together and soon form a mat. Moss leaves are not waterproof, and by growing in thick mats they keep moisture around themselves.

How do ferns grow?

Ferns do not have flowers, so they cannot produce seeds. Instead they have spores on the underside of the leaves. The spores fall to the ground and grow into little discs. The discs contain male and female cells, which later come together and grow into young ferns. Some ferns, like bracken, also spread from rhizomes, or underground stems.

▲ The stinkhorn is well named. Hungry flies swarm towards this smelly fungus, hoping for a meal. They fly off, carrying the stinkhorn's spores.

▼ Under the fern's fronds are sporangia, lined with spores. A spore is blown away and grows into a prothallus, from which a young fern soon develops.

Do plants have clocks?

Many plants know what time of year it is with amazing accuracy. Some flowering plants bloom at exactly the same time every year. Like many animals, plants prepare for winter by storing food in their underground stems and roots. Their 'clock' is controlled by the length of day and night, which changes all year round.

Can plants eat insects?

Insect-eating plants, like the sundew and Venus flytrap, live in poor, often boggy soil. The soil has few minerals to feed the plants. The plants have therefore developed traps to catch insects as an extra food source. The sundew's leaves are covered in sticky-tipped tentacles. The Venus flytrap catches insects in traps on the end of its leaves. Each trap snaps shut when an insect touches one of its trigger hairs. The insect is crushed and the plant breaks down its body with acid to obtain the food chemicals it needs.

Why do plant stems grow up and roots grow down?

Plants react to the Earth's gravity. No matter which way you plant a bean seed, the root always grows downwards. The stem grows upwards, seeking the light.

Fern

Sporangia

Prothallus

Young sporophyte

New fern

What kind of tree is used for making baskets?

Many baskets are made from the thin branches of the willow or osier. The bark is taken off to give white wood, or the branches may be boiled with the bark on, which dyes the wood. The branches are soaked so that they will bend easily for weaving into baskets. When they dry, they become firm but are still pliable, so that they do not easily break. Willow wood has many other uses because it is both light and strong.

What is a pollarded tree?

If the top of a young deciduous tree is cut off about 2 metres from the ground, it will send out fresh shoots from the new top. This is called pollarding. Willows may be pollarded to encourage the growth of suitable branches for basket-making.

Why should cattle not graze near yew trees?

Farmers stop cattle, horses and sheep from grazing under yew trees because their leaves, bark and fruit are poisonous. The animals do not try to graze on the yew trees themselves. But they will eat pieces that have fallen off the trees.

How do trees act as the Earth's 'lungs'?

Trees play a vital part in keeping the Earth's atmosphere fit for animals and people to breathe. Tree leaves take up carbon dioxide gas from the air and give off oxygen. We could not live on Earth if the air had too much carbon dioxide or not enough oxygen.

TREE FACTS

■ Travellers in Madagascar can take a drink from the traveller's tree. This tree stores water at the base of its long leaf stalks.

■ The tree with the thickest trunk is a Montezuma bald cypress growing in Mexico. It is 12 metres around!

■ The ombu tree of Argentina is very hardy. It needs little water. Its wood is so moist it will not burn, and so spongy that it is impossible to chop down!

■ The coco-de-mer palm tree of the Indian Ocean has the largest seeds of any tree. The nuts of the coco-de-mer can weigh as much as 20 kg.

■ In Arizona's petrified forest there are logs of prehistoric trees turned to stone millions of years ago.

▼ The spindle tree gets its name because its wood was used to make spindles. It has attractive flowers.

How is a palm different from most other trees?

Palms are unlike most other trees because they do not grow side branches. They do not grow thicker, but only taller. A pattern of scars may be seen all the way up the trunk of a palm tree. The scars mark the places where old leaves once grew. New leaves grow in a cluster at the top of the trunk. If this cluster is cut off, no more new leaves can grow, and the palm will die. The trunk of a palm tree does not have growth-rings like other trees. Palm trees are very useful. They provide nuts for food, and leaves for use as building materials.

Why is a spindle tree so named?

The spindle tree grows in Europe and North America where it is sometimes called the wahoo. The wood of this tree used to be used to make spindles. The spindle was used to wind wool which was spun by hand. This method of spinning is still used in some parts of the world.

BODY BASICS

What is the human body made of?

About two-thirds of the human body is water. The remaining third is an extremely complicated mixture of chemicals. The water-and-chemical mix is arranged into structures called cells. These are tiny, but you can see them using a microscope. Each part of the body is made of a completely different kind of cell. Heart cells, skin cells, bone cells and blood cells all are different. Brain cells are among the very smallest.

▼ This is what a cell's inside looks like. All cells are made up in the same basic way, though they are different shapes and sizes.

What is a cell?

Cells are the small building blocks of the body. They have a very thin outer layer, called the cell membrane, which lets in food and oxygen and lets out waste. Much of the cell is a jelly-like substance called cytoplasm. Activity inside the cell is controlled by the nucleus. There are over 50 thousand billion cells in the human body. There are tubular, round, flat and square cells. Female egg cells are the largest, just big enough to be seen without a microscope.

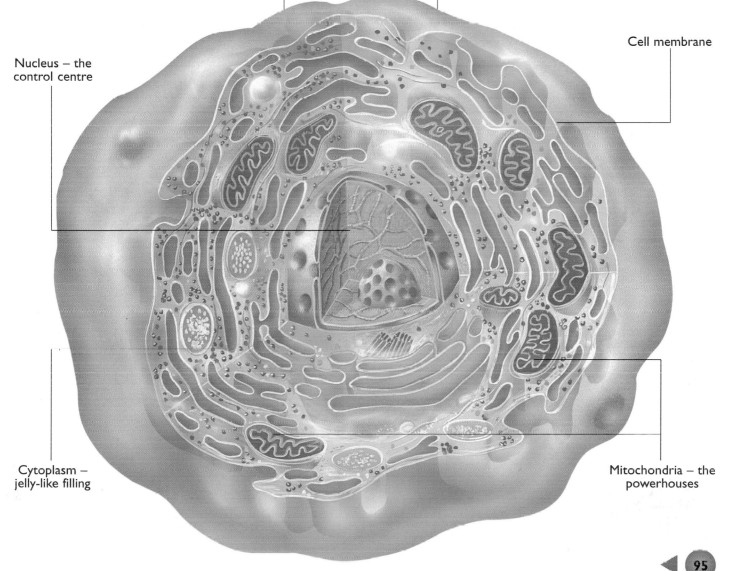

Nucleus – the control centre

Cell membrane

Cytoplasm – jelly-like filling

Mitochondria – the powerhouses

SKELETON AND MOVEMENT

How many bones are there in the body?

Adults have about 206 bones. The number may vary slightly from person to person because some people have an extra pair of ribs, and some have more bones in their hands and feet.

Bones support the soft parts of the body. Without bones, we would

be a messy heap. They also protect vital organs in our body from physical damage. For example, the skull protects the brain and eyes, and the ribcage protects the lungs and heart.

Which is the smallest bone?

In the middle ear is a tiny bone called the stirrup. It is only 3 millimetres long and weighs about 3 milligrams. It passes sound vibrations to the liquid in the inner ear.

Your funny bone isn't a bone at all. It's a nerve just under the skin in each elbow. If you bang your elbow, the nerve sends a message to your brain, and you get a funny feeling!

Which is the largest bone?

The largest bone is the thighbone, or femur. Its special design means it is also the strongest bone. A man who is 1.8 metres tall will have a femur about 0.5 metres long, accounting for almost a third of his height. Our bones grow as we do. When you were born, you had about 350 bones. But by the time you finish growing, there will be only 200 or so bones inside you! As you grow, some of the smaller bones in your body join together to make bigger ones.

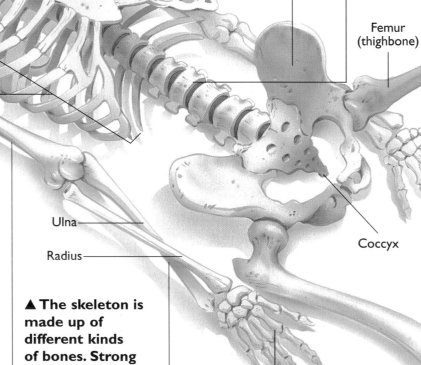

Cranium (skull)

Clavicle (collarbone)

Costa cartilage

Sternum (breastbone)

Spine (backbone)

Pelvis (hipbone)

Femur (thighbone)

Mandible (jawbone)

Scapula (shoulder blade)

Ribcage

Humerus

Ulna

Radius

Coccyx

Metacarpals (hand bones)

▲ The skeleton is made up of different kinds of bones. Strong bones protect important organs (like the brain and the heart).

What is inside a bone?

The outer layer of bone is called compact bone. This is hard and very strong. The inner layer of bone contains lots of spaces, and so is called spongy bone. This bone is also strong but is fairly light, so it keeps down the overall weight of the skeleton, and makes it easier to move. In the middle of bone there is a cavity, filled with a substance called bone marrow. The marrow inside a child's bones is red. As it ages, the marrow in some bones becomes yellowish.

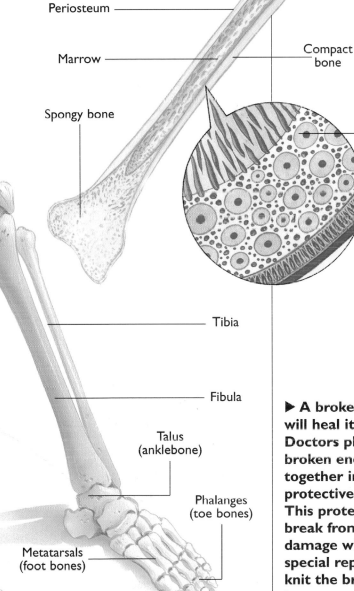

Periosteum

Marrow

Spongy bone

Compact bone

Haversian canals

Tibia

Fibula

Talus (anklebone)

Phalanges (toe bones)

Metatarsals (foot bones)

▼ A bone has a hard outer layer, or periosteum. Beneath this is the compact bone, where food and oxygen move along blood vessels in the Haversian canals.

▶ A broken bone will heal itself. Doctors place the broken ends together inside a protective cast. This protects the break from further damage while special repair cells knit the broken bone together.

How strong is bone?

For its weight, bone is as strong as steel and four times stronger than the same amount of reinforced concrete.

The hard part of bone is made up mainly of the mineral calcium phosphate. Through this run fibres of a protein called collagen. Calcium phosphate gives bone its strength and collagen gives bone its bendiness. If you boil a chicken bone, the collagen is removed so that the bone becomes brittle. If a chicken bone is put in strong vinegar, the calcium dissolves and so the bone becomes rubbery.

How do broken bones mend?

When a bone is cracked or broken, bone cells at the injury grow and multiply, spreading through the damaged region to close up the break. If the two broken ends of the bone are lined up and held still inside a plaster cast, the bone will heal. In children and young adults, this healing process takes 12 weeks or less for bones in the arm or leg. More complicated breaks, known as compound fractures can be more serious. Doctors sometimes insert pins into the bone to hold the broken parts together.

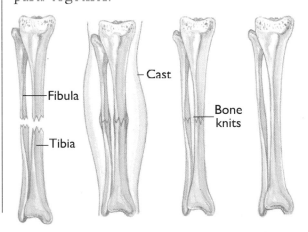

Fibula

Tibia

Cast

Bone knits

Where are the vertebrae?

The vertebrae (just one is a vertebra) are the bones that make up the spine. There are 33 altogether, linked in a flexible chain that runs from the neck to the lower back (the bottom nine vertebrae are fused). The top two vertebrae, the atlas and axis vertebrae, have a different structure from the others, so they can work as a pair to let the head nod and turn. Between each pair of vertebrae a cartilage disc cushions against any jarring. If a disc slips out of place, it can be painful until it is replaced.

Atlas vertebra

Axis vertebra

▲ The atlas vertebra twists on the axis vertebra. This allows you to turn your head sideways.

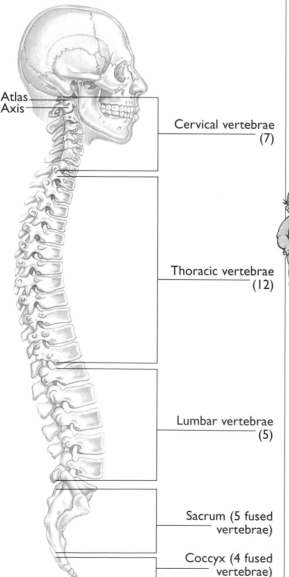

Atlas
Axis

Cervical vertebrae (7)

Thoracic vertebrae (12)

Lumbar vertebrae (5)

Sacrum (5 fused vertebrae)

Coccyx (4 fused vertebrae)

Your bones are partly made of a mineral called calcium. It's rather like stone, but your bones are very much alive. They get bigger as you grow.

◀ Your backbone is a flexible column, held upright in its S-shaped curve by muscles and ligaments. There are 33 vertebrae in the spine.

What are ribs for?

The ribs form a protective cage around the heart and lungs. You can feel your ribcage extending from the flat bone in the middle of your chest, right around your sides to your spine. The ribs also swing up and down when you breathe to inflate and deflate your lungs.

How do bones grow?

In a foetus (unborn child) the bones are made of cartilage. By the time the baby is born, most of the cartilage has turned to bone, in a process called ossification. Growth areas still remain near the ends of the bone. This is where new bone cells are formed. These growth areas disappear when the skeleton reaches full size. Even then, the bone can still alter its shape slightly and repair itself.

Why do people shrink as they grow old?

As people get older, the cartilage pads that protect the bones of the spine become thinner and this leads to height loss. Because people's muscles become weaker with age, their posture changes and this makes them look smaller too. Bones are probably at their strongest when we are in our late twenties. Many people over 60, women in particular, suffer from a condition known as osteoporosis. The bones lose some calcium and become more brittle. Eating fresh green vegetables, milk and milk products should supply enough calcium for most people's needs, but in some cases taking extra calcium may be recommended by a doctor.

What is a joint?

A joint is a place where two or more bones meet. A joint may be fixed (the skull), or movable (the knee). Joints allow us to twist, turn and move our bones. Muscles are attached to and move the bones across a joint. Usually only one bone at a joint moves, relative to another. Strong, elastic straps of tissue called ligaments hold bones together at joints.

What is cartilage?

Cartilage is a slippery bluish-white substance found at the ends of bones, which allows bones to move against one another without causing damage. Cartilage is more slippery than ice. Cartilage is flexible and gives when bones are jarred, so it makes a good shock absorber. The knee has two extra pieces of cartilage, because the knee joint is always under a substantial amount of stress.

▼ This is how your hip joint works. The synovial fluid lubricates the joint, to reduce rubbing between bones.

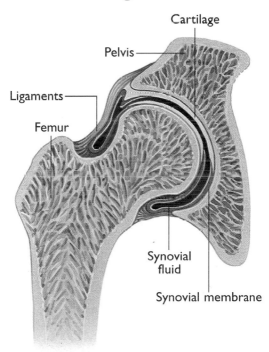

- Cartilage
- Pelvis
- Ligaments
- Femur
- Synovial fluid
- Synovial membrane

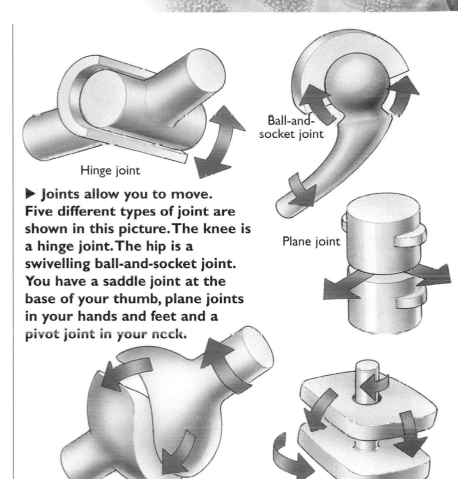

Hinge joint

▶ Joints allow you to move. Five different types of joint are shown in this picture. The knee is a hinge joint. The hip is a swivelling ball-and-socket joint. You have a saddle joint at the base of your thumb, plane joints in your hands and feet and a pivot joint in your neck.

Ball-and-socket joint

Plane joint

Saddle joint

Pivot joint

BONY FACTS

■ Bones weigh surprisingly little. Bone makes up only about 12 percent of your body weight.

■ The only movable joints in your head are those that join the lower jaw to the skull. The hips are the strongest joints.

■ There are 29 different bones in the skull.

■ Hinge joints move in only one direction, a bit like a door hinge. You can find hinge joints in your elbow and between the bones of your fingers, as well as in your knee.

■ The marrow inside a bone can make up to 5 billion red blood cells each day. It also makes the white blood cells.

How many joints do we have?

We have over a hundred joints altogether. There are four main types. Ball-and-socket joints are found at the hip and shoulder. They give free movement in many directions. Hinge joints such as those at the knee and elbow, allow movement in only one direction, rather like a door hinge. Suture joints join together bones in the skull and pelvis. These joints are rigid. Swivel joints, which are found between vertebrae in the spine, allow small tilting and turning actions. Some joints are lubricated, not with oil as in an engine, but with a liquid called synovial fluid that is sandwiched between the bones.

How do muscles help us move?

Joints allow the skeleton to move, but muscles produce the movement, by pulling the bone into a new position. Here is what happens when you bend your elbow. The biceps muscle is attached to your shoulder blade at one end and to a bone in the forearm at the other. The triceps muscle is also connected to the shoulder blade and forearm. When the biceps contracts (shortens), the triceps is relaxed (lengthens) and the elbow bends. When the triceps contracts and the biceps is relaxed, the elbow joint straightens and so does your arm.

What are muscles made of?

Muscles are made of thousands of cells called muscle fibres, which shorten when a muscle contracts. The cells are held together by a layer of connective tissue. The pulling power of a muscle varies since not all the fibres shorten at once.

How many muscles do you have?

You have about 650 muscles, with over 50 in your face alone. You use 17 muscles to smile, over 40 to frown.

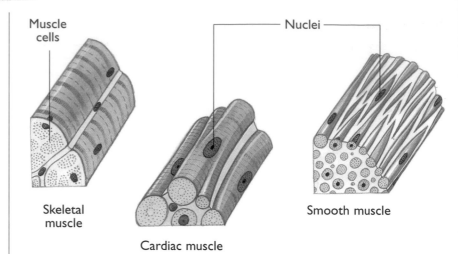

Muscle cells

Nuclei

Skeletal muscle

Cardiac muscle

Smooth muscle

▲ The three types of muscle are made up of different muscle cells. Skeletal muscle cells are the longest, and have several nuclei, whereas cardiac and smooth muscle cells have only one nucleus.

Is there more than one sort of muscle?

There are three main muscle types: skeletal, smooth and cardiac (heart). Skeletal muscles are voluntary, which means we can control them by thinking. The other two types of muscle are involuntary, which means they work automatically. Smooth muscle moves food along the digestive system. Cardiac muscle produces the pumping of the heart and never stops working.

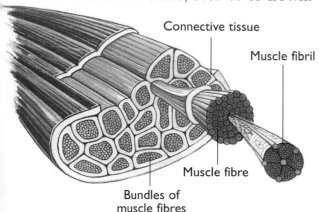

Connective tissue

Muscle fibril

Muscle fibre

Bundles of muscle fibres

◄ Muscles consist of bundles of fibres. The fibres contain rods, which slide over each other to shorten the fibre when the muscle contracts.

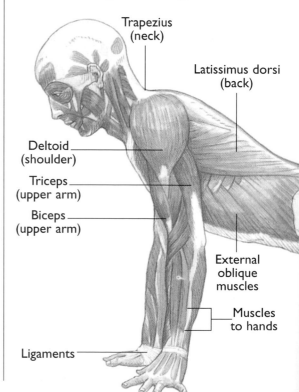

Trapezius (neck)

Latissimus dorsi (back)

Deltoid (shoulder)

Triceps (upper arm)

Biceps (upper arm)

External oblique muscles

Muscles to hands

Ligaments

Why do most muscles work in pairs?

Muscles can only pull, or contract, they cannot push. Either another muscle, or gravity, must pull a muscle out into a longer shape when it is relaxed. That is why most muscles come in pairs and work against each other. We call such muscles an antagonistic pair.

Which is the strongest muscle?

Size for size, the strongest muscle in your body is the masseter. One masseter is located on each side of the mouth. Together they give a biting force of about 70 kilograms.

Which is the largest muscle?

This is the gluteus maximus, the muscle that runs from the buttock to the back of the thigh. However, in women, one muscle may show a dramatic increase in size. During pregnancy, the uterus (womb) increases in weight from 30 grams to more than 1 kilogram.

You get cramp when your muscles are tired. You may have to stamp, stretch or rub the leg to get rid of the pain.

MUSCLE FACTS

■ Muscles account for around 40 percent of your body weight.

■ You use about 200 different muscles when you walk.

■ Even when you are not moving, some of your muscle fibres have to contract to keep you standing up or sitting down.

■ The smallest muscle is the stapedius, which is in the middle ear. It is less than 0.27 mm long.

Your biggest muscles are the ones you sit on.

Which is the most active muscle?

It has been estimated that the eye muscles move more than 100,000 times a day. Many of these movements take place during dreaming. Cardiac (heart) muscle keeps contracting 70 or so times a minute, while the smooth muscle in your gut moves all the time.

Why do muscles get tired?

When a muscle works very hard, it makes some of the energy it needs by breaking down stored food without using oxygen. This process is called anaerobic respiration. It causes a waste substance called lactic acid to build up inside the muscle, stopping it from working properly.

What causes cramp?

When too much lactic acid builds up, it causes the muscle to contract strongly and painfully. This is cramp. Cramp occurs when you start to exercise a little-used muscle, or if you have been sitting or standing in an uncomfortable position. The best way to deal with cramp it to massage and gently stretch the painful muscle.

What are the benefits of regular exercise?

Exercise helps you to look good, feel good and stay healthy. It strengthens your muscles and helps to maintain good muscle tone. It can improve your body shape and posture. Exercising strengthens the heart muscle, helps to keep a good blood-flow and can also relieve stress.

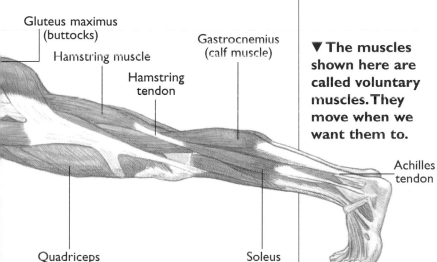

Gluteus maximus (buttocks)

Hamstring muscle

Hamstring tendon

Gastrocnemius (calf muscle)

▼ The muscles shown here are called voluntary muscles. They move when we want them to.

Achilles tendon

Quadriceps

Soleus (lower leg)

LUNGS AND HEART

What happens when we breathe?

When we breathe in, we draw air in through our nose or mouth. The air is mainly nitrogen (78 percent), with about 21 percent oxygen and 0.04 percent carbon dioxide. This mixture of gases travels down the windpipe, or trachea, into two large tubes called bronchi, one leading to each lung. From here the air travels into a system of smaller air passages called bronchioles and finally reaches millions of tiny air sacs, called alveoli, inside each lung.

Fold your arms across your chest. Now breathe in. You'll feel your lungs getting bigger as they fill up with air.

▼ **When you breathe in, your lungs fill with air. Air passes down the windpipe, through two bronchial tubes into the lungs. The rib cage protects the lungs and heart.**

When we breathe out, air takes the reverse route from the air sacs to our nose or mouth. But the content of the air is slightly different. The air we breathe out contains much less oxygen than before and more carbon dioxide and more water vapour. A large sheet of muscle called the diaphragm, situated just below the lungs, contracts and expands to pull air in or push air out of the lungs.

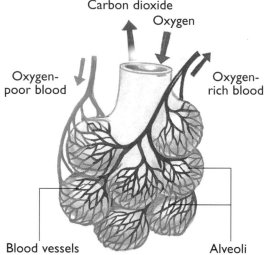

Carbon dioxide

Oxygen

Oxygen-poor blood

Oxygen-rich blood

Blood vessels

Alveoli

▲ **Inside the lungs, oxygen from the air is exchanged with waste carbon dioxide gas from the blood. The oxygen is carried to the body cells in the blood.**

Why do we breathe faster when we exercise?

When we exercise, our muscles do more work and therefore need more energy. They get this energy from food, which is broken down during respiration. Respiration uses up oxygen and so we breathe faster to supply the extra oxygen our muscles need when we exercise.

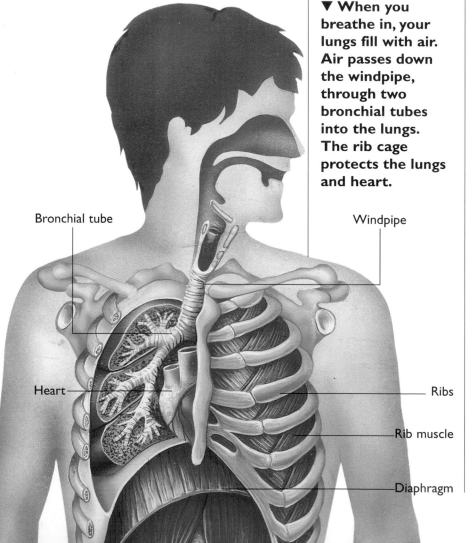

Bronchial tube

Windpipe

Heart

Ribs

Rib muscle

Diaphragm

When we are sitting or standing, we breathe in and out only about 10 percent of the air in our lungs. When we exercise hard, this figure goes up to about 60 percent.

Why is it better to breathe through your nose?

Air breathed in through your nose is warmed to a comfortable temperature for your lungs, and moistened and cleaned more effectively than air breathed in through your mouth. Small hairs in the nose filter out dirt. Mucus inside the nose traps some of the dirt, and tiny hairs called cilia push this to the throat where it is swallowed. Like the nose, the air passages in the lungs have mucus and cilia to help clean the air breathed in.

Why is breathing harder on top of a mountain?

The higher up you climb, the thinner the air becomes. This means that with each breath you are taking in much less oxygen than you would normally. Breathing is therefore more difficult on a high mountain. Exercise becomes difficult because you have to breathe much more heavily to get the oxygen you need.

What can a chest X-ray show?

Doctors use chest X-rays to look for signs of disease in the lungs. The infections that cause bronchitis, pneumonia or tuberculosis, or more serious conditions such as lung cancer, can show up on the X-ray picture as dark patches.

DID YOU KNOW!

■ A baby is born with pink lungs. As we get older, our lungs darken because we breathe dirty air.

■ A person at rest breathes in and out about 13 times a minute. With each breath, about 500 cc of air is taken in.

■ On average, the lungs of an adult man can hold about 6 litres of air.

■ A woman's lungs hold slightly less air, about 4.5 litres.

■ In ancient times, people thought that a person's breath was the life spirit.

Why do we pant after running fast?

When you pant after a sprint, you are paying the 'oxygen debt'. Exercise that helps your body take in more oxygen causes a build up of lactic acid, a waste product. Once the exercise is over, the liver processes the lactic acid using oxygen to break it down. The oxygen debt is the amount of oxygen you must take in to process the lactic acid that has built up.

Why do we yawn?

A yawn seems to be the body's way of getting more oxygen to the brain to make us feel more lively. When we yawn we take in air slowly and deeply and then breathe it out. We seem to yawn most when we are tired or bored, or sitting in a stuffy room. Yawning can be a sign that a person needs more air. A drink or washing the face in cold water can stop us yawning.

▲ It is almost impossible to stop yourself yawning. Animals yawn too.

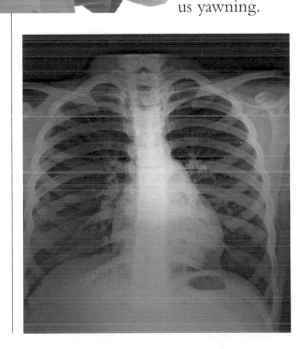

▶ An X-ray photo of a person's lungs, showing the ribs and spinal column. Doctors use X-rays to check for signs of lung disease.

What happens when you cough?

Just before you cough, you tightly close your vocal cords and tense your chest muscles. Then, when you release your vocal cords, the air comes shooting out of your lungs. Coughing is important because it removes irritating particles from your throat and air passages.

Why do we sneeze?

Sneezing is a way of getting rid of something that is irritating the sensitive parts of the nose. Air is forced out of the lungs through the nose. Sneezing helps stop dust or pollen from reaching our lungs.

What makes a lump in the throat?

It feels like a lump, but it is actually a tightening of muscles in the throat, a side effect of the hormone adrenaline, which is released when we feel sad.

THROATY FACTS

■ Your Adam's apple is the lump in the front of your throat. It is formed by the voice box or larynx.

■ Inside the larynx are two bands of cartilage called vocal cords.

■ People snore when soft tissues in the throat collapse during deep sleep. The soft tissues partly block air passing in and out of the lungs. Vibrations are set up, producing the snores.

▶ **Blood circulates around the body. Arteries take blood from the heart to the cells of the body. Veins carry blood back to the heart.**

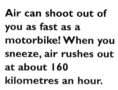

Air can shoot out of you as fast as a motorbike! When you sneeze, air rushes out at about 160 kilometres an hour.

◀ **If dust or germs get into your nose, your body makes you sneeze to get rid of them. Your lungs shoot out air.**

How does the voice work?

When you speak or sing, air from your lungs passes out across your vocal cords and makes them vibrate. If you almost close the space between your vocal cords, you get a high-pitched sound. If you open the space, you get a lower-pitched sound. A fast outbreath produces a loud note.

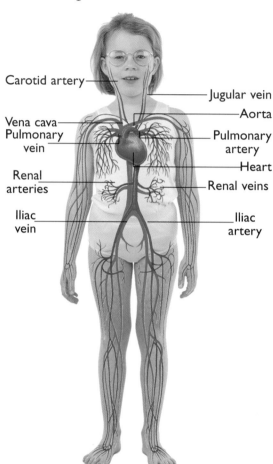

Carotid artery

Jugular vein

Aorta

Vena cava
Pulmonary vein

Pulmonary artery

Heart

Renal arteries

Renal veins

Iliac vein

Iliac artery

What is your circulation?

Your circulation is the system that carries blood around your body. It consists of a pump, called the heart, and a branching system of tubes, called blood vessels. There are three main types of blood vessel. Arteries carry blood away from the heart. Veins carry blood back to the heart. Capillaries are the tiny blood vessels that connect arteries with veins. They go to every part of the body.

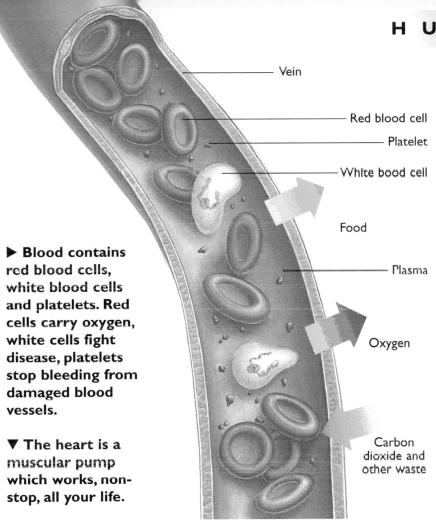

Vein

Red blood cell

Platelet

White bood cell

Food

Plasma

Oxygen

Carbon dioxide and other waste

▶ **Blood contains red blood cells, white blood cells and platelets. Red cells carry oxygen, white cells fight disease, platelets stop bleeding from damaged blood vessels.**

▼ **The heart is a muscular pump which works, non-stop, all your life.**

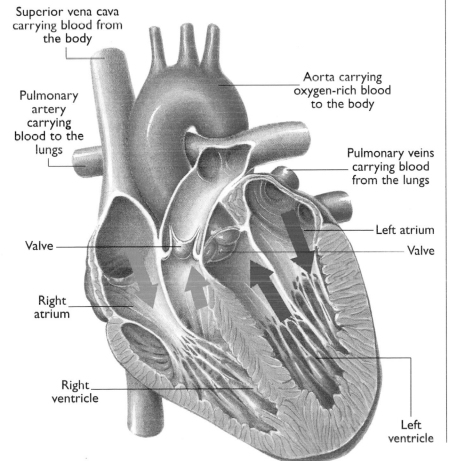

Superior vena cava carrying blood from the body

Pulmonary artery carrying blood to the lungs

Valve

Right atrium

Right ventricle

Aorta carrying oxygen-rich blood to the body

Pulmonary veins carrying blood from the lungs

Left atrium

Valve

Left ventricle

How does blood get around the body?

Blood is pumped around the body by the heart. When the heart squeezes, blood is pushed out under high pressure into the arteries. Arteries have thick muscular walls to cope with this pressure. As the blood travels around the body, it gradually loses its pressure and so flows more slowly through the veins. Veins have thinner walls and contain one-way valves to direct the blood back to the heart.

How does the heart work?

Each side of the heart has two chambers. The top chambers, called atria (singular: atrium), receive blood from large veins. When the atria squeeze, they pump blood into the bottom chambers, or ventricles. The ventricles then squeeze, pumping blood out along large arteries. The right ventricle sends blood to the lungs. The left ventricle sends it round the body.

How can I measure my heart rate?

The easiest way to measure your heart rate is by measuring your pulse. The pulse is a regular throb or beat which can be felt beneath the skin at certain points, such as the inside of your wrist. Your heart rate is the number of pulses counted in one minute.

What is blood made of?

Blood consists of a liquid called plasma, which contains red and white blood cells, and cell fragments called platelets. Dissolved in the plasma are thousands of different substances.

What does blood do?

Blood carries useful materials around the body and takes away waste products. Blood helps with communication, by delivering chemical messengers, called hormones, to parts of the body. Blood protects the body from germs, by sealing cuts with thickened, or clotted, blood and by attacking germs with white blood cells. Body temperature can be controlled by directing blood to or away from the skin to warm or cool it.

What do red blood cells do?

The main function of red blood cells is to deliver oxygen around the body. The haemoglobin in red blood cells combines with oxygen, which is picked up in the lungs and then delivered to all body tissues. Haemoglobin is a very efficient oxygen-carrier. It allows blood to carry 60 times more oxygen than could be dissolved in the blood plasma. Red blood cells are packed full of haemoglobin.

A baby has less than 1 litre of blood, not quite enough to fill a milk carton. When you grow up, you will have enough blood to half-fill a bucket – about 5 litres.

FACTS ABOUT THE HEART AND BLOOD

■ Your heart is only roughly similar in shape to a 'love heart'.

■ The left side of the heart is bigger than the right.

■ A heartbeat is the sound the heart makes when the heart valves open and close. A doctor can listen to the sounds by placing a stethoscope on your chest.

■ There are four blood groups: A, B, AB and O.

■ It takes about a minute for a drop of blood to travel from the heart to your toes and back again.

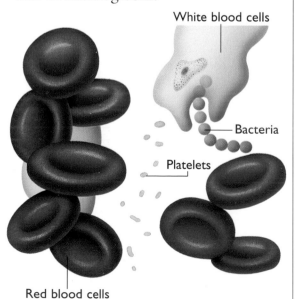

White blood cells

Bacteria

Platelets

Red blood cells

◄ Red blood cells look like doughnuts. They carry oxygen to all parts of the body. White cells fight harmful bacteria. Platelets stop bleeding and seal wounds.

What do white blood cells do?

White blood cells help to protect the body from disease. About two-thirds of white blood cells are phagocytes, which defend the body by eating up invading germs. The remaining white cells are lymphocytes. They produce chemicals called antibodies, which destroy harmful germs. White blood cells are much larger than red blood cells, but they are far fewer in number (approximately 1:600).

Where in the body gets the most blood?

Size for size, the kidneys get more blood than other organs. The kidneys have a vital role in filtering and cleaning the blood. However, during hard exercise muscles get more blood. The body supplies the muscles with up to five times more blood than they get when the body is at rest. Blood is diverted from other organs to feed the muscles. Only the blood supply to the brain is constant throughout.

Why do cuts stop bleeding?

Cuts stop bleeding because blood quickly forms a clot that plugs the wound and seals off the damaged vessels. At the site of an injury, the platelets in the bloodstream stick together, as well as to the edges of the cut, making a thin seal. The platelets, and cells damaged by the injury, release substances that react with clotting factors in the blood to form fibres. Blood cells get caught up in the tangle of platelets and fibres, and form a clot that plugs the leak.

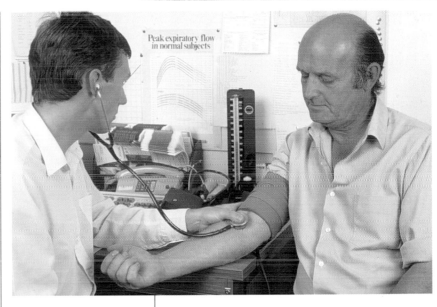

How does blood deal with germs?

When we cut or graze our skin, blood vessels are broken. Blood leaks out and helps to wash away harmful germs from the site of the injury. Platelets help to form a clot, which then becomes a scab and seals up the injury. At the same time, the phagocytes (the white blood cells) move in and eat up any germs that may have entered the body, while other white cells called lymphocytes knock out the germs by producing disease-fighting chemicals, which are called antibodies.

What is a blood group?

A blood group is the name given to a type of blood. Blood groups vary from person to person. The two main systems for grouping blood are the ABO and Rhesus systems. There are four blood groups in the ABO system, the most common blood grouping. They are O, A, B and AB.

What is a blood transfusion?

A blood transfusion is the transfer of blood from a healthy person (the donor) into the body of someone who lacks enough blood, either because of disease or injury. The donor's blood must be matched to the patient's blood group.

A blood donor volunteers to give blood so that hospitals can have a supply stored, ready for operations and emergencies. A donor can give about 0.5 litres of blood without any ill effects and many people who are blood donors give blood regularly.

▲ Taking a person's blood pressure is a routine method for checking that the heart and circulation are working properly.

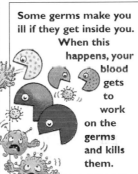

Some germs make you ill if they get inside you. When this happens, your blood gets to work on the germs and kills them.

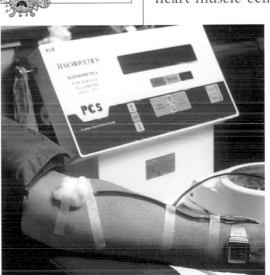

What is blood pressure?

Blood pressure is the pushing force given to blood by the heart. A doctor usually measures blood pressure using a special arm cuff attached to the gauge. The first reading gives blood pressure during heartbeats: the second, pressure between heartbeats.

What is a heart attack?

A heart attack happens when the heart can no longer cope with the demands made upon it. Heart attacks are usually caused by a blood clot blocking a coronary artery. Some heart muscle cells become starved of food and oxygen, and die. Many people recover from heart attacks.

◀ People who give blood are called donors. They attend donor centres where blood is taken from the arm and then stored until it is needed for a transfusion.

FOOD AND WASTE

Why do we need food?

Food contains different kinds of substances, which our bodies need, but they are not in a form that the body can use. They must first be broken down in a process called digestion. The food is first chewed into smaller pieces, then broken down chemically in the stomach and intestines by acids and proteins called digestive enzymes.

Your body tells you it needs food by making you feel hungry. Food smells, or just thinking about food, can make your mouth water.

▼ The digestive system starts in the mouth. Food passes through the stomach and the intestines. Finally, waste leaves the body.

Teeth

Salivary glands

Oesophagus

Gall bladder

Duodenum

Colon

Liver

Stomach

Pyloric sphincter

Pancreas

Ileum

Rectum

Which foods give us energy?

Foods that contain carbohydrates are a good source of energy. Sugars, and a substance called starch, found in bread and potatoes, are carbohydrates. Fats give us energy too. Butter, margarine and oils are very rich in fats, and are best eaten in small amounts.

Why do we need vitamins and minerals?

Although we need only tiny amounts of vitamins and minerals, they are essential for many functions in the body. Lack of the mineral iron, for example, leads to a shortage of red blood cells, causing anaemia. Vitamin B helps wounds to heal and keeps the gums healthy. Calcium and vitamin D help to make bones strong. Vitamin D is found in fish and cheese and is made by the skin in sunlight.

What is a balanced diet?

A balanced diet is one that supplies the different types of foods that you need in the right amounts – not too much and not too little of each. It gives you the raw materials and energy for a healthy, active life. The amount of food you need each day depends on your age, size and sex, as well as your general level of activity. A tall teenage boy who plays a lot of sport will need a lot more food each day than a small elderly woman. In general, adult men need more food-energy than women.

Fats

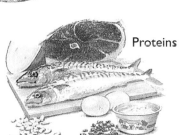

Proteins

Carbohydrates

Fibres

◀ **For good health, it is important to eat a balanced diet, including some of each of the foods shown: fruit, vegetables, carbohydrates (for fuel), fibre (to aid digestion), fats (for energy) and proteins.**

Why do we get hungry?

Our eating is controlled by an area deep in the brain. When this 'hunger centre' receives signals from parts of the body saying that we need to eat, we get hungry. Painful sensations, such as stomach cramps, can also sometimes prompt us to eat.

How much water do we need every day?

An adult needs about 1.5 to 2 litres of water a day. Much of this will come from food. For example, bread is about 40 percent water.

We feel thirsty when the normal amount of water in the blood starts to drop, and the blood gets very slightly thicker. Part of our brain senses this and sends signals to the body that tell us we need more fluid.

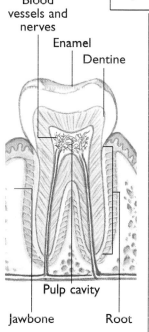

Blood vessels and nerves

Enamel

Dentine

Pulp cavity

Jawbone   Root

▲ **The centre of a tooth is a space full of nerves and blood vessels. Around it is a wall of dentine and on top, a layer of hard enamel.**

Why are teeth different shapes?

Teeth are different shapes because they have different jobs to do. The incisor teeth at the front of your mouth are shaped like chisels. They are used for biting and gnawing. The canines, just behind the incisors, are pointed teeth used for tearing food. The premolars and molars at the back are shaped for grinding food.

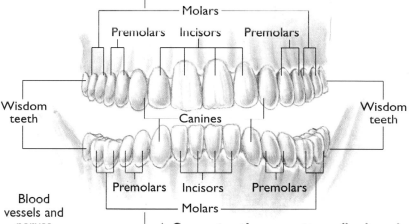

Molars — Premolars — Incisors — Premolars — Wisdom teeth — Canines — Wisdom teeth — Premolars — Incisors — Premolars — Molars

▲ **Some teeth are cutters (incisors). Others are grinders (molars). The wisdom teeth are the last to appear.**

What are teeth made of?

Each tooth consists of a visible part, called the crown, and a root, which attaches it to a socket in the jawbone. The outer, off-white part of the tooth is made of enamel, the hardest substance in the body. Underneath the enamel is dentine, which is similar to bone, but harder.

How do teeth grow?

Teeth grow from small patches of tissue covering the bone of the upper and lower jaws. Teeth start growing before we are born, but they only begin to come through the gum about six months after birth.

Why does your mouth water?

The taste, smell and sometimes even the thought of food causes the salivary glands to send saliva (a colourless fluid) along little ducts into the mouth. Sometimes jets of saliva squirt out into your mouth, so that your mouth 'waters'. Saliva is mostly water, with some mucus. It also contains an enzyme, which starts off the digestive process by breaking down starch, a carbohydrate.

What happens when you swallow?

Swallowing is a complicated process. When you swallow, your tongue squeezes against the roof of your mouth and pushes the food or drink up and back. At the same time, the soft part at the top of your mouth moves up, closing off the nasal passages so that nothing goes up your nose. Finally, your epiglottis flaps down and your larynx (voice box) moves forwards and upwards. This closes off the windpipe and opens up the gullet, or oesophagus. The food or drink is squeezed into your throat and down the oesophagus to the stomach.

What happens in the stomach?

The stomach looks like a bag. It has muscular walls, and is closed by valves. In the stomach, food is churned up and mixed with stomach juices containing digestive enzymes and acid. The acid also kills most of the germs in food. The mushy food is then delivered gradually to the small intestine.

If air comes back up the tube from your tummy, you make a sound called a burp. Fizzy drinks often make people burp.

MORE BODY FACTS

■ An average person eats 50 tonnes of food and drinks more than 40,000 litres of liquid in a lifetime.

■ When you are resting, about a quarter of your blood is in your liver. When you begin to move about, some of this blood is immediately sent to other organs.

■ Indigestion is a pain in the stomach. It can be caused by eating too fast, or by the stomach producing too much acid.

■ If you eat food that is bad, or just eat too much, you may vomit. Muscles in your diaphragm and stomach contract and force the contents of your stomach back up and out of your body.

■ About two-thirds of your body is water. You might live 2 to 3 weeks without food, but you could die in 2 or 3 days without water.

▶ The liver is the body's largest organ. Its activity produces enough heat to keep your insides warm. The pancreas makes the hormone insulin. Bile is stored in the gall bladder.

Why does your tummy sometimes rumble?

The stomach and intestines are very active – the stomach churns food and the intestines squeeze it along. All this activity means that your stomach makes noises most of the time. When you are hungry your stomach contains a little liquid and a lot of gas. Because there is a lot of gas in your stomach, its rumblings are louder.

What does the liver do?

The liver has many different roles. It checks the amount of digested food in the blood. If there is more food than the body needs it changes the extra into sugar and stores it. The liver also stores some vitamins and iron. It helps the body to get rid of some poisons and cleans the blood by removing dead red blood cells. The liver makes bile which is stored in the gall bladder before being pumped into the digestive system where it breaks down fats.

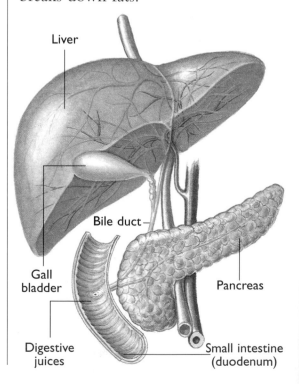

Liver

Bile duct

Gall bladder

Pancreas

Digestive juices

Small intestine (duodenum)

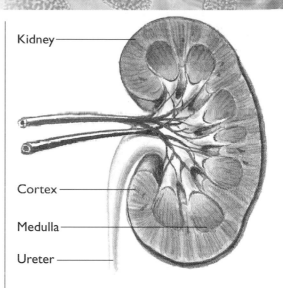

Kidney

Cortex

Medulla

Ureter

How long does it take to digest a meal?

It takes about 24 hours to completely digest a typical meal. Food spends about four hours in your stomach. This is followed by up to six hours in the small intestine, six or seven hours in the colon and six or seven hours in the rectum, before the residue is expelled as faeces (solid waste).

What are the body's waste substances?

The body's main waste substances are the gas carbon dioxide (produced during respiration), urea (from breaking down excess proteins), and water and salts that the body does not need. The excretory organs excrete waste. They are the lungs, the kidneys, the liver and the skin. The lungs, for example, get rid of carbon dioxide. The kidneys get rid of water and other substances, such as salts. Waste products from the liver are taken to the kidneys and excreted in urine, or they are excreted in bile, and expelled through the gut.

Why do we have an appendix?

No one knows. The appendix is a dead-end tube at the point where the small and large intestines join. It is not used in human digestion, although it is an important organ in animals that eat grass. The appendix can sometimes cause trouble, if it becomes infected and inflamed. This condition is known as appendicitis, and the appendix may have to be removed in hospital. People without their appendix never notice any difference.

▶ **You have two kidneys. These organs filter the blood, remove waste (urea) made in the liver and send it as urine to the ureter.**

When you go to the toilet, your body is getting rid of water it doesn't need. This waste water is called urine. Urine is usually a yellowish colour.

DID YOU KNOW!

■ Diarrhoea may be caused by food poisoning or by an infection in the intestines. You need to drink a lot to make up for the water you lose when you have diarrhoea.

■ You can swallow upside-down, though it isn't a good idea. It is possible because food is pushed along the oesophagus by bands of muscles.

■ The walls of the stomach are protected by a layer of mucus. This prevents the enzymes and strong acid from trying to digest the stomach itself!

■ Your kidneys filter all the blood in your body about 300 times each day.

■ People can live with one kidney. If one kidney is diseased or damaged, it can be removed and the other kidney will do the job of two kidneys.

■ Urine is yellow because it contains substances formed by the liver when it breaks down haemoglobin from old blood.

What do the kidneys do?

The kidneys are a pair of very hard-working filters. They purify the blood, taking out waste substances and making sure that useful substances are kept in. The kidneys produce urine, a fluid that contains waste substances filtered from the blood. Urine is passed to the bladder, where it is stored until it leaves the body through a tube called the urethra.

How does a kidney machine work?

A kidney machine filters blood by a process called dialysis. It is used to help people whose own kidneys are not working properly. A tube inserted into an artery in a patient's arm carries blood to the machine, where it is pumped through cellophane tubing in a container of liquid. Wastes in the blood pass through the walls of the tubing into the liquid, and substances that the body needs pass from the liquid into the blood. The clean blood is then returned to the patient through a tube connected to a vein in their arm. Blood must pass through the machine 20 times or more.

SKIN AND HAIR

Why do we have skin?

Skin is a waterproof, flexible covering that protects us from the outside world and helps to keep out harmful germs. Our skin is sensitive to touch, heat, cold and pain, and so it allows us to sense what is happening around us. Skin helps protect us from harmful rays in strong sunlight, and uses some sunlight to make vitamin D. Skin contains sweat glands, body hairs and tiny blood vessels which help to control our body temperature.

Hair

Pore

Sebaceous gland

Blood vessel

Dermis

Granular layer

Epidermis

Hair root

Erector muscle

Hypodermis

Sweat gland

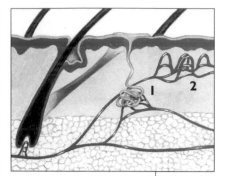 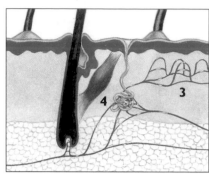

▲ Beneath the skin: sweat glands (1); skin capillaries which widen (2) to let heat escape and narrow (3) to reduce heat loss; hair erector muscles (4) which make 'goose pimples'.

▲ The skin has two main layers: a tough outer layer called the epidermis and beneath it, the dermis. Sebaceous glands give off oil to stop the skin drying out.

Why are people's skins different colours?

Melanin is a dark brown substance, or pigment, that protects the skin from the Sun's harmful ultraviolet rays. The colour of skin depends on how much melanin there is in the epidermis.

Where does sweat come from?

Sweat is a salt-water liquid, which also contains small amounts of the body's waste substances. Sweat is produced by glands in the dermis and is released onto the skin through tiny openings called pores. As the sweat dries, it cools the body. There are many sweat glands under the arms, in the groin and on the hands, feet and face. Stale sweat smells. It is important to wash regularly to remove it.

Why do bruises change colour?

A bruise is a purplish mark that appears when tiny blood vessels in the skin break, generally after a hard knock. Bruises are first dark purple, then change through blue, green and yellow before fading away altogether. These colour changes are a result of the blood being broken down and reabsorbed as the damage heals and the normal skin colour returns.

HUMAN BODY

How does skin heal itself?

Cut or injured skin heals itself automatically. If someone cuts themselves and starts to bleed, the blood soon forms a clot that stops further bleeding. The clot dries to form a scab, which prevents germs from entering the damaged skin. Beneath the scab, new skin cells grow across the wound, and when the skin is healed the scab drops off.

How does skin tan?

In strong sunlight, the skin produces extra melanin to protect it from harmful ultraviolet rays. This melanin spreads through the epidermis, in the form of tiny black grains. Eventually skin turns darker, producing a tan. Every skin colour turns darker with exposure to sunlight.

What are nails made of?

Nails are made of dead cells that contain keratin, the protein found in the outer layer of skin. Nails grow by being pushed out of a pit in the skin called the nail-bed, which lies horizontal to the skin. As the nail grows it slides along the surface of the nail-bed to the fingertip. Most of the nail is pink, because the blood vessels underneath it show through.

HAIR FACTS

- Most people have about 100,000 hairs on their head alone.
- Hair goes grey because as we get older some hairs lack pigment.
- Hair is very strong. A rope made from about 1,000 human hairs could support an adult.
- The average person loses 50 to 100 hairs a day, but these are continually replaced.
- Some men go bald because the male hormone, testosterone, seems to affect the hair follicles so that lost hair is not replaced.
- Dandruff is dead skin that flakes off the scalp.

▲ Whether your skin is pale or dark, too much sunlight can burn you. When you are in the sun, wear a hat and put on a layer of suitable sun protection cream.

What is hair for?

Hair helps to prevent heat loss from the body, because it is able to trap a layer of warm air next to the skin. Hairs in our nostrils filter out dirt, to keep our lungs clean. Hair has two parts: the root and the shaft. The hair root is embedded in the skin and is enclosed in a tiny pit, called a hair follicle. The hair shaft contains the pigment that gives hair its colour. Hair is made of keratin, the same substance found in nails and skin.

Why is hair different colours?

Hair colour is determined by the mixture of pigments that it contains. Hair-producing cells can produce a mixture of black, red and yellow pigments. For example, dark-haired people have predominantly black pigment and fair-haired people have mostly yellow pigment.

What makes hair curly?

Hair is curly, wavy or straight depending on the shape of the follicles it grows from. Straight hair grows from round follicles, wavy hair from oval follicles, and curly hair from flat follicles.

Why do we have eyelashes?

Eyelashes act as protection for our eyes. Our eyelashes help stop dust and other particles from reaching the delicate surface of the eye and irritating it. Our eyebrows, however, are probably used to make signals, as a means of non-verbal communication, rather than as protection for our eyes.

113

NERVES AND SENSES

How are the body's actions co-ordinated?

Co-ordination is the way different activities in the body are linked together. The body relies on two systems to co-ordinate its actions. The nervous system sends messages to and from the brain as electrical signals along nerves. The hormonal (endocrine) system sends chemical messengers called hormones around the body. The hormones travel in the bloodstream through the arteries.

What are hormones?

Hormones are chemicals produced in one part of the body, that have an effect on another part. For example, the hormone insulin is produced by the pancreas and affects the functioning of the liver and other tissues in the body.

There are over 30 hormones. They are produced by structures called endocrine glands, which are found in the head, neck and torso. Hormones have an enormous effect on many bodily processes, from our growth to the workings of our reproductive system.

Which is the most important gland?

The pituitary gland is the most important, because it produces hormones that control most of the other endocrine glands. Height is controlled by a growth hormone produced by the pituitary gland. Too

BRAIN FACTS

■ The brain probably contains 10 billion nerve cells.

■ Each of these cells can have as many as 25,000 connections to other cells.

■ It is estimated that the brain can store as many as 100 million bits of information in a lifetime.

■ Brains are getting heavier. In 1860 the average man's brain weighed 1,370 grams. Today it weighs 1,420 grams.

■ Messages travel along large nerves at more than 90 metres a second (about 320 km/h).

■ Messages go much more slowly through the smaller nerves, such as those in the digestive system.

People's brains are different sizes. Bigger brains don't make people more clever – any more than big feet make them better runners!

much can make a person very tall, and too little can stunt their growth. On the whole, however, most people reach the same sort of height as their parents and grandparents.

What makes up the nervous system?

The nervous system is made up of billions of nerve cells, which carry electrical messages all around the body. It has two main parts: the central nervous system (CNS), made up of the brain and the spinal cord; and the peripheral nervous system (PNS), made up of all the nerves that run through the central nervous system to the rest of the body.

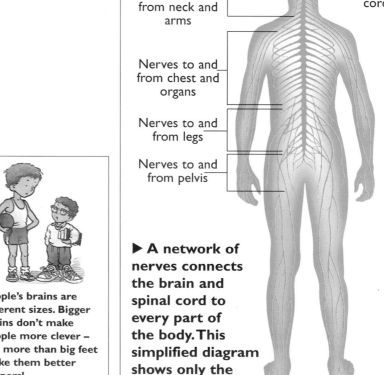

Brain

Spinal cord

Nerves to and from neck and arms

Nerves to and from chest and organs

Nerves to and from legs

Nerves to and from pelvis

▶ A network of nerves connects the brain and spinal cord to every part of the body. This simplified diagram shows only the main nerves.

How many nerves do you have?

Running between your brain and the sense organs and muscles in your head are 24 large nerves – the cranial nerves. These include nerves from your eyes, nose and ears. A further 62 nerves, the spinal nerves, run from your spinal cord to the rest of the body.

▼ A typical muscle nerve cell, or neuron, has a star-shaped control centre. The axon carries messages. Dendrites receive messages. Neurons communicate with one another at synapses.

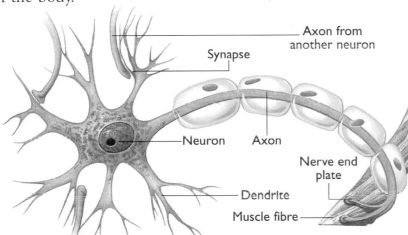

Synapse
Axon from another neuron
Neuron
Axon
Nerve end plate
Dendrite
Muscle fibre

How does a message travel along a nerve?

A message is picked up by a nerve cell at its dendrite end. The message travels through the cell as a small electrical current, called a nerve impulse. When the message gets to the end of the axon it is then passed to the next cell.

▼ We use our five senses all the time. They tell us what is going on and help us communicate.

What is a reflex?

When you react to something without thinking, your action is a reflex. For example, if your hand touches something hot, you will jerk it away without stopping to think about it. Most reflexes are controlled by your spinal cord and hardly involve your brain at all.

How do nerves pass on messages?

One nerve cell does not actually touch the next. The message has to be carried by chemicals across a gap called the synapse. The branched ends of axons send out chemicals called neurotransmitters when triggered by a nerve impulse. The chemicals stimulate the next-door cell, setting up a new nerve impulse so that the message carries on its way.

What are our five senses?

Our five senses are sight, hearing, smell, taste and touch. Our sense organs, such as our eyes, contain special cells called sensory receptors. These cells pass information about the outside world to nerve cells, which then transmit a message to the brain. Sensory receptors in the eye receive information in the form of light rays.

Sight

Hearing

Touch

Smell

Taste

How do our eyes work?

The eyes are two tough balls of tissue containing transparent jelly. At the front of each eye is a transparent covering called the cornea. The coloured part of the eye is called the iris. It surrounds the pupil, a dark hole through which light enters the eyeball. Six muscles connect the eyeball to the bones in the eyesocket and move the eyeball around. The optic nerve runs out of the back of the eye and goes to the brain.

Light rays enter the eye and pass through the pupil to the lens. Both the curved surface of the eye and the lens bend the rays and focus them into a clear image onto the retina. Cells in the retina send messages along the optic nerve to the brain.

EYE FACTS

- You blink on average about 6 times a minute.

- The human eye can detect 10 million different colour shades.

- In bright light, muscles in the iris make the pupil shrink, protecting the sensitive retina.

- Tears keep our eyes shiny and moist. Tears are made by a gland above the eyeball.

- Tear fluid also contains a chemical that kills germs.

- Two-thousandths of a second after light hits the retina, your brain has formed an image!

- We all have one eye that we use more than the other – just as people are right-handed or left-handed.

What gives your eyes their colour?

Your eye colour is produced by a pigment called melanin. Eyes can be brown, blue, grey, green or somewhere in between. The colour depends on how much melanin is present in the iris – brown eyes contain much more than blue eyes.

How do we see colours?

There are three types of cone cell, each sensitive to one of three colours: red, blue or green. We see other colours when a combination of cone cells are triggered. For example, when both red and green cones are stimulated, we see yellow.

Are two eyes better than one?

Yes. Two eyes see over a bigger area, and because our eyes are set slightly apart, they see objects from slightly different angles. The brain fits the two images together to give a 3-D image, which helps us judge distances better.

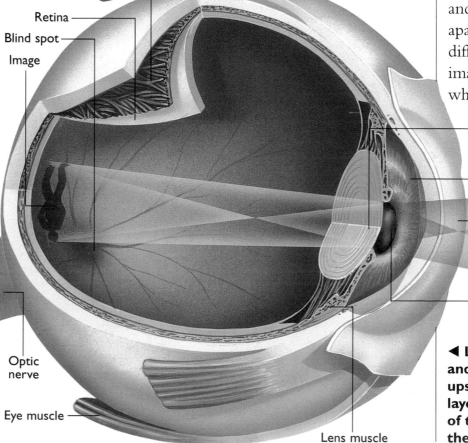

Blood vessels

Retina

Blind spot

Image

Optic nerve

Eye muscle

Lens muscle

Lens

Iris

Light rays

Cornea

Pupil

◄ **Light rays pass through the pupil and are focused by the lens as an upside-down image on the retina, a layer of light-sensitive cells at the back of the eye. Your brain turns the image the right way up.**

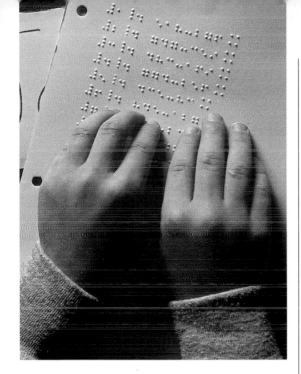

How do blind people read with their fingers?

Blind people often compensate for their lack of sight by developing other senses – hearing, smell and touch in particular. They may learn to read by touch, using a system called Braille, in which small dots raised from the surface of the paper represent letters and punctuation. Blind people can read about 100 words a minute by passing their fingertips over the page.

What causes pain?

Any stimulus that is strong enough to cause tissue damage is likely to trigger pain; for example, strong pressure, swelling, muscle spasm, and the presence or absence of certain chemicals. Other sensory receptors will also give pain signals if the stimulus they respond to is strong enough. For example, temperature receptors will give a feeling of pain if the temperature is too hot or too cold. Pain can be useful – it tells us that something is wrong and stops us hurting ourselves more seriously.

◄ Blind people can read using Braille. The tips of the fingers are especially sensitive and a skilled blind reader can read a Braille book as fast as most sighted people can read a printed page.

Pain tells you if something is wrong. It warns your body to take care and protect itself. It hurts when you stub your toe because your body is telling you to stop – something is in the way!

▶ Some parts of your body have more nerve cells than others. If the size of the various parts of your body corresponded to the number of nerve cells in them, this is what you would look like!

Which are the most sensitive parts of the body?

The lips are most sensitive to touch and texture, while the small of the back is the least sensitive. The most sensitive parts for pressure are the fingertips, and the least sensitive is the bottom! The lips and fingertips are so sensitive because they have more nerve endings. Our fingers and toes need to be more sensitive, as we use them to explore the world around us. Our lips are very sensitive too, as you can see from the picture below.

Why do we itch sometimes?

Little is known about why we itch. Sometimes we can see a cause, such as a scab or an insect bite. Stimulating pain receptors can cause itching, but no nerve-endings have been specifically connected with itching alone. Thinking about an itch can bring on the urge to scratch, but the reason for this is a mystery.

REPRODUCTION AND GROWTH

How does a new life begin?

Every baby begins life when a single egg cell from the mother and a tiny sperm cell from the father join together inside the mother's body. This is called fertilization. The fertilized egg grows and divides, and after nine months the baby is born.

Where do eggs come from?

Eggs are made in two almond-shaped organs in the woman's body, called the ovaries. About once a month, from puberty (10 to 14 years) until the age of 45 to 50, an egg is released from one of the two ovaries.

Where do sperm come from?

A man's reproductive organs are the penis and testes (singular: testis). Sperm are made in the testes. They are manufactured in tiny tubes and are then stored in a long tube called the epididymis which is coiled on the surface of the testis. The sperm travel to the urethra inside the erect penis through two tubes called sperm ducts to pass to the woman's body. Sperm look like microscopic tadpoles. Only one sperm can fertilize the egg. Each sperm has a head containing a nucleus, which fuses with the egg when fertilization takes place. The tail stays outside.

DID YOU KNOW?

■ About 50 million sperm are made in each testis every day.

■ Menstruation occurs roughly every 28 days. Bleeding usually lasts for four to five days.

■ A sperm lashes its tail to push itself along as it moves towards the egg.

■ 300 million sperm may be released, but only a few hundred get close to the egg and only one will fertilize it – if fertilization happens.

▼ The female and male reproductive organs. During sexual intercourse, sperm travel from the penis through the vagina and womb to the Fallopian tube to reach the egg.

Where does fertilization take place?

Sperm enter the woman's body during sexual intercourse. The man's penis becomes stiff and is put inside the woman's vagina. Semen, a fluid containing the sperm, is squirted from the penis into the woman's vagina. An egg may be fertilized as a result. The sperm fertilizes the egg in a tube called the Fallopian tube which joins each ovary to the womb. The fertilized egg travels on to the womb, where the baby grows.

What is the menstrual cycle?

Women have a monthly cycle, or period. Every month a mature egg is released from the ovaries and the lining of the womb develops so that it can receive a fertilized egg. If the egg is not fertilized the womb lining breaks down. This is called the

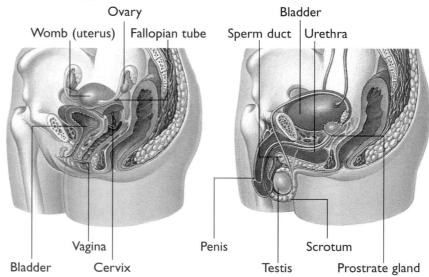

Womb (uterus)   Ovary   Fallopian tube   Bladder   Sperm duct   Urethra

Bladder   Vagina   Cervix   Penis   Testis   Scrotum   Prostrate gland

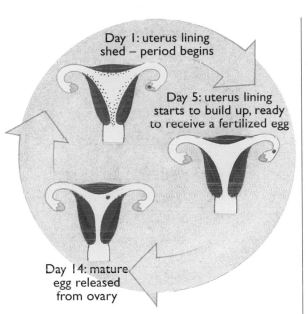

Day 1: uterus lining shed – period begins

Day 5: uterus lining starts to build up, ready to receive a fertilized egg

Day 14: mature egg released from ovary

◀ A girl begins to have menstrual periods at puberty. Every month, the ovaries release an egg cell. The most likely time for an egg to be fertilized is between the fourteenth day and the eighteenth day of her cycle.

LIFE FACTS

■ At 4 weeks, the embryo is no bigger than a grain of rice. It has a head and a tail.

■ At 16 weeks, the mother feels the baby kicking.

■ By the 20th week, it has eyebrows and fingernails.

How quickly does the embryo develop?

The embryo grows very quickly. Between the fourth and eighth week of pregancy, its hands, feet and facial features develop. By twelve weeks, the embryo looks human and its major organs are developing.

When is a baby an embryo?

An unborn baby is called an embryo up to eight weeks after fertilization. The embryo forms from part of the ball of cells implanted in the mother's womb. Its life-support system is the placenta, a disc-shaped organ with many blood vessels, connected to the baby by the umbilical cord through which the baby feeds.

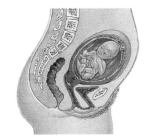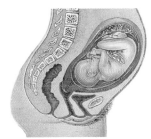

8 weeks

12 weeks

28 weeks

menstrual cycle. It usually takes about 28 days, although the length of time varies from person to person. The cycle is controlled by hormones from the pituitary gland and the ovaries.

What is contraception?

Contraception is another name for birth control. It refers to the variety of methods that prevent a woman becoming pregnant. 'Barrier' methods prevent the sperm from meeting the egg. The condom, for example, is a rubber sheath worn over the penis, which stops sperm reaching the womb. Women can also take a contraceptive pill which stops the ovaries making mature eggs.

What happens if the egg is fertilized?

If the egg is fertilized, its outer membrane swells into a jelly-like barrier to keep out other sperm. The fertilized egg travels down the Fallopian tube to the womb. As it does so it divides, first into two cells, then four, then eight. It arrives in the womb as a ball of about 100 cells.

▶ The foetus grows inside its mother's womb. It gets food and oxygen from its mother through the umbilical cord. By 12 weeks, it looks human and has fingers and toes. At 38 weeks, the baby's head is near the opening of the womb. The baby is ready to be born.

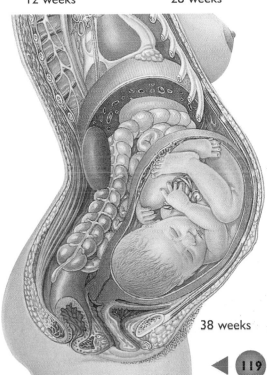

38 weeks

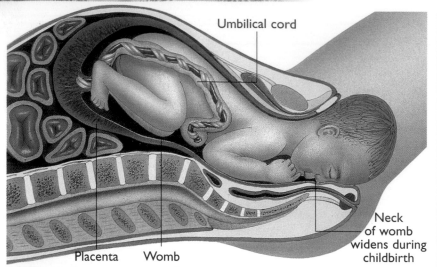

Umbilical cord

Placenta   Womb

Neck
of womb
widens during
childbirth

What happens when a baby is born?

Birth usually takes place around the 38th week of pregnancy. The process of giving birth usually lasts between six and twelve hours. The mother pushes hard with her abdominal muscles and the baby is gradually pushed through the cervix and vagina (birth canal), out into the world.

What are twins?

If two eggs are released by the mother's ovaries and both are fertilized, two foetuses develop with separate placentas. These are called fraternal twins. Identical twins come from the same egg and sperm, and so have exactly the same genes. The single fertilized egg splits at an early stage, producing two foetuses that can grow into identical twins.

▲ **When a baby is ready to be born, the neck of the womb stretches and opens, and the baby is pushed out. The baby starts to breathe and the umbilical cord is cut.**

As soon as a baby is born, it takes a big gulp of air and begins to breathe. The umbilical cord is cut, leaving a small scar – the tummy button.

◄ **Identical twins come from one egg, which splits to produce two foetuses that grow into two babies that look alike.**

What is a multiple birth?

When a pregnant woman gives birth to more than two children, it is called a multiple birth. The highest number of children ever produced from a multiple birth is ten.

What is a test-tube baby?

The world's first test-tube baby was born in England on 25 July, 1978. A test-tube baby does not grow inside a test tube. Eggs are taken from the woman and mixed in a small glass dish with sperm from the man. The eggs are fertilized and the young embryos are kept alive for a few days before they are placed in the woman's womb. The resulting babies are called test tube babies. Such treatments are used to help people who cannot have children normally.

What can a newborn baby sense?

A baby has a good sense of smell, much better than its sense of hearing or sight. It first learns to recognize its mother by smell.

What happens in the first week of life?

In the first week of a baby's life many changes are taking place. For example, the blood, which originally flowed through the umbilical artery, is re-routed through the lungs, liver and the heart. A hole between the two sides of the heart seals up so the heart can function properly. A newborn baby has several reflex actions. It automatically turns its head towards the breast and will grasp any object placed in its palm.

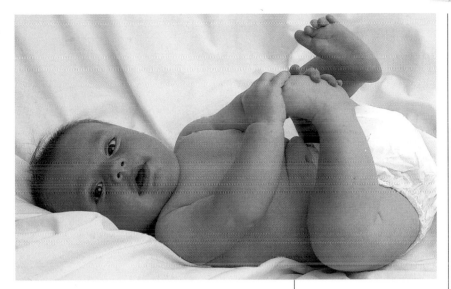

What can a baby do at three months?

At three months, a baby usually spends most of its time lying on its back. It can raise its head slightly, smile at its parents and will turn towards a noise. It can hold a rattle and will try to reach for toys, but its movements are jerky.

What is a baby like at twelve months?

The baby is now three times its weight at birth. It crawls mostly, but can usually stand with support and walk a little while holding on to furniture. It is able to pick up objects carefully between finger and thumb, and has learned to let go of objects. The baby can now recognize its name and say a few simple words.

▲ A baby has a large head to hold its brain. It needs a large brain to learn about its surroundings and respond to them.

GROWTH FACTS

■ At 6 months a baby has doubled its birth weight and can sit propped up.

■ Children grow very quickly during the first two years of life.

■ From age 3 to 10 growth is slower. A new growth spurt begins at puberty.

■ Boys may carry on growing until they are 23.

■ Most girls are fully grown by the age of 20.

◀ At 12 months, a toddler is beginning to stand and to take a few steps with assistance.

How do we grow?

Most of our growth is due to an increase in the number of cells in our body. Cells divide to form other cells. This process continues until we are fully grown. Growth is controlled by a hormone produced by the pituitary gland. You actually grow a little faster at night, since this is when levels of the growth hormone are highest.

What is puberty?

Puberty is the period in our life when the sex organs mature and other physical changes occur so that we develop into men and women.

At puberty, a girl's ovaries mature and her menstrual cycle begins. Her breasts develop and her hips widen. Body hair develops under the arms and in the groin area. Her voice becomes lower. Boys and girls start to lose their 'puppy fat'.

At puberty, a boy's penis and testes get larger and he starts producing sperm. His body shape changes and his torso gets larger. He can grow a beard and his body hair becomes thicker, particularly under his arms and in the groin area. His voice box (larynx) develops and his voice gets deeper, or 'breaks'.

What triggers the changes of puberty?

In both boys and girls, puberty is triggered by the pituitary gland in the brain. This gland stimulates other glands to release sex hormones. In boys, the changes are triggered by testosterone, which is produced by the testes. In girls, they are triggered by oestrogen, produced by the ovaries.

BRAIN AND MIND

What does the brain look like?

From above, the brain looks rather like a giant walnut, pink-grey in colour and wrinkled. It has the consistency of blancmange.

What is the brain made of?

The brain is a mass of over 10 billion nerve cells. These are surrounded and supported by cells called glia, which supply them with nutrients.

What does the brain do?

The brain is the body's control centre. It sends messages to and receives them from organs and tissues all over the body. The brain gives us our ability to learn, reason and feel. As well as our voluntary, or conscious, activities it controls involuntary activities, too. For example, it controls heartbeat and digestion.

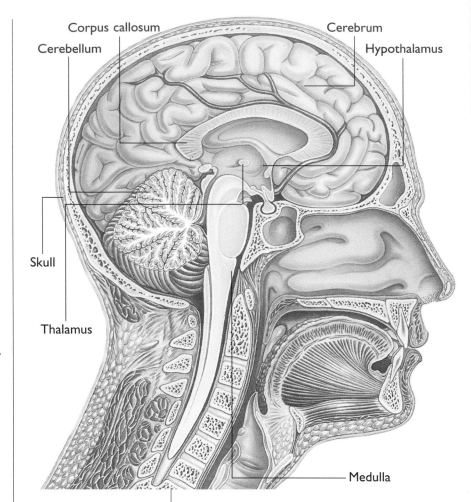

Corpus callosum

Cerebellum

Cerebrum

Hypothalamus

Skull

Thalamus

Medulla

▲ The brain is protected by the bony skull. The biggest part of the brain is the cerebrum. This is the conscious part of the brain.

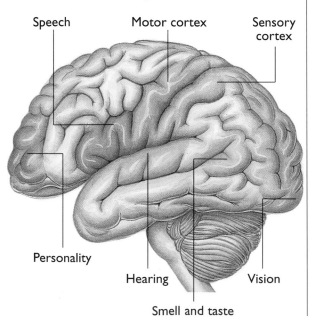

Speech

Motor cortex

Sensory cortex

Personality

Hearing

Vision

Smell and taste

◄ Different parts of the brain process different types of information.

How is the brain protected?

The skull protects the brain from most physical injuries. The brain is also protected by three layers of tissue called meninges, which are wrapped around it. The inner layer acts as a barrier to prevent bacteria reaching the brain. The middle layer contains cerebrospinal fluid. This supplies the brain with food and oxygen and acts as a shock absorber, cushioning the brain against damage. The outer layer lines the cranium. The skull itself consists of several bones which are fused together.

How is the brain like a computer?

Like a computer, the brain is made up of circuits that carry electrical signals, but these circuits are made up of nerve cells. As in a computer, some of the circuits in the brain form a memory to store information, and others are used to process incoming information and respond to it.

What are the main parts of the brain?

The three main parts are the cerebrum at the top, the medulla on the underside, and the cerebellum at the back. The largest part is the cerebrum (about 85 percent of the brain's weight). It gives us intelligence and emotions. We use it to think, feel and remember.

Why are most people right-handed?

The left side of the brain is connected to the right side of the body. The nerve cells that carry messages from the brain cross over at the base of the brain. Signals from the left go to the right side of the body, and vice versa. In most people, the left side of the brain is dominant over the right side. As the left brain controls movement in the right side of the body, most people therefore have better control with their right hand.

Do the right and left halves do different jobs?

Yes, they do. In most people the left side seems to control speaking, writing and logical thinking. The right side is more artistic and creative.

Our brain is so important that a quarter of all the blood pumped by the heart is pushed into the brain. The brain's capacity for storing information is quite extraordinary. A person of 80 can often remember with great accuracy an event that happened in their early childhood. Scientists still do not know how the 10 billion cells in our brain manage this remarkable feat.

BRAIN FACTS

■ A human brain weighs on average 1.4 kg: that's about 2.5 percent of body weight.

■ By the age of 5, a child's brain has reached 90 percent of its full weight.

■ The brain is roughly shaped like a cauliflower.

■ The brain has over 10 billion nerve cells in it.

■ The outer edge of the cerebrum (the 'thinking zone') is about the size of a newspaper page, but is all scrunched up.

■ Grey matter is the part of the brain and spinal cord that contains the nerve cell bodies.

Are girls' brains different to boys'?

There is evidence that girls' and boys' brains are slightly different. As a general rule, most boys are better at tasks that require 'spatial ability' – picturing the shape and position of objects or patterns. Girls are better at using words and usually learn to read at an earlier age than boys.

What is the mind?

The mind is the part of us that gives rise to our thoughts, memories and feelings. Most people believe that the mind is situated in the brain.

How many things can we remember?

We can remember a list of about seven things at the same time. This is why most people have difficulty in remembering a telephone number with more than seven figures. If the numbers are grouped, it makes them easier to remember because your memory can hold about seven 'packets' or groups of information at one time. Memory is located in more than one area of the brain.

How do we learn?

We learn in many different ways. When we learn facts for a classroom test, we may soon forget them. When we learn a skill like riding a bicycle, or swimming, it may stay with us for a lifetime. Much of our early learning comes from copying other people. Animals learn in the same way, from their parents. Humans also learn from passed-on information – for example, from books.

What is body language?

Body language is non-verbal communication; that is, everything other than what we say. This includes the pitch of the voice, our facial expression, our gestures and hand movements, and posture. Hand gestures can mean different things in different cultures. The thumbs-up sign means 'OK' in English-speaking countries. In France it also means 'zero' and in Japan it means 'money'. In some countries it is a rude gesture.

What is social behaviour?

Social behaviour is the way we act when we are with other people. In particular, it is the behaviour of someone in a group, such as a family, a group of friends or a class at school. Group, or peer, pressure is the pressure a group of people put on an individual to behave in a particular way. For example, in a group of friends you may feel under pressure to like the same music and clothes as the others, or to go to the same places. It is fun to be one of the crowd sometimes, but it's also good to have your own ideas and values.

SLEEP FACTS

■ On average, most people sleep about 8 hours a day. So in your lifetime, you will probably spend about 20 years sleeping!

■ Our bodies grow and repair themselves during 3-4 hour periods of deep sleep, called orthodox sleep.

■ We dream during rapid eye movement (REM) sleep (about 2-3 hours a night).

■ During REM sleep our eyes flick back and forth under our eyelids.

■ Some people suffering from a rare condition called total insomnia have gone without proper sleep for many years.

■ Babies sleep most of the time because they are growing so quickly.

■ We sleep more when we are ill, because our bodies need time to rest and get better.

Why do we need to sleep?

No one is exactly sure why we need to sleep. Of course, sleeping rests the body and it is thought that during sleep we repair our tissues, grow new cells and recover from the day's activities. Our brains are still very active while we sleep and some people think that the brain sorts through the day's events during this time, organizing new information and fitting it in with previous information. This may help us to learn from new experiences. A newborn baby needs 16 hours of sleep each day; a person aged 65 needs only 6 hours.

Some people sleepwalk. Nobody knows what causes sleep-walking. Parts of the brain that control movement and speech stay awake. The person may speak, sit up, and even walk, but they do not recall anything when they wake up.

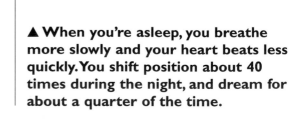

▲ When you're asleep, you breathe more slowly and your heart beats less quickly. You shift position about 40 times during the night, and dream for about a quarter of the time.

AFRICA

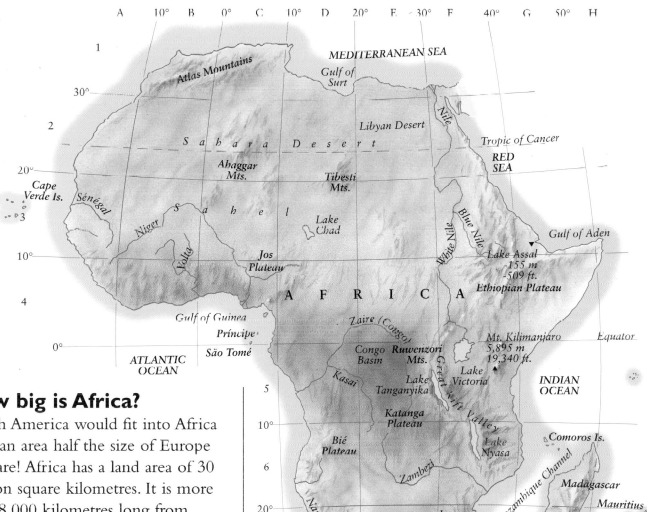

A 10° B 0° C 10° D 20° E 30° F 40° G 50° H

MEDITERRANEAN SEA

Atlas Mountains

Gulf of Surt

30°

1

Nile

Libyan Desert

2

S a h a r a   D e s e r t

Tropic of Cancer

RED SEA

20°

Ahaggar Mts.

Tibesti Mts.

Cape Verde Is.

Sénégal

S   a   h   e   l

Niger

Volta

Lake Chad

White Nile

Blue Nile

Gulf of Aden

Lake Assal
-155 m
-509 ft.

3

Jos Plateau

10°

Ethiopian Plateau

4

A   F   R   I   C   A

Gulf of Guinea

Príncipe

São Tomé

ATLANTIC OCEAN

0°

Zaire (Congo)

Congo Basin

Ruwenzori Mts.

Mt. Kilimanjaro
5,895 m
19,340 ft.

Equator

Kasai

Lake Tanganyika

Lake Victoria

Great Rift Valley

INDIAN OCEAN

5

10°

Katanga Plateau

Lake Nyasa

Comoros Is.

6

Bié Plateau

Zambezi

Mozambique Channel

Madagascar

Mauritius

Namib Desert

20°

Kalahari Desert

Limpopo

Tropic of Capricorn

Réunion

7

Orange

Drakensberg Mts.

mi.
0   500

30°

8

Cape of Good Hope

Cape Agulhas

0   500
km

How big is Africa?

North America would fit into Africa with an area half the size of Europe to spare! Africa has a land area of 30 million square kilometres. It is more than 8,000 kilometres long from north to south, and more than 6,000 kilometres wide from east to west.

Africa is mostly a huge jungle: true or false?

False. Most of Africa is either desert (40 percent) or grassy savannah (40 percent). Forests cover less than a fifth of Africa. Most of this African forest is wet tropical rainforest.

Where are the Mountains of the Moon?

The Ruwenzori Mountains are on the border between Uganda and

▲ The map of Africa shows how much of the continent is desert. There are also large expanses of grassland. The rainforests are in central and western Africa.

Zaire (Dem. Rep. of Congo) in central Africa. These peaks are over 5,000 metres high. They were named the Mountains of the Moon by the early geographer Ptolemy, who in AD 150 drew a map showing the river Nile beginning its journey in these mountains. The river has several sources, including Lake Victoria.

◀ Tourists walk along the crest of a huge sand dune in Namibia. The Namib is one of Africa's driest deserts.

Is there much desert in Africa?

About 40 percent of Africa is desert. The Sahara Desert covers much of the northern third of the continent. Other deserts are the Namib and the Kalahari in the southwest.

What is the Great Rift Valley?

The Great Rift Valley is one of Africa's outstanding natural features: a series of valleys that cuts through eastern Africa. The Great Rift Valley is the result of enormous volcanic movement. In places, the rift in the Earth is over one and a half kilometres deep and 40 kilometres wide. In other places, the rift has filled with water creating some of Africa's greatest lakes (Mobutu Sese Seko, Edward, Nyasa and Tanganyika), as well as the Red Sea.

How high is the land in Africa?

Compared to Asia or North America, Africa is fairly flat. The north, west and centre of the continent are mostly below 600 metres. Most of northern Africa is the plateau of the Sahara. The highest land in Africa is in the east and south. This area includes the Great Rift Valley and the grassy plains of the Eastern Highlands.

▲ Boats carry goods and passengers along the Nile. This mighty river is the lifeblood of Egypt, and has been for thousands of years.

Like all rivers, the Nile is hard to measure because its course constantly changes. It is about 6,670 kilometres long.

▶ Tugela River tumbles over a series of falls, creating a spectacular, natural wonder.

Which are Africa's greatest rivers?

Africa's biggest rivers are the Nile (the longest river in the world), followed by the Zaire (Congo), the Niger and the Zambezi.

Where is the Tugela Falls?

The Tugela Falls is a series of five waterfalls on the Tugela River in South Africa. The highest fall is 410 metres high and in all, the five falls drop 947 metres. Tugela is the second highest waterfall in the world.

Is there any snow in Africa?

Africa's highest mountain is in Tanzania in eastern Africa. It is Kilimanjaro or Uhuru ('Freedom') and is 5,895 metres high. Kilimanjaro is an extinct volcano. Although very near the Equator, the summit is always covered with snow.

Which is Africa's largest island?

The island of Madagascar, off the eastern coast of Africa, covers 587,000 square kilometres. It is the fourth biggest island in the world and is separated from the mainland by the Mozambique Channel. Madagascar has animals found nowhere else in the world, such as lemurs and rare birds. Most of its people rely on agriculture.

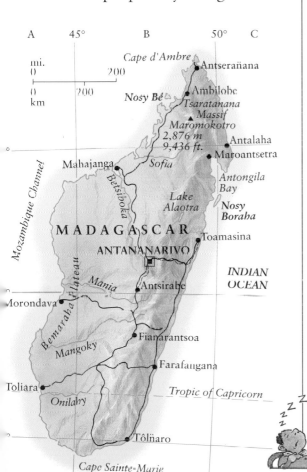

▲ Kilimanjaro's snow-capped peak can be seen from far away. The mountain towers above the vast plains where elephants and many other animals roam.

◀ Central Madagascar is a high plateau. There are lowlands in the east and south. Much of the island's natural forests have been cut down.

On the island of Madagascar, a man makes a speech to his bride-to-be before she will marry him. If the speech is no good, he pays a fine and starts all over again!

When did people first live in Africa?

Africa was where human beings first evolved. Scientists have found bones and other remains of human-like creatures that are older than any remains found elsewhere. These creatures lived more than 4 million years ago. About 2 million years ago the first true humans lived in Africa, hunting animals, gathering plants and making the first stone tools. These people are known as *Homo habilis* ('skilful human').

▼ The human-like creature *Australopithecus* lived in Africa over 4 million years ago, and may have used sticks and stones as tools.

ASIA

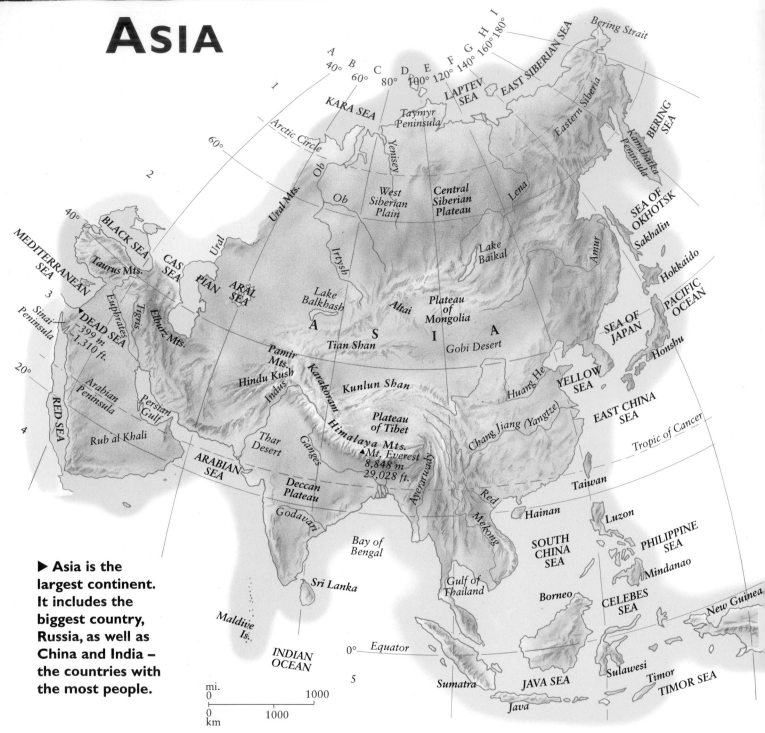

A
40°
B
60°
C
80°
D
100°
E
120°
F
140°
G
160°
H
180°
I

Bering Strait

KARA SEA

LAPTEV SEA

EAST SIBERIAN SEA

Taymyr Peninsula

Arctic Circle

60°

Ob

Yenisey

West Siberian Plain

Central Siberian Plateau

Eastern Siberia

BERING SEA

Kamchatka Peninsula

Ob

Ural Mts.

Lena

SEA OF OKHOTSK

Sakhalin

40°

BLACK SEA

CAS PIAN SEA

Ural

Lake Baikal

Amur

Hokkaido

PACIFIC OCEAN

MEDITERRANEAN SEA

Taurus Mts.

ARAL SEA

Irtysh

Altai

Plateau of Mongolia

SEA OF JAPAN

Honshu

Euphrates

Elburz Mts.

Lake Balkhash

A   S   I   A

Sinai Peninsula

DEAD SEA
−399 m
−1,310 ft.

Tigris

Tian Shan

Gobi Desert

Huang He

YELLOW SEA

20°

Arabian Peninsula

Persian Gulf

Pamir Mts.

Hindu Kush

Karakoram

Kunlun Shan

Chang Jiang (Yangtze)

EAST CHINA SEA

RED SEA

Indus

Himalaya Mts.

Plateau of Tibet

Tropic of Cancer

Rub al Khali

Thar Desert

Ganges

▲Mt. Everest
8,848 m
29,028 ft.

Ayeyarwady

Red

Taiwan

ARABIAN SEA

Deccan Plateau

Godavari

Mekong

Hainan

Luzon

PHILIPPINE SEA

Bay of Bengal

SOUTH CHINA SEA

Mindanao

▶ Asia is the largest continent. It includes the biggest country, Russia, as well as China and India – the countries with the most people.

Sri Lanka

Gulf of Thailand

Borneo

CELEBES SEA

New Guinea

Maldive Is.

INDIAN OCEAN

0°   Equator

Sulawesi

Timor

TIMOR SEA

mi.
0   1000

Sumatra

JAVA SEA

Java

0   1000
km

How big is Asia?

Asia is the biggest continent. Its area of 44 million square kilometres is greater than North and South America put together, and four times greater than Europe. The coastline of Asia is almost 130,000 kilometres long – more than three times the distance around the world.

Some mountains get smaller all the time as they are worn away. The Himalayas are getting higher, pushed up by movements in the Earth's crust.

What are Asia's main features?

Asia's natural features are very varied, from the world's highest mountains (the Himalayas) to long rivers (such as the Chang Jiang), lakes as big as seas (the Caspian) and deserts like the Gobi. There are hot jungles, cold forests, grasslands and snowy tundras.

Where are Asia's high and low points?

Asia has the highest and lowest points on the Earth's land. Mount Everest (over 8,800 m above sea level) is the highest point. The shores of the Dead Sea (almost 400 m below sea level) are the lowest points to be found anywhere on land.

Where are Asia's deepest gorges?

The deepest gorges cut by rivers are those made by the rivers Indus, Brahmaputra and Ganges which flow through India and Pakistan. In places, these rivers cut gorges that are more than five kilometres deep.

Does Asia have more people than any other continent?

Yes. As well as covering one-third of the Earth's land surface, Asia has about three-fifths of the world's people. More than 3.5 billion people live in Asia, in 49 countries.

▲ In the Dead Sea, you can float while reading the paper! This is because the water is unusually salty and supports your weight.

ASIA FACTS

- Area: 44,380,400 sq km.
- Population 3.5 billion people.
- Number of countries: 49.
- Longest river: Chang Jiang (Yangtze), 6,300 km.
- Largest lake: Caspian Sea, 372,000 sq km.
- Highest mountain: Everest 8,863 m above sea level.
- Largest country: Russia (partly in Europe).
- Country with most people: China.
- Largest city: Tokyo (Japan), where over 26.5 million people live.

Which country has the most languages?

India has 14 major languages and more than 160 others. There are also 700 dialects (local or regional variations). Hindi is the official language of India and many Indians also speak English.

Where is the Khyber Pass?

The Khyber Pass is in northwest Pakistan. Here the land is rugged and hilly. The pass is a route through the mountains to Afghanistan.

What is the Tonlé Sap?

The Tonlé Sap is a large lake in Cambodia, in Southeast Asia. During the summer floods, its waters cover some 10,000 square kilometres. The lake is formed by water from the Mekong River, the longest river in Southeast Asia (4,500 km) and the fifth longest in Asia.

▼ The Tonlé Sap is a large lake in Cambodia. People in this region use the rivers and the lakes for transport and fishing.

NORTH AND CENTRAL AMERICA

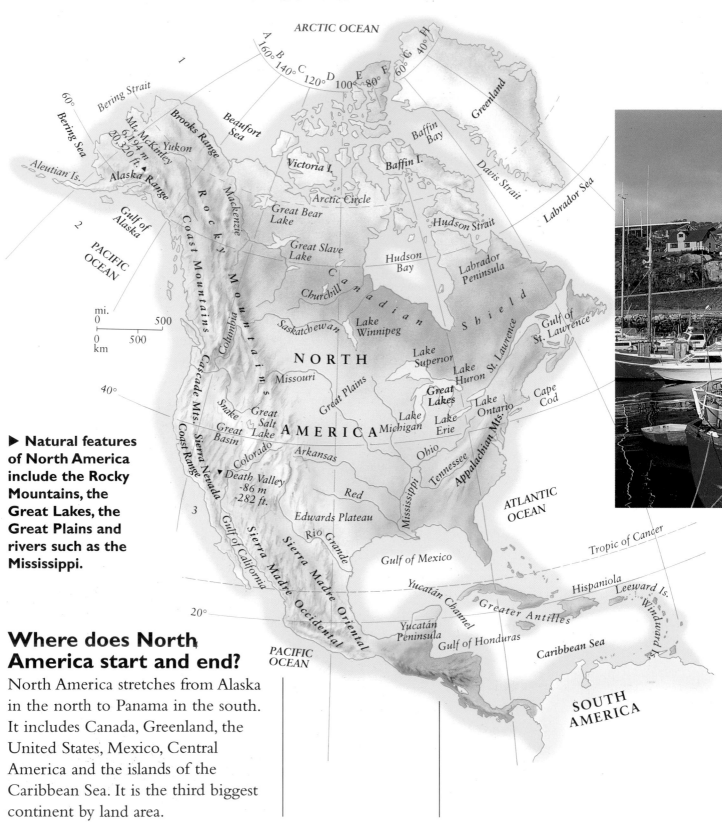

ARCTIC OCEAN

A 160° B 140° C 120° D 100° E 80° F 60° G 40° H

1

60°

Bering Strait

Bering Sea

Aleutian Is.

Brooks Range

Beaufort Sea

Mt. McKinley 6,194 m 20,320 ft.

Yukon

Alaska Range

Gulf of Alaska

Greenland

Baffin Bay

Baffin I.

Davis Strait

Labrador Sea

2

PACIFIC OCEAN

Victoria I.

Arctic Circle

Great Bear Lake

Coast Mountains

Mackenzie

Great Slave Lake

Hudson Strait

Hudson Bay

Labrador Peninsula

Rocky Mountains

Churchill

C a n a d i a n

S h i e l d

Gulf of St. Lawrence

mi.
0   500
0   500
km

Columbia

Saskatchewan

Lake Winnipeg

Lake Superior

St. Lawrence

Cape Cod

40°

NORTH

Missouri

Great Plains

Lake Huron

Lake Ontario

Cascade Mts.

Snake

Great Salt Lake

Great Basin

AMERICA

Lake Michigan

Lake Erie

Appalachian Mts.

Coast Range

Sierra Nevada

Colorado

Arkansas

Ohio

▶ Natural features of North America include the Rocky Mountains, the Great Lakes, the Great Plains and rivers such as the Mississippi.

▼ Death Valley -86 m -282 ft.

Red

Tennessee

Mississippi

ATLANTIC OCEAN

3

Edwards Plateau

Rio Grande

Tropic of Cancer

Gulf of California

Sierra Madre Occidental

Sierra Madre Oriental

Gulf of Mexico

Yucatán Channel

Greater Antilles

Hispaniola

Leeward Is.

Windward Is.

20°

Where does North America start and end?

PACIFIC OCEAN

Yucatán Peninsula

Gulf of Honduras

Caribbean Sea

North America stretches from Alaska in the north to Panama in the south. It includes Canada, Greenland, the United States, Mexico, Central America and the islands of the Caribbean Sea. It is the third biggest continent by land area.

SOUTH AMERICA

Which is North America's largest country?

Canada. It covers more than 9,970,000 square kilometres. The United States of America is smaller, covering 9,373,000 square kilometres. Yet only 29 million people live in Canada compared to over 268 million in the United States.

Is Greenland part of North America?

Greenland is a self-governing part of Denmark, a country in Europe. Yet geographically this enormous island is part of North America.

Which is North America's biggest city?

Mexico City, with over 20 million people, is the biggest city in North America. The largest city in the United States is New York, with a population of over 16 million.

More people live in Mexico City than in any other city in the world. The United Nations calculate that by the year 2000, Mexico City will have more than 25 million people.

◀ Julianehaab is a port in southern Greenland. Ice covers 80 percent of this high island.

▼ This map shows the different climate regions of North America, from the Arctic north to the tropical south.

Which is North America's smallest country?

Of the 23 independent North American countries the smallest is St Kitts and Nevis, an island state in the Caribbean. The islands have a combined area of 269 square kilometres and only 44,000 people live there. There are even smaller island states in the region but they are not self-governing.

What is the climate of North America like?

North America has every kind of climate. The far north is ice-covered all year round. The interior has mostly cold winters and either warm or cool summers. The southeast is warm and moist. The southwest is mostly dry with great ranges of temperature and areas of desert. In the far south, in Central America, there are hot, wet tropical forests.

Climate Regions of North America

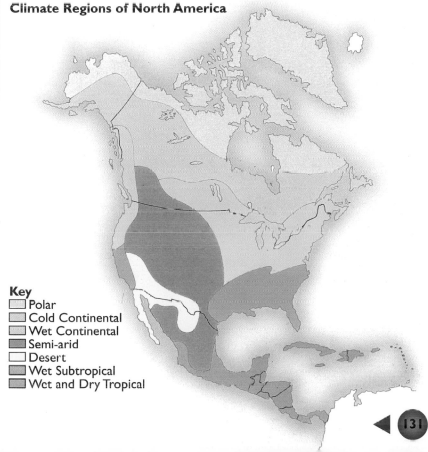

Key
- Polar
- Cold Continental
- Wet Continental
- Semi-arid
- Desert
- Wet Subtropical
- Wet and Dry Tropical

Where is the Capitol?

To Americans, the Capitol in Washington, DC is one of the most familiar buildings in the country. The Capitol is the seat of the United States Congress.

Which US cities have the tallest buildings?

New York City and Chicago have long been rivals in the skyscraper contest. New York boasts the twin towers of the World Trade Center, and the Empire State Building, while Chicago (which claims to be the home of the skyscraper) has the even taller Sears Tower, the second highest building in the world.

Where are yellow cabs a familiar sight?

Visitors to New York City may travel around the city in one of its famous yellow cabs. Or they may ride on one of the city's three subway systems. New York City also has two of the best-known railway stations in the nation: Grand Central Terminal and Pennsylvania Station. Thousands of commuters travel to the city each day.

The president of the United States lives in the White House in Washington D.C. It earned its colour after the building was burned by British troops in 1814 and the smoke-stained walls were painted white.

▼ An Inuit. The name Eskimo (also used for the Inuit) is a Native American word meaning 'eaters of raw meat'.

◀ New York's Times Square is one of the city's many famous sights, with its bright lights and yellow cabs.

In which part of North America is French more common than English?

In the Canadian province of Quebec. Most of the people of Quebec are French Canadians. Montreal, the largest city in Quebec, has more French-speakers than any other city in the world after Paris in France.

Why do people come to watch the Calgary Stampede?

This is one of the most exciting rodeo shows in the world. It takes place in July every year in Calgary, a city in Alberta, Canada. Large crowds pack the arena to watch the famous chuckwagon race, which is one of the highlights of the rodeo.

Where do the Inuit live?

The Inuit are people who live in the Canadian Arctic. Here, most of the ground is covered in snow in winter. The Inuit traditionally lived by hunting and fishing, but the modern world has brought changes, including the mining of oil and gas. Many Inuit now have regular jobs or make craft goods to sell to tourists. They want more control over their ancient lands.

Where do people store corn in pyramids?

In Mexico. Cone-shaped silos looking rather like pyramids can store a year's corn (maize) harvest. The Mayan people grew corn as their main food crop in Mexico as early as 3,000 years ago, and it is still an important source of food, forming the basis of many Mexican dishes.

Where is Chichén Itzá?

Chichén Itzá is an ancient city in Mexico, built by the Mayan people over 1,000 years ago. The city's ruins include a tall limestone pyramid with a temple on top, and a huge plaza or open space where there was a steam bath and a ball game court. The ruins are now an important archaeological site and tourist attraction.

Where do people celebrate the Day of the Dead?

The Day of the Dead is a Mexican holiday which takes place every year on November 2, All Souls' Day. People remember dead friends and relatives, taking flowers and candles to their graves and having picnics there.

◀ The stone Chacmool, or messenger of the gods, at Chichén Itzá was used in sacrificial ceremonies.

FACTS ABOUT NORTH AMERICA

■ Mexico's most popular sport is soccer. Mexicans also enjoy bullfights.

■ A favourite dish in Newfoundland, Canada, is flipper pie (made from fish, not seals).

■ The first people to settle North America came from Asia more than 15,000 years ago.

■ The first Europeans known to visit North America were Vikings, about AD 1000.

■ The United States is the fourth biggest country by area – after Russia, Canada and China.

■ The national bird of the USA is the bald eagle, shown on the Great Seal, the official symbol of the United States.

▼ Mexicans make painted papier-mâché skeletons to celebrate the Day of the Dead. The skeletons wear hats too!

Where is Central America?

Central America is the narrow land bridge joining North and South America. It extends from Guatemala and Belize in the north as far as Panama in the south. There are seven countries in Central America, the largest being Nicaragua.

Who built pyramids in Central America?

The native peoples of Central America developed remarkable civilizations. The Mayan people built great stepped pyramids. On top of each pyramid was a small temple. The Maya built cities such as Tikal, in what is now Guatemala. The great age of Mayan civilization lasted from AD 250 to 900.

How did the Caribbean Sea get its name?

The Caribbean Sea is to the east of Central America. Its name comes from the Caribs, a people who lived on some of the islands of the West Indies and in South America. When Christopher Columbus sailed to America in 1492, the Spanish sailors called the sea Mar Caribe – Caribbean Sea.

Where is cigar-rolling an important industry?

Cuba is famous for its cigars. Workers roll Havana cigars by hand. These cigars are named after Havana, the capital city of Cuba. Cuba has had a communist government since 1959, when Fidel Castro overthrew the dictator Fulgencio Batista.

SOUTH AMERICA

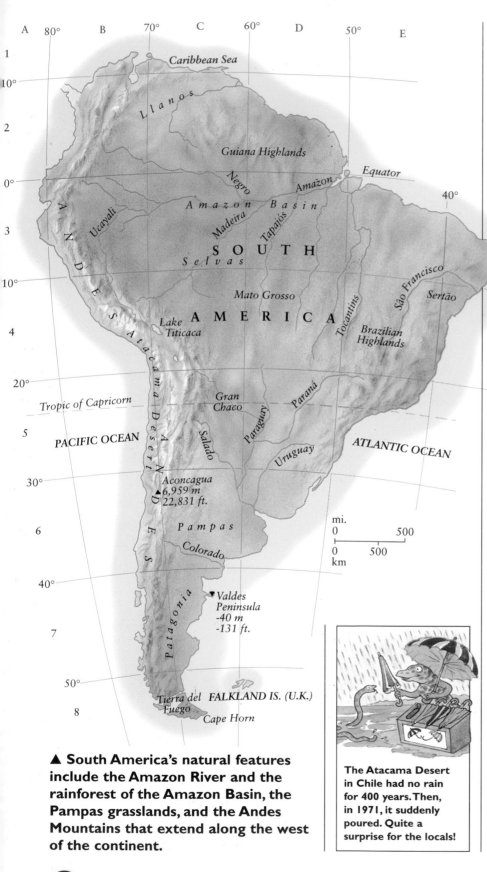

South America's natural features map showing coordinates A–E and 1–8

- Caribbean Sea
- Llanos
- Guiana Highlands
- Negro
- Amazon
- Equator
- Amazon Basin
- Ucayali
- Madeira
- Tapajós
- SOUTH
- Selvas
- A N D E S
- Atacama Desert
- Mato Grosso
- São Francisco
- Sertão
- Lake Titicaca
- AMERICA
- Tocantins
- Brazilian Highlands
- Gran Chaco
- Paraná
- Tropic of Capricorn
- PACIFIC OCEAN
- Salado
- Paraguay
- Uruguay
- ATLANTIC OCEAN
- Aconcagua ▲ 6,959 m 22,831 ft.
- Pampas
- Colorado
- mi. 0 — 500
- 0 — 500 km
- Patagonia
- ▼ Valdes Peninsula -40 m -131 ft.
- Tierra del Fuego
- FALKLAND IS. (U.K.)
- Cape Horn

▲ **South America's natural features include the Amazon River and the rainforest of the Amazon Basin, the Pampas grasslands, and the Andes Mountains that extend along the west of the continent.**

The Atacama Desert in Chile had no rain for 400 years. Then, in 1971, it suddenly poured. Quite a surprise for the locals!

Is South America south of North America?

The South American continent is actually southeast of North America, not directly south. New York, on the east coast of North America, is farther west than Valparaiso, Chile, on the west coast of South America.

How big is South America?

South America covers an area of nearly 18 million square kilometres, so it is roughly twice as big as Canada. South America has the world's biggest rainforest, in the Amazon River Basin and the high Andes Mountains.

Where is Cape Horn?

Cape Horn is at the southernmost tip of South America. Most of South America lies within the tropics, yet Cape Horn is less than 1,000 kilometres from Antarctica.

Who were the first people to live in South America?

When Europeans arrived in South America in the late 1400s, they discovered that people had been living there for thousands of years, including the great Aztec, Inca and Mayan civilizations. Today, most South Americans are of mixed ancestry. They share many traditions, but local cultures reflect their African, American Indian and European background.

Which are South America's most important rivers?

There are four mighty river systems in South America. They are the Magdalena, Orinoco, Amazon and Paraná–Paraguay.

Why is Quito not so tropical?

Quito is the capital of Equador. It is only 25 kilometres south of the Equator so it should be hot. However, it is almost 3,000 metres above sea level, which means it has a mild climate – 'higher' means 'cooler'.

Where is Patagonia?

Patagonia is a bleak desert region at the very southern tip of Argentina. When Spanish explorers reached there in the 1500s they met local Indians who stuffed their boots with grass for extra warmth. The name Patagonia comes from a Spanish word meaning 'big feet'.

▶ **La Paz in Bolivia holds the record as the world's highest national capital.**

SOUTH AMERICA FACTS

- Area: 17,817,000 sq km.
- Population: 458,000,000 people.
- Number of countries: 12.
- Longest river: Amazon, 6,448 km.
- Largest lake: Maracaibo, 13,512 sq km.
- Highest mountain: Mount Aconcagua (Argentina), 6,959 m above sea level.
- Largest country: Brazil.
- Country with most people: Brazil.
- Largest city: São Paulo (Brazil).

▶ **Glaciers flow down from the Andes Mountains. This is a glacier in Patagonia, seen from a viewing platform.**

Which is the highest capital city in the world?

La Paz, the capital of Bolivia, is 3,600 metres above sea level. High in the Andes Mountains, it is the world's highest capital. Lhasa in Tibet is higher by about 50 metres, but Tibet is not now an independent country.

Which is the biggest lake in South America?

South America has fewer large lakes than other continents. The biggest lake is Lake Maracaibo (13,512 square kilometres) in Venezuela. This lake has valuable oil reserves beneath it and is also a busy waterway.

How big is the Amazon rainforest?

The Amazon forest is one of the wonders of the natural world. The Amazon River Basin, in which the rainforest grows, covers about 7 million square kilometres. That's twice the size of India. Although much of the forest has been destroyed by logging and burning, it is still by far the biggest forest anywhere on Earth. Conservationists are trying to save as much as possible of the remaining forest from destruction.

What is the Selva?

The Selva is a region of tropical rainforest in the Amazon River Basin. It is one of four regions in the central plains of South America. The other three are the Llanos grasslands of the north, the Gran Chaco scrubforest and the southern Pampas grasslands.

Where do gauchos live?

Gauchos are South American cowboys. Huge herds of cattle roam the grassy plains of Brazil, Uruguay and Argentina. The gauchos used to be horsemen who rounded up wild cattle. Now they are ranch workers.

▶ **The Amazon rainforest is amazingly rich in plant and animal life. Each layer of the forest teems with life, from the dark forest floor to the sunlit treetops.**

▼ **Gauchos look after enormous herds of cattle on the grassy plains of Argentina. They ride tough, well-trained horses.**

Liana

Monkey

Frog

Toucan

Macaws

Butterfly

Ants

MORE FACTS ABOUT SOUTH AMERICA

■ Much of South America is thinly populated but cities such as São Paulo are fast-growing, with many poor people living in shanty slums.

■ Coastal Peru and northern Chile are among the driest places on Earth.

■ Cape Horn at the tip of South America is only 970 km from Antarctica.

■ Spanish is spoken in most of South America, except in Brazil where Portuguese is spoken.

■ The Amazon holds 20 percent of the world's fresh water.

■ Lake Titicaca in Bolivia is the highest lake in the world used by boats. It is 3,821 m above sea level.

Why is South America a youthful continent?

South America has more than 450 million people. The population now is three times greater than 50 years ago. Many people have large families and about a third of all South Americans are under 15 years old.

Which is the biggest city in South America?

São Paulo, in Brazil, with a population of more than 16 million is the largest South American city, yet it is not Brazil's capital. Brasilia, a new city with 400,000 people in the country's centre, replaced Rio de Janeiro as the capital in 1960.

Is South America rich in minerals?

Yes, the continent has large reserves of metals such as copper, iron ore, lead, zinc and gold. Venezuela is the chief South American oil producer. Bolivia has tin mines. Guyana, Surinam and Brazil mine bauxite (which is aluminium ore).

What does Cotopaxi do?

From time to time it erupts, for Cotopaxi is one of the world's largest active volcanoes. It has erupted 25 times in the past 400 years, the last time in 1975. Cotopaxi is in Ecuador and is 5,897 metres high.

Where is South America's low point?

On the east coast of Argentina. The Valdés Peninsula is about 40 metres below the level of the sea.

EUROPE

20° A 10° B 0° C 10° D 20° E 30° F 40° G 50° H 60° I 70°

ARCTIC OCEAN

North Cape

BARENTS SEA

Arctic Circle

Iceland

NORWEGIAN SEA

Faeroe Is.

Shetland Is.

WHITE SEA

Northern Dvina

60°

Ural Mountains

Scandinavian Peninsula

Gulf of Bothnia

Lake Onega

Lake Ladoga

Ireland

NORTH SEA

Lake Vanern

Western Dvina

Volga

50°

Great Britain

BALTIC SEA

Ural

Thames

Vistula

EUROPE

English Channel

Elbe

Oder

NORTH ATLANTIC OCEAN

Seine

Rhine

Dnepr

Don

CASPIAN SEA

Loire

Bay of Biscay

Carpathian Mts.

SEA OF AZOV

Mt. Elbrus 5,642 m 18,508 ft.

-28 m -92 ft.

Massif Central

Rhône

Alps

Po

Hungarian Plain

Crimea

Caucasus Mts.

Duero

Pyrenees

Dinaric Alps

Danube

BLACK SEA

Iberian Peninsula

Corsica

Apennines

ADRIATIC SEA

Balkan Peninsula

Tagus

Meseta

Sardinia

Balkan Mts.

mi.
0   500

Balearic Is.

TYRRHENIAN SEA

0   500
km

Strait of Gibraltar

MEDITERRANEAN SEA

IONIAN SEA

AEGEAN SEA

Sicily

Malta

Crete

Where do Europe and Asia join?

Europe is part of the Asian landmass, for no sea divides it from Asia. In the east, several natural land barriers form a boundary between Europe and Asia. These barriers include the Ural Mountains, the Ural River and the Caspian Sea. Since Europe and Asia are joined, the two together are sometimes referred to as Eurasia. Europe is smaller than all the other continents except Australia.

▲ The map of Europe shows how the continent has water on three sides. Its natural features include mountain ranges such as the Pyrenees, Alps, Carpathians and Urals. Europe's rivers include the Danube, Rhine and Volga.

Which is Europe's longest river?

The longest river in Europe is the Volga. It flows for 3,531 kilometres across Russia and empties into the Caspian Sea.

Why is western Europe ice-free in winter?

Although much of the coast of Norway lies in Arctic waters, it is not ice-bound in winter. Norway, like the rest of northwest Europe, has milder winters than places in North America which are equally far north. This is because the Gulf Stream's warm waters flow across the Atlantic. The warm ocean current warms the winds blowing from the sea across western Europe, keeping winters in coastal areas (such as the United Kingdom) mild with ice-free oceans.

Where is Scandinavia?

Scandinavia is a region of northern Europe. Three countries are part of Scandinavia, though not all of them are on the Scandinavian peninsula: Denmark (the most southerly), Norway, and Sweden. Iceland (an island in the Atlantic Ocean) and Finland are often included.

Where is Lapland?

Lapland is the part of Scandinavia and Finland north of the Arctic Circle. It is not a country, but takes its name from the Lapps, or Sami, a people who traditionally roam the area with their herds of reindeer.

► The Black Forest in Germany is a reminder that in the past much of western Europe was covered by dense forest.

EUROPE FACTS

■ Area: 10,534,600 sq km.

■ Population: 713,000,000 people.

■ Number of countries: 47.

■ Longest river: Volga, 3,531 km.

■ Largest lake: excluding Caspian Sea (Europe-Asia border) Lake Ladoga in Russia, 17,703 sq km.

■ Highest mountain: Mount Elbrus, 5,633 m above sea level.

■ Largest country: Russia (part in Asia).

■ Country with most people: Russia.

■ Largest city: Moscow (Russia), 8,957,000 people.

◄ The Lapps still herd reindeer. These hardy people use the animals to draw sleds across the snow-covered ground.

Where is the Black Forest?

The Black Forest, or Schwarzwald in German, is a region of mountains and coniferous forest in southwest Germany. The Danube River rises there and the Rhine River flows along its western edge. The Black Forest, with its dark-leaved trees, is a remnant of the much larger forests that once covered most of northern Europe.

Why has the Mediterranean Sea been so important?

The Mediterranean Sea has been a trading area for thousands of years. Civilization spread across the sea from Egypt and Mesopotamia. Greece and Rome became powerful and later Italian city-states such as Venice grew rich from Mediterranean trade. Today the Mediterranean is still important for trade, especially with the oil fields in the Middle East, and is also a popular tourist area. Around its sunny shores are busy ports, picturesque villages and modern holiday resorts.

◀ **Italy is shaped rather like a boot. The north is cooler than the south, and more industrialized. The islands of Sicily and Sardinia are part of Italy.**

Is all of Italy warm?

Parts of Italy have a Mediterranean climate with mild winters and hot, dry summers. The south, especially Sicily, can be very hot. However, areas of northern Italy around the Po Valley and in the Alps have cold winters.

How high are the Scottish Highlands?

In the Highlands of Scotland are the highest mountains in Britain. They are ancient and have been worn and weathered over many millions of years, giving them a smooth, rounded appearance. The highest mountain, Ben Nevis, is only 1,343 metres high.

▼ **Outside its famous film festival, Cannes has a quiet, genteel mood.**

Where is the Cote d'Azur?

In the south of France, the summers are dry and hot and there are usually many sunny winter days. The French call part of their Mediterranean coast the 'sky-blue coast', or Cote d'Azur, for this reason.

Which European country has reclaimed nearly half its land from the sea?

The Netherlands. The name Netherlands means 'low countries' and this part of Europe is very flat and low-lying. Sea walls called dykes hold back the sea. Pumps drain the flat land and a network of canals carry the water away. Large areas of marsh have been reclaimed from the sea and turned into good farmland.

Which countries share the Iberian Peninsula?

Spain and Portugal. This square-shaped peninsula is in the southwest corner of Europe.

▲ The Netherlands is sometimes known as Holland. Its capital is Amsterdam.

Where is the Camargue?

The Camargue is the delta, or mouth, of the Rhône River in southeastern France. Formed by sedimentation, it is flat, lonely marshland, with numerous shallow lagoons. Rich in bird life, it was once known for its herds of horses and fighting bulls. Today farmers grow vines and rice there.

How many countries make up the British Isles?

Two: the United Kingdom and the Republic of Ireland. The United Kingdom consists of Great Britain (England, Wales and Scotland) and Northern Ireland.

◄ This map shows the main natural features and cities of the United Kingdom. The capital is London.

AUSTRALASIA AND THE PACIFIC

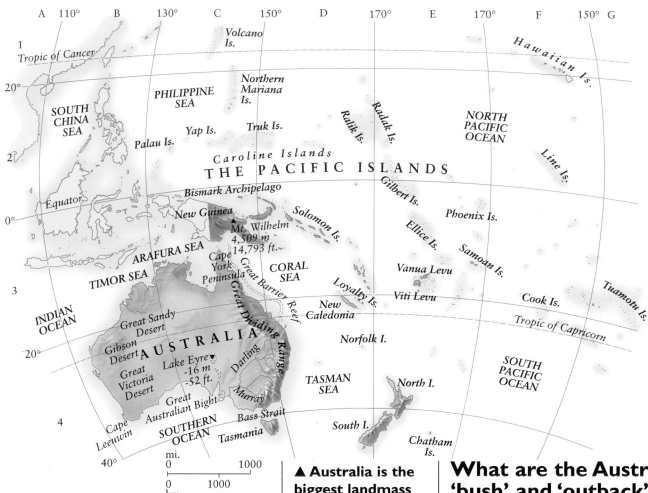

A 110°   B   130°   C   150°   D   170°   E   170°   F   150° G

1 Tropic of Cancer

Volcano Is.

Hawaiian Is.

20°

PHILIPPINE
SEA

Northern
Mariana
Is.

SOUTH
CHINA
SEA

Yap Is.

Truk Is.

NORTH
PACIFIC
OCEAN

Palau Is.

2

Caroline Islands
THE PACIFIC ISLANDS

Ralik Is.

Radak Is.

Line Is.

Equator

Bismark Archipelago

Gilbert Is.

New Guinea

Phoenix Is.

0°

▲ Mt. Wilhelm
4,509 m
14,793 ft.

Solomon Is.

Ellice Is.

Samoan Is.

ARAFURA SEA

Cape
York
Peninsula

CORAL
SEA

Vanua Levu

Tuamotu Is.

TIMOR SEA

Great Barrier Reef

Loyalty Is.

Viti Levu

Cook Is.

3

INDIAN
OCEAN

Great Sandy
Desert

Great Dividing Range

New
Caledonia

Tropic of Capricorn

Gibson
Desert A U S T R A L I A

Norfolk I.

20°

Great
Victoria
Desert

Lake Eyre ▼
-16 m
-52 ft.

Darling

SOUTH
PACIFIC
OCEAN

Great
Australian Bight

Murray

TASMAN
SEA

North I.

Cape
Leeuwin

SOUTHERN
OCEAN

Bass Strait

4

South I.

Tasmania

Chatham
Is.

40°

mi.
0   1000

0   1000
km

Where is Australasia?

Australia, New Zealand and neighbouring islands in the Pacific Ocean make up Australasia. Papua New Guinea is also included. Australia is sometimes treated as a continent on its own because it is so big. The islands without Australia are called Oceania. The whole area covers vast parts of the Pacific Ocean, from the warm seas north of the Equator to the icy waters around Antarctica.

▲ Australia is the biggest landmass in the island region of the southern Pacific. There are thousands of other islands.

What are the Australian 'bush' and 'outback'?

Most Australians today live in towns and cities. They call the countryside the bush and the vast, near-empty interior of their country the outback. The outback has a few mining and farm settlements, but no large cities. Most outback farms are cattle or sheep ranches, called 'stations'. Some are huge, covering more than 2,500 square kilometres – bigger than a city the size of London or New York. Ranchers use trucks and helicopters and keep in touch with the outside world by radio.

Where is Tasmania?

Tasmania is an island about 200 kilometres off the coast of southern Australia. The Bass Strait separates the island from the mainland. Tasmania was part of the mainland until about 12,000 years ago. It became an island when the sea rose, filling what is now the Bass Strait.

Which lake in Australia disappears?

A map of Australia shows Lake Eyre, an apparently large lake in South Australia. Yet most years the lake is dry. It fills with water only after unusually heavy rains. Most of the time it is a bed of salt. The salt forms a crust over four metres thick.

The prickly-pear cactus, introduced to Australia, escaped from gardens and spread over thousands of kilometres. The caterpillars of the Cactoblastis moth finally destroyed it.

▶ The bed of Lake Eyre is a thick coating of salt. The salt forms lumps and patterns on the surface of the lake which is usually dry.

Which is Australia's longest river?

The Murray (2,589 kilometres) is Australia's longest permanently flowing river. The Darling is 2,740 kilometres, but much of it is dry in the winter. Early explorers had hoped to find greater rivers flowing from the vast heart of the country.

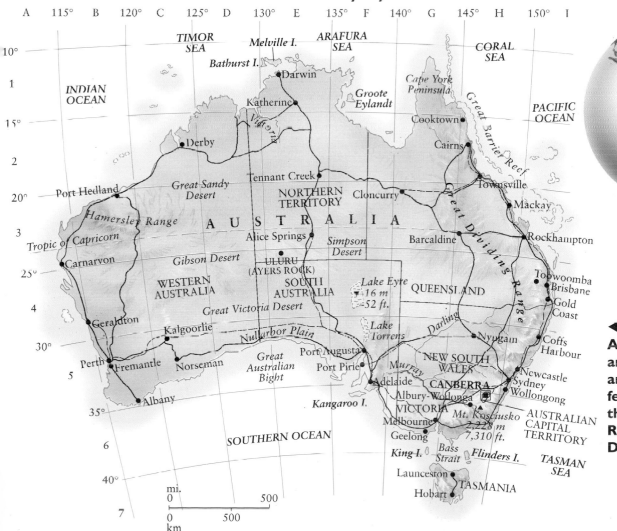

◀ This map shows Australia's states and territories, and natural features such as the Great Barrier Reef and Great Dividing Range.

ANCIENT WORLD

What is Stonehenge?

Stonehenge is an ancient monument in southern England, and it was constructed at various times between 2800 BC and 1500 BC. It was probably used as a temple, or to observe the movements of the Sun and Moon to make calendars.

Why were the pyramids of Egypt built?

The pyramids were built as tombs for the pharaohs (rulers) of Ancient Egypt, and they had chambers that contained the remains of the pharaohs. However, these chambers were later robbed of their treasures. The biggest pyramid, the Great Pyramid at Giza, was 146.5 metres high when built in about 2600 BC.

▼ The Seven Wonders of the World were listed by writers in ancient times. They were visited by travellers who marvelled at their size and magnificence. The pyramids were the oldest and by far the biggest of the Wonders.

What were the Seven Wonders of the World?

The Seven Wonders were structures of the ancient world. They were considered to be the seven most wonderful ever built. The Great Pyramid in Egypt is the only one still standing. The other six were the Hanging Gardens of Babylon; the Temple of Diana at Ephesus; the Tomb of Mausolus at Halicarnassus; the statue of Zeus at Olympia; the Pharos Lighthouse at Alexandria; and the Colossus of Rhodes, a statue beside the harbour entrance. There are no reliable pictures of the six vanished Wonders, only descriptions by historians and travellers.

Hanging Gardens of Babylon (Iraq)

The Great Pyramid at Giza (Egypt)

The Pharos Lighthouse at Alexandria (Egypt)

The Tomb of Mausolus at Halicarnassus (Turkey)

The Colossus of Rhodes (Greece)

The Temple of Diana at Ephesus (Turkey)

The statue of Zeus at Olympia (Greece)

◀ **Alexander the Great led his armies as far east as India. In a short but brilliant life, he was never defeated in battle.**

Who was Cleopatra?

Cleopatra was an extremely beautiful queen of Egypt. She was born in 69 BC. The Roman leader Julius Caesar, fascinated by her, made her queen. After Caesar's death, Cleopatra captivated Mark Antony, his successor. Antony left his wife Octavia for Cleopatra, provoking a battle for control of Rome with Octavian, who was Octavia's brother. Octavian met Antony and Cleopatra in battle in 31 BC and won. Defeated, Antony killed himself and Cleopatra soon also took her own life, possibly with an asp (a poisonous snake).

Who founded the ancient city of Alexandria?

The city of Alexandria in Egypt was founded in 331 BC by the Greek emperor Alexander the Great. By conquest, Alexander built up a great empire that extended from Greece as far as India and Egypt, and was as big as the United States. The empire brought Greek civilization to the ancient world, and Alexandria became its centre of learning.

Who was the first Roman emperor?

Augustus, who lived from 63 BC to AD 14, was the first emperor of Ancient Rome. Before Augustus, Rome was a republic governed by consuls, who were elected to power. After the death of Julius Caesar, Augustus – then called Octavian – held power with Mark Antony. Octavian defeated Mark Antony, and in 27 BC declared that Rome would henceforth be an empire with himself as the first emperor. He took the name Augustus, and Rome reached its greatest glory under his rule. The month of August is named after him.

◀ **Cleopatra lived in great splendour in Egypt. She was a descendant of one of Alexander the Great's generals.**

DID YOU KNOW?

■ The Greek philosopher Aristotle was Alexander the Great's tutor.

■ Cleopatra married two of her brothers, sharing the throne with them.

■ She had a son by Julius Caesar, and twins by Mark Antony.

■ Hadrian's Wall had gates where soldiers kept a check on all people travelling in and out of Roman Britain.

Why did the Romans build a wall across England?

Hadrian's Wall is a famous landmark in the north of England. It is a huge wall, 118 kilometres long, that runs across the whole country from coast to coast. It was built by the Roman emperor Hadrian between AD 123 and 138 to keep Scottish raiders from invading England, then a province of the Roman Empire.

◀ 145

Who took elephants across the Alps?

Hannibal commanded the forces of Carthage against Rome, and used elephants in war to scare his enemies. Hannibal took the Romans by surprise by marching over the Alps in 218 BC, taking the elephants with him. Once in Italy, Hannibal harried the Romans for years but he did not defeat them.

▼ Hannibal's army and war elephants crossed the Alps.

When did the Mayan Empire flourish?

The Mayan Empire was at its height in southern Mexico and Central America from about AD 250 to the 900s. The Maya built huge stone cities, had elaborate religious ceremonies, and developed a system of picture writing. The great Mayan cities were abandoned in the 900s. Nobody knows why.

Who was China's first emperor?

For 260 years the states of eastern China fought each other for control of the whole country. The struggle was eventually won by Ch'in, one of the westernmost states. Its leader was Prince Cheng, known as the 'Tiger of Ch'in'. When Ch'in won, Cheng proclaimed himself Shih Huang-ti, which means 'the first emperor'. Shih Huang-ti also ordered the building of the Great Wall of China to keep out invaders from the north.

Who were the Incas?

The ancestors of the Incas lived among the mountains of Peru possibly as long as 4,000 years ago. The Incas began building up their country in about AD 1200.

From 1438 to 1493, two kings, Pachacuti and his son Topa Inca, expanded the Inca Empire. It eventually covered large parts of present-day Ecuador, Bolivia, Chile and Argentina.

The Mayan people of Central America chewed gum. The rubbery gum was called chicle and they collected it from the sapodilla tree. Chicle is still used to make chewing gum.

Who were the Celts?

The Celts were a group of peoples living in central Europe in the 500s BC. Many migrated west. They were warriors and farmers. Their language survives in Welsh, Gaelic and Breton.

▶ The Inca ruler Pachacuti led his army into battle to expand his empire.

When was the Han dynasty founded?

The Han dynasty overthrew the Ch'in dynasty in 202 BC. It ruled China for more than 400 years. During the Han dynasty the Chinese Empire expanded. Han scholars studied higher mathematics and astronomy. Paper was invented during this period, and Han traders visited Persia and Rome.

▼ The Ancient Chinese built large cities. People from the countryside brought vegetables and farm animals into town to sell in the market. Travellers from the West were amazed by Chinese cities, and the orderly life that went on in them.

▼ Vikings fighting at sea. Their wooden longships were fast and easy to steer.

Who were the Vikings?

The Vikings were pirates from Scandinavia. They were bold and skilful navigators, who sailed the European seas in their long ships. Each ship had a large, square sail, but could also be driven by oars.

From AD 793 onwards, Vikings from Norway raided England. They began to settle there in the late 800s. Other Vikings attacked France and settled there. They were known as Northmen, or Normans, and gave their name to Normandy. Other Vikings reached Spain, Sicily, Italy and Russia, leaving their mark.

Who was Attila?

Attila was the leader of the Huns, a warlike group of tribes from central Asia which terrorized Europe in the AD 400s. He forced the rulers of the eastern Roman Empire to pay him a large annual fee to leave them alone. He then led a large army of Huns into Gaul (France). The Romans defeated Attila at Châlons-sur-Marne in 451. He died two years later.

Who was Confucius?

Confucius was a Chinese philosopher who lived nearly 2,500 years ago. The real name of Confucius was K'ung ch'iu. He became known as K'ung-fu-tzu, which means great master Kung; Confucius is a westernized form of that title.

DID YOU KNOW?

■ The Vikings were feared as warriors. They hired themselves out as paid soldiers.

■ Much of what we know about Ancient China comes from tombs. Clay models of houses, soldiers and horses have been found in Chinese tombs.

■ The Holy Roman Empire lasted until the early 1800s. But it was never very powerful after the Middle Ages.

■ Confucius believed in order, family and good government. His ideas had a great influence on Chinese life.

■ The Huns were one of a number of 'barbarian' peoples who attacked the Roman Empire. The Romans regarded these peoples as uncivilized.

What was the Holy Roman Empire?

The Holy Roman Empire was a group of small German and neighbouring states that were powerful in the Middle Ages. It was intended to be a second Roman Empire built of Christian states. The Empire was founded by Charlemagne, or Charles the Great, who was crowned the first Holy Roman emperor by the Pope in Rome on Christmas Day, AD 800.

EXPLORERS

Who discovered America, but thought it was Asia?

The first European explorer known to have reached America was Christopher Columbus, who was born in Italy, but explored for the Spanish. He sailed from Spain to the Bahama Islands off the coast of North America in 1492. Columbus was trying to find a new route to India or the Indies (then a name for the East), and thought he had got there. He therefore called the people he found there Indians.

Who sailed across the Pacific on a raft?

In 1947, a team of scientists led by Thor Heyerdahl, who was born in Norway in 1914, sailed across the Pacific Ocean on a raft called the Kon-Tiki. The raft was of an ancient design, and the expedition showed that the people of the South Sea Islands could have got there by raft from South America.

Who is America named after?

America is named after the Italian explorer Amerigo Vespucci, who lived from 1451 to 1512. Vespucci explored South America after Columbus reached America. Unlike Columbus, Vespucci believed that a new land had been discovered, and it was named America after him. The name was given to the two new continents – North and South America.

Christopher Columbus

▲ Columbus set out with three small ships across the Atlantic. The journey to the New World took 30 days.

In Columbus's time, many people believed the world was flat. They feared that he and his ships would sail too far west and fall over the edge!

▶ Marco Polo followed the ancient trade routes across Asia to China. Travellers rode horses and camels over mountains and deserts.

Where did Marco Polo travel?

Marco Polo and his family were the greatest European travellers of the Middle Ages. Marco was born in Venice, Italy. His father and uncle were traders and had visited China, where they met the Emperor Kublai Khan. In 1271 they set off again, with Marco. The travellers did not return until 1295. During all this time, they travelled throughout China and southern Asia. They were amazed by the sights they saw.

Who named a huge country after a village?

This was the French explorer Jacques Cartier and the country is Canada. Although he was not the first European to reach Canada, Cartier was the first to explore much of it. From 1534 onwards, he made three voyages to Canada. Cartier tried to find out what the Indian name for the country was. However, the Indians he asked thought he was enquiring about their village. So they said 'kanada' which meant 'village'.

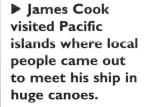

▶ James Cook visited Pacific islands where local people came out to meet his ship in huge canoes.

▼ The Aztecs of Mexico thought Cortes was a pale-skinned god and welcomed him with gifts.

Who were the conquistadors?

The conquistadors were the Spanish invaders who conquered the Indian civilizations in Central and South America in the 1500s. Conquistador is the Spanish word for 'conqueror'. The conquistadors sought the gold treasures made by the Indians but destroyed their civilizations. The best-known of the conquistadors are Hernando Cortes, who plundered Mexico, and Francisco Pizarro, who laid waste the Inca Empire of Peru. The invaders destroyed the way of life of the peoples they conquered.

DID YOU KNOW?

■ Magellan had 277 men under his command when he set sail in 1519.

■ One ship and 19 men returned home in 1522 after the historic round-the-world voyage.

■ The first European to see the Pacific Ocean was the Spaniard Vasco Nuñez de Balboa.

■ In 1513 Balboa crossed Panama from the Atlantic coast and saw the Pacific.

■ Europeans had been to North America before Columbus. In AD 1000, the Viking Leif Ericsson sailed from Greenland to Newfoundland.

Who first explored the South Seas?

The South Seas are the southern part of the Pacific Ocean, and are dotted with many tropical islands. This part of the world was first thoroughly explored by Captain James Cook, a British explorer who made three voyages there between 1768 and 1779. He also explored Australia and New Zealand, and he realized that a great unknown continent (Antarctica) must exist to the south, though he never reached it. Cook was one of the greatest of all explorers. He made maps of the coastlines he sailed along and on his ships were artists who drew the people, animals and plants they saw. On his third voyage, Cook was murdered by islanders in Hawaii.

Who was Abel Tasman?

In 1642 sailors on board a Dutch ship sighted New Zealand. The ship's captain was Abel Janszoon Tasman, the first European explorer to reach New Zealand and the island of Tasmania (named after him). Tasman was searching for an unknown South Land. He actually sailed around Australia without realizing it, and thought neither New Zealand nor Tasmania worth further voyages.

FAMOUS EVENTS

What does the Bayeux Tapestry show?

The Bayeux Tapestry is a very long piece of embroidery. It shows in pictures the invasion of England by Duke William of Normandy (William the Conqueror) in 1066. Bayeux is a small town in northern France and the tapestry is in a museum there. It is rather like a strip cartoon, and it starts with King Harold of England's visit to Duke William, probably in 1064. It ends with the Battle of Hastings in 1066 when Harold was killed by an arrow that pierced his eye, and his troops were defeated.

▶ **Disguised as Native Americans, colonists threw British tea into the water. This was one of the acts that led to the American War of Independence.**

Which war began with a tea party?

In 1773, when America was still a British colony, a Tea Act was passed in Britain which allowed the East India Company to send tea directly from London to America without using American merchants. In Boston, a group of patriotic Americans boarded the tea ships and threw the tea into the harbour. This event is known as the Boston Tea Party. Soon after, the the War of Independence began.

Sheep were brought to Australia by the early settlers. Today there are about 147 million sheep, nearly nine times the number of people in Australia!

▲ **Norman soldiers on horseback charge into battle. This scene is part of the long Bayeux Tapestry which tells the story of William's invasion of England in 1066.**

Why is the year 1901 important in the history of Australia?

On January 1, 1901, the Commonwealth of Australia came into being. Before this, Australia consisted of a number of separate colonies. By the Commonwealth Act of 1900, the colonies became a federation. The formation of the Commonwealth marked the beginning of Australia as a full nation.

What was the charge of the Light Brigade?

Between 1854 and 1856 the Crimean War was fought between Russia on one side and Turkey, England, France and Sardinia on the other. In October 1854 the Russians tried to seize the British base at Balaklava. Owing to a misunderstanding of orders the Light Brigade, an army division, charged the main Russian position. The soldiers were heavily outnumbered by the Russians and many were killed, but the brave survivors got through and captured the enemy position.

What caused the American Civil War?

Political differences between the northern states (the Union) and the southern states (the Confederacy). The turning point came in 1860 when Abraham Lincoln became president. The South, which depended on slaves for labour, feared Lincoln would abolish slavery. In 1861, 11 southern states seceded (separated) from the Union because they thought that states, not Congress, should decide their own laws. After four years of fighting, the South surrendered, preserving the Union.

When was the Battle of Gettysburg?

The Battle of Gettysburg was a turning point in the American Civil War. It lasted from July 1 to July 3, 1863. Gettysburg is a little town in Pennsylvania, in the North. The Confederates led by Robert E. Lee were defeated by the Union army under George Meade.

▲ **During the Great War, recruiting posters urged men to join the army. Many died in trench warfare in France and Belgium.**

▼ **The Battle of Agincourt (1415) was an English victory over a larger French army during the long Hundred Years' War.**

Which war became known as the Great War?

World War I (1914–1918) became known as the Great War. This was because, at the time, there had never been a war in which so many different countries took part. More people were killed than ever before in a war, and more buildings were destroyed. But when World War II took place (1939–1945), it was even bigger and more destructive.

What was the Hundred Years' War?

France and England were at war from 1337 to 1453. This is more than a hundred years but the period is known as the Hundred Years' War. It was eventually won by France.

HISTORY

Which event does the Eiffel Tower commemorate?

The Eiffel Tower, designed by Alexandre Eiffel, was built for the Paris Exhibition of 1889. This exhibition commemorated the French Revolution, which began a century before. The Revolution started on July 14, 1789, when a mob of angry people attacked the Bastille, a prison in Paris. They pulled the building down stone by stone. The anniversary of the destruction of the Bastille is a national holiday in France.

Which 'unsinkable' ship sank on its first voyage?

This ship was the *Titanic*, a British passenger liner. At the time, the *Titanic* was the world's largest ship, and experts believed that it was unsinkable. But on the night of April 14, 1912, during its first voyage, it hit an iceberg in the middle of the Atlantic Ocean. It sank and, out of more than 2,200 people on board, over 1,500 were drowned.

▲ **Discontent helped start the French Revolution. In Paris, crowds attacked the Bastille prison and freed all of the prisoners.**

▶ **Sitting beside his wife Jacqueline, President Kennedy was driven through the streets of Dallas to meet the cheering crowds. Moments later he was shot by an assassin. People still argue about who killed him.**

In the 1780s French people were angered by a new tax on salt, which they used to keep meat fresh. The tax made salt too expensive.

Who was shot in 1865 at Ford's Theater, Washington, DC?

Abraham Lincoln, sixteenth president of the United States, was shot on April 14, 1865 at Ford's Theater, Washington, DC. He died the next day. He was shot by an unsuccessful actor called John Wilkes Booth, who wanted to kill Lincoln because the Confederate States had been beaten in the American Civil War.

When was President Kennedy assassinated?

President John F Kennedy of the United States was assassinated by a gunman in Dallas, Texas, on November 22, 1963. The president was being driven in an open car.

Who won the Battle of the Little Bighorn?

The battle was fought on June 25, 1876 between the Sioux and a US cavalry column led by Colonel George A Custer. Trouble had begun in 1874 when the United States government sent miners and soldiers into the Black Hills of South Dakota, a region sacred to the Sioux. The Sioux refused to sell the land, so the government decided to drive them out. Custer split his force of 650 troops into three columns. His own column fell into a Sioux ambush led by Chief Sitting Bull. Custer and his men were all killed.

▼ On D-Day, June 6, 1944, Allied troops landed in France. The massive air, sea and land invasion was the biggest in history.

What happened at Pearl Harbor?

On the morning of December 7, 1941, Japanese bombers attacked the United States naval base at Pearl Harbor, Hawaii. They destroyed six warships, damaged 12 others and destroyed 174 aircraft. The Japanese attacked while their officials were negotiating in Washington, DC about causes of dispute between Japan and the United States. The Pearl Harbor attack took the United States into the war against Japan and its allies Germany and Italy.

When did World War II start?

World War II began with the German invasion of Poland on September 1, 1939. On September 3, Britain and France declared war on Germany. Australia, New Zealand, India, Canada and South Africa supported Britain. By 1940 Germany had overrun much of Europe. Japan and Italy joined in on Germany's side. Italy invaded Yugoslavia, Greece and much of North Africa. Germany then attacked Russia in 1941, the year the United States entered the war. In 1944 Allied forces invaded western Europe while Russia attacked from the east. Germany was defeated by May 1945. Japan surrendered in August 1945.

▼ Genghis Khan's Mongol warriors rode into battle on horseback. Each man was a skilled rider and fighter.

Which empire was ruled by Genghis Khan?

Genghis Khan was the leader of the Mongols, a warlike group of people from the plains of central Asia. He was one of the greatest conquerors in history, leading a vast army of horsemen against China in 1211, into Russia in 1223, and even threatening to overrun eastern Europe. Genghis Khan created a Mongol empire. His grandson Kublai Khan ruled China.

What was the Spanish Armada?

The Armada was an invasion fleet of galleons packed with soldiers sent from Spain to attack England in 1588. Spain was then Europe's mightiest power. The English fleet fought off the Armada in a series of battles in the English Channel, but did not seriously damage it. However, the Spanish could not join forces with an invasion army waiting in the Netherlands, and their ships were driven north around Britain by strong winds. Many were wrecked in storms off the coasts of Scotland and Ireland.

When did the Pilgrim Fathers land in America?

In 1620 a group of Puritans left England on a ship called the *Mayflower*. They were bound for new lives in America. They sailed from Plymouth in Devon and landed in Massachusetts. The Pilgrim Fathers, as they became known,

▲ The great galleons of the Spanish Armada were out-sailed by the smaller English ships at the Battle of Gravelines in the English Channel.

founded the second English colony in North America, the first was founded by people who went to America seeking religious freedom. Those who survived the first hard winter in America gave thanks with a feast, which was the first Thanksgiving.

When did France become a republic?

In 1792, after revolution had overthrown the monarchy. The French Revolution began in 1789, as a movement to make government in France more democratic. But the revolution rapidly became more extreme and violent. People accused of being enemies of the republic were executed. In 1799, a soldier named Napoleon Bonaparte seized power, and he soon made himself emperor.

◄ The Pilgrim Fathers were helped by Native Americans as they built homes and planted crops in their new land.

When was the Russian Revolution?

In 1917, revolutionaries forced the tsar (emperor) of Russia to give up his supreme power. A group of communist extremists, known as Bolsheviks, seized power from the liberal democratic politicians. Their leader was Vladimir Lenin (Vladimir Ilyich Ulyanov). By 1921, Lenin had made Russia a communist state, the largest of the newly created Union of Soviet Socialist Republics.

Who led India to independence?

Mohandas Karamchand Gandhi (1869-1948) was the most influential leader of the movement that won India's independence from British rule in 1947. Gandhi was a lawyer, who preached a policy of non-violence as he campaigned for India's freedom. After independence, Gandhi tried to stop the fighting that broke out between India's Hindus and Muslims. He was assassinated in 1948 by a Hindu who disliked Gandhi's tolerance of all religions.

GREAT EVENTS

■ Greece fought a war for freedom against Turkey from 1821 to 1829.

■ Spain's colonies in South America won their independence between 1809 and 1825.

■ 1848 became known as Europe's Year of Revolutions.

■ In 1860 Guiseppe Garibaldi led a victorious army from Sicily through southern Italy to join up with Victor Emmanuel's army from the north. When Rome was captured, Italy became a united country.

■ Fidel Castro led the Cuban Revolution of 1959 which overthrew the dictator Fulgencio Batista.

■ In 1900 only two African countries – Ethiopia and Liberia – were truly independent. By the 1990s all the major territories of Africa were self-governing.

◄ **Gandhi first practised non-violent protest in South Africa. He took his beliefs to India and inspired other protestors around the world.**

► **South Africa's Nelson Mandela with Queen Elizabeth II of Great Britain. Mandela won praise for his courage and statesmanship.**

When was Germany reunited?

Germany was divided by the victorious Allies after its defeat in World War II (1939-1945). East Germany came under communist rule and Russian domination, while West Germany was rebuilt by the Western democracies as a prosperous, free country. In 1961 the building of the Berlin Wall symbolized the division of the two Germanies. In 1989, the collapse of communism in Eastern Europe began. The government in East Germany fell, the Berlin Wall was torn down, and in 1990 Germany became one country again with a democratic government.

Who was South Africa's first black president?

From the 1950s, all South Africans were classified by race. Whites ruled, while blacks had few freedoms. Nelson Mandela, a leader of the African National Congress, was jailed from 1962 until 1990 for opposing the government. As the old system broke down, he was freed, and in 1994 he was elected South Africa's first black president.

INDEX

ACKNOWLEDGEMENTS

The publishers wish to thank the artists who have contributed toward this book. These include the following:

Susanna Addario; Hemesh Alles; Marion Appleton; Hayward Art Group; Craig Austin; David Barnett; Peter Bull; Vanessa Card; Tony Chance; Kuo Kang Chen; Harry Clow; Stephen Conlin; Peter Dennis; Richard Draper; Eugene Fleury; Chris Forsey; Mark Franklin; Terry Gabbey; Sheila Galbraith; Mark George; Jeremy Gower; Ruby Green; Ray Grinaway; Nick Harris; Nicholas Hewetson; Adam Hook; Christian Hook; Christina Hook; Richard Hook; Tony Kenyon; Mike Lacey; Claire Littlejohn; Mick Loates; Bernard Long; Alan Male; Shane Marsh; Jamie Medlin; Nicki Palin; Alex Pang; Roger Payne; Mel Pickering; Maurice Pledger; Bryan Poole; Sebastian Quigley; Claudia Saraceni; Guy Smith; Tony Smith; Michael Steward; Simon Tegg; Ian Thompson; Ross Watton; Steve Weston; Linda Worrall; David Wright.

Photographs

The publishers wish to thank the following for supplying photographs for this book:

Page 10 (BC) Corbis; 17 (BR) Corbis; 18 (TR) Corbis; 29 (TR) ZEFA; 32 (TR) Corbis; 36 (C) Mehau Kulyk/ Science Photo Library; 39 (CL) Firework Ltd; 43 (TR) Geoff Tompkinson/ Science Photo Library; 45 (BC) Corbis; 48 (TL) Yves Baulieu/ Publiphoto Diffusion/ Science Photo Library; 51 (TL) Corbis; 64 (CR) Ford; 78 (TL) Bill Coster/ NHPA; 84 (BR) G.I. Bernard/ Oxford Scientific Films; 91 (BL) Stan Osolinski/ Oxford Scientific Films; 103 (BR) Science Photo Library; 107 (TR) Simon Fraser/ Science Photo Library; 107 (BR) Jeremy Mason/ Science Photo Library; 117 (TL) Will & Deni McIntyre/ Science Photo Library; 120 (BL) Ian West/ Bubbles; 121 (TL) Jeremy Bright/ Robert Harding Picture Library; 121 (BL) Robert Harding; 126 (TL) Peter Lambert/ Tony Stone Worldwide; 126 (BR) The Hutchison Library; 127 (TR) c 1996 Corel Corp.; 129 (TL) Hugh Sitton/ Tony Stone Images; 129 (BR) Spectrum Colour Library; 130/1 (CR) Spectrum Colour Library; 132 (BL) Rohan/ Tony Stone Images; 133 (TL) ZEFA; 135 (TR) ZEFA; 135 (BR) D. Saunders/ Trip; 139 (TR) ZEFA; 139 (BL) Jaemsen/ ZEFA; 140 (BR) Spectrum Colour Library; 143 (CR) Spectrum Colour Library; 150 (TR) The Hulton Getty Picture Collection Ltd.; 152 (CR) Corbis; 155 (BR) Simon Krectmem/ Reuter Popperfoto